SOCIAL MARKETING STRATEGIES

Conservation Issues and Analysis

DONALD L. PERRY

Southern Illinois University
Carbondale, Illinois

GOODYEAR PUBLISHING COMPANY
Pacific Palisades, California

Library of Congress Cataloging in Publication Data

Perry, Donald L.
    Social marketing strategies.

    Bibliography: p.
    Includes index.
    1. Environmental policy.   2. Conservation of natural
resources.   3. Marketing—Social aspects.   I. Title.
HC79.E5P45   301.31   75-13477
ISBN 0-87620-865-0

CONTENTS

PART THREE: THE SOLUTION

PREFACE

Marketing literature is comprised of concepts, principles, theories, studies, and relationships borrowed from other disciplines. The fields of economics, behavioral sciences, communication theory, quantitative analysis, anthropology, business administration, and others have been the sources of substantial contributions to the development of marketing thought. This acquisitive trait has, in turn, led marketing academicians and practitioners to broaden the scope and role of marketing's place in our society. Quite naturally, the great issues of the contemporary world became an integral part of distribution thought and practice.

The virtual explosion of environment-oriented literature, within the broad spectrum of social science and scientific studies, is having a profound impact on distribution theory and business policy-making throughout industry. The environment comprises an awesome array of complex ecological, scientific, and social issues; the absolute interdependency of earth's natural life-giving processes is causing man to re-evaluate his historic place in our finite world.

Social marketing embraces the environmental issue; it is here that socioecologic relationships emerge that link ecological balances to socioeconomic demands on the natural system. One basic theme that runs through scientific and social science literature is that behavior modification will be an absolute requirement for civilization if mankind is to avoid a "Club of Rome" collapse by the turn of the century. Because mankind is capable of modifying a course of action, environmental calamities can be largely avoided through prudent programs.

One approach most prominently mentioned today is *conservation*. The conservation of natural resources requires an across-the-board commitment from all segments of society. Conservation concepts are interwoven into many facets of environmental and socioeconomic behavior. The conservation ethic is more than preservation; it should be viewed as a broad scenario of ecological, social, and economic considerations functioning in context with long-range resource policies. Science and technology play key roles in cleaning up the environment, improving fuel use efficiency, controlling toxic agents, repairing cumulative damage to the landscape, and improving or upgrading raw material supplies.

Social Marketing Strategies: Conservation Issues and Analysis occupies a unique niche in distribution literature; the book is presented to readers in an integrative and uncluttered manner. Within these pages, ecology is discussed in the context of basic relationships that can be comprehended by students, practioners, and other readers who lack foundational courses in ecology and environmental systems.

Donald L. Perry

INTRODUCTION

Social marketing is a dynamic and emerging branch of marketing. Its primary focal point is the analysis of social aspects and their interfaces with income distribution, the ecology, resources and raw materials, and social politics. These relationships in turn affect purchasing power, spending patterns, life-style choices, and market freedoms. Marketing is constantly adjusting to major shifts in society and the economy.

Management is challenged in the present era to evaluate social and economic changes on an equal par with company profit planning. The rate of change has accelerated to the point that few business leaders are experienced in coping with the fast-developing shifts in our social system. Traditional practices, growth policies, and attitudes seem strangely out of date in this period of confusing cross-currents of change.

The future is being evaluated under assumptions quite different from those of the 1960s. Fundamental changes or modifications in life-styles and economic growth policies are now centered around the need to conserve natural resources and strategic raw materials. Material acquisition and exponential growth threaten to deplete the nation's stockpile of energy and metals; conservation measures are considered essential if the nation is to avoid severe economic and ecological calamities by the year 2000.

The conservation ethic has found its way into our social thought; and it has filtered into industrial planning rooms. Consumers, industry, and government agencies are viewing the future with confidence that conservation measures can adjust demand rates with supply capacities. This will, as many now admit, mean the end to opulant dreams that we once held. Instead, the nation must consider standard-of-living choices that the economy and the ecosystem can sustain in the long run.

If we elect to employ resources wisely, the "zero-growth" alternative can be avoided. The choice lies somewhere between exponential growth calamity and zero-growth policies. Living within an economic and ecological budget that allows the economy to grow is a realistic goal if conservation and pollution controls are built in to the system.

Marketing and ecological issues have become the subject of several books and journal articles. George Fisk *(Marketing and the Ecological Crisis* and Frederick E. Webster, Jr. *(Social Aspects of Marketing)* discuss in considerable depth the interfaces between marketing systems and the ecology. These works have aided the profession in relating the distribution system to societal problems that seem destined to alter our standard of living.

Marketing practices can be altered to correct societal deficiencies in the distribution system. Government, consumers, business, and the public are clearly responsible for determining these national goals. A more promising behavior modification role for marketing (as well as for other segments of our society) lies in constructing a positive strategy for change. In this strategy the conservation ethic, pollution controls, and resource policies should harmonize into programs that allow technology, science, economic policies, and social requirements to effect positive solutions. New products, for example, can be made more efficient, can be made more "recyclable," and can use fewer resources. New products can be directed to perform a social job, such as to control pollution. Social services may well provide business with the next innovative growth market for the future.

Social Marketing Strategies: Conservation Issues and Analysis presents a resource strategy for the nation. The complex issues and the limits and opportunities relating to these strategy choices are presented. Literature from environmental sources provides contemporary views on resource management. Cases and discussion questions provide further insights into the resource issue and its ecological implications.

PART ONE

THE ISSUES

CHAPTER ONE

ECONOMIC GROWTH

STRATEGIES

DEFINING THE AMERICAN DREAM

The "American dream" essentially consists of material acquisition goals, strong infusions of technological innovations, and cultural adaptation to change. Economic expansion is associated with the quality of life that affluent families identify with the dream. This material emphasis requires not only cultural changes, but alterations in the environment. Affluence depletes natural resources from the finite planet earth. Processing, manufacturing, distribution, and consumption activities provide essential products and services. These functions have characteristically resulted in delivering the material goods that are central to the American dream. The environmental interfaces with American life style and economic expansion policies have, until recently, received little attention by society.

The growing concerns about pollution and resource depletion are reshaping the basic concepts concerning economic growth and material acquisition. Affluence and convenience shaped the American dream; they continue to produce a profound influence on the nation's people. Today, it may be said that convenience has become ". . . a natural right of citizens of the richest nation of the world."[1] While the dream is not being abandoned, it is being redefined and incorporated in a much larger scenario involving environmental and economic growth limits. One aspect of the large issue at stake is illustrated in Figure 1-1, which depicts the raw material and product flow within a distribution system.

FIGURE 1-1 Raw Material-Product Flow Chart

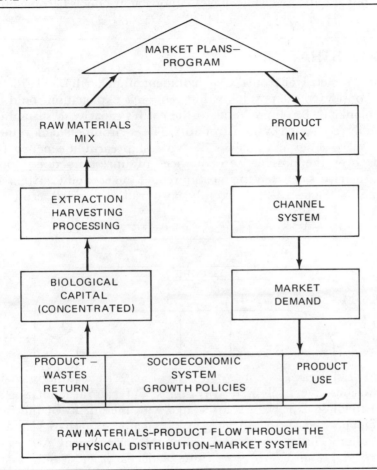

Product decisions involve a broad cross section of socioeconomic factors. Biological capital (natural resources in concentrated deposits) provides a source of primary raw materials for industry. But product decisions determine the finished goods mix that society consumes. Waste products in the post-consumption phase are returned to the natural environment or are recycled into the production system.

Science and technology have made affluence and convenience not only possible, but well within reach of the average citizen. Increased productivity, new products, new techniques, and new advances in medical science have made our life more complex, demanding, and varied. Along with the technological improvements have come the excitement of change and the adjustments to new communities, neighbors, gadgets, and laws. Life as measured against once familiar guideposts has become more temporary and subject to sudden obsolescence.[2] Unfortunately, in our haste to grow economically, Americans have left the environment polluted; displaced resources have escaped into the land, water, air, and our bodies. Our life styles determine not only the *amount* of materials we acquire, but also the rate with which fashionable products become obsolete.

GROWTH STRATEGIES

Affluence extracts a toll from the environment; until Earth Day 1970, few persons considered the possibility that economic exploitation could endanger mankind. But finite limits to the earth's capacity to sustain life were readily recognized by the astronauts. The environmental movement and the space program's analysis of "spaceship earth" deepened our concerns over the possible consequences of unrestrained economic growth. Interfaces between the biosphere and the economic system are illustrated in Figure 1-2. Currently, two rather divided economic

FIGURE 1-2 Biological-Economic Interfaces—The Pollution and Purification Cycle

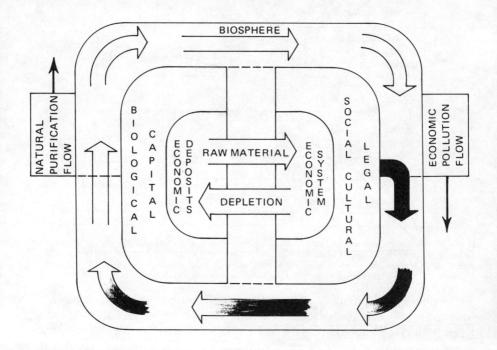

Natural resources provide raw material for industry, and in turn, pollutants enter the environment as industrial by-products. To a certain extent, natural processes filter out pollutants, but natural filtration processes may become overloaded.

strategies are widely discussed:

1. No absolute limit exists on natural resource availability because the definition of resources changes over time, with new discoveries, and with new abilities.
2. No rate of production of a resource, renewable or nonrenewable, material or energy, can go on increasing exponentially without end.[3]

No-Limits Strategy

Science and technology make it possible to locate, mine, and process mineral and metal deposits that were once uneconomical. Previous civilizations were largely dependent on mineral and metal deposits of high-grade ore located on or very near the surface of the earth. Highly improved methods of transportation now make it possible to move low-

FIGURE 1-3

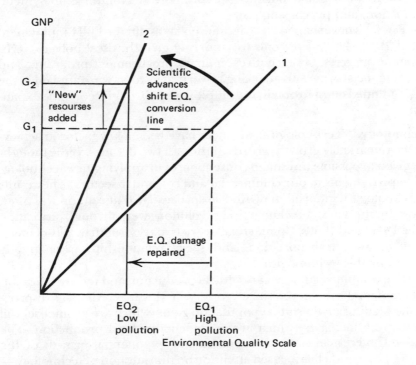

Under this model, science is given the task of not only stimulating economic growth, but of cleaning up the environment as well. Using an economic-environmental (growth-pollution) conversion line, one may note that a major scientific breakthrough in resource management and pollution control shifts the conversion line from 1 to 2. This stimulates new growth and lowers the E.Q. pollution levels. The system becomes more efficient, even with high growth rates. Can the system continue even with exponential expansion without encountering some limit?

grade ores great distances to processing centers. Exploration and mining ventures are now moving into once-unknown reaches of the globe in search of new ore deposits. Proponents of the no-growth-limit viewpoint project that well before the earth's supply of nonrenewable resources is exhausted, technology capable of converting ordinary rocks and water into minerals, metals and energy at economical prices will be available.[4] This reasoning is shown in the graph in Figure 1-3. The combinations of technology and supportive economic growth policies are key elements in the no-limit strategy.

Full Employment Act of 1946.   Fearful of another depression and the new economic challenges of the post–World War II period, Congress passed a major legislative commitment to economic growth and development. In this act, "The Congress hereby declares that it is continuing policy and responsibility of the federal government to use all practicable means consistent with its needs and obligations and other essential considerations of national policy . . . to promote maximum employment, production, and purchasing power."[5]

Few laws have shaped an economic policy as did the Full Employment Act of 1946. The major tools for spurring growth, fiscal policies, technological progress, tax incentives, military procurement programs, and sweeping social programs attacking poverty at its roots were applied in the single-minded quest to obtain full employment through economic expansion.

Technology.   Technological advances have been a key factor in achieving the remarkable growth records of the past two decades. Little thought was given to possible unwanted consequences in applying new technological improvements to our commercial and consumer sectors. The results of technological innovation proved so spectacular that caution was often thrown to the wind. A technological revolution swept through our nation in the 1950s and 1960s. Commercial districts, parks, suburbs, city centers, urban sprawls, transportation, and social relationships were greatly marked by this technological era.

The combined gains in agricultural production and industrialization that mankind has achieved since World War II were credited as disproving the Malthusian thesis that population gains (which are geometric) will outstrip the increases (which are arithmetic) in food production. The renewed interest in natural resources and exponential growth of the world's population has focused attention on the question of technology — whether it has resolved mankind's struggle to survive the population race, or whether it has merely postponed temporarily the ultimate day of reckoning. The viewpoint that one takes determines the relative optimism or pessimism that he assigns to the future. Utopians view the future in terms of great technological flexibility, where raw materials can be extracted from common substances. Survival certainly is more assured if technology can successfully resolve the pollution issue, as Figure 1-4 shows.

FIGURE 1-4 Industrial-Consumer Pollution Loops

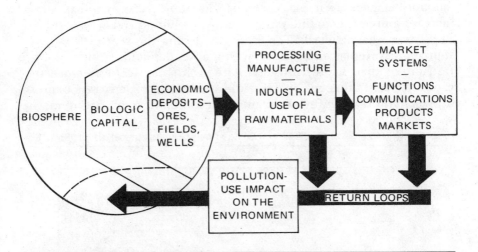

Economic wastes loop back into the environment. The biosphere becomes polluted and biological wealth vital to mankind's future (i.e., sea foods, grains, livestock, fibers, forest products, etc.) are threatened by toxic substances. Resulting ecological imbalances further hasten the destruction of finite renewable resources. One may project that technology will eventually control pollution emissions and restore the environment.

Our spectacular increases in agricultural production during the past 20 years are cited by this no-growth-limit school as evidence that improvements in capital equipment, chemical weed controls and fertilizers, grains, livestock, and farm operations keep us well ahead of population increases.[6] When viewed over the past 30 years, foods and fibers have responded well to scientific selective breeding and plant hybridization research projects designed to increase yield and reduce the length of time between planting and havesting dates.

Is pollution considered a temporary transitional problem that will be brought under control by new technology? Those who believe that technology can conquer pollution speak of the future in terms of a clean, prosperous, and wonderous age in which man's ancient enemies —hunger, poverty, disease, and crippling social conflicts—will be eliminated. Our unique affluency strongly influences these utopian-like projections among chemists, architects, engineers, planners, and space-age technocrats.[7] Technological capability, which could achieve numerous new breakthroughs in resource management and life-style choices, has lagged well behind this concept of the "model society."

Growth-within-Limits Strategy

Economic expansion, as measured by the real GNP, strongly advanced between the years 1958 and 1974. From Figure 1-5, one may note how closely total energy consumption correlates with real GNP. Our economy is dependent on abundant energy supplies. As the economy continues to require not only energy but other natural resources in exponential amounts, science, technology, and world trade patterns will be under increasing pressures to find ways to control pollution and to discover new deposits of raw materials. For example, during the years 1973–74, resource pressures became intense, with market demands rising at a much faster pace than supply capacity. Although some factories worked at capacity levels, other producers could neither fill orders nor obtain resources required for further plant expansion.[8] In turn, strong market

FIGURE 1-5   Increases in Real GNP and Energy Use—Correlation Analysis for 1958–1974

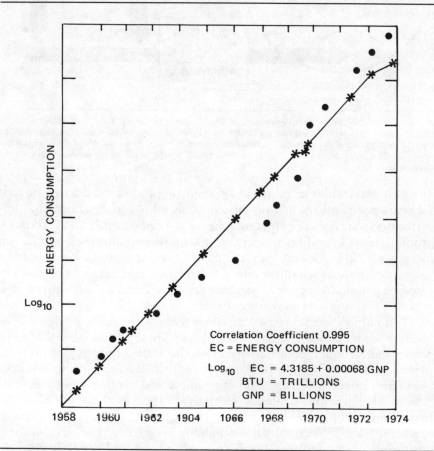

Correlation Coefficient 0.995
EC = ENERGY CONSUMPTION

Log_{10} EC = 4.3185 + 0.00068 GNP
BTU = TRILLIONS
GNP = BILLIONS

Real GNP in billions 1958 dollars.

demand drives up prices for finished goods; the problems of supply are further troubled by consumers hoarding goods and by panic buying.

In the final analysis, economic wealth is derived from natural wealth; financial capital, managerial skills, an efficient distribution system, technological improvements (real), and a viable social order harmonize to make economic specialization work. Affluence is the result of complex combinations of variables. The measure of economic success that we achieved within the past two decades resulted from not one sensational development but from a broad sweep of improvements in numerous science and social science subject areas. The willingness of a nation to alter its behavior and to innovate new solutions to problems is as important to future advancement as are technological and scientific tools. Conversely, if a nation becomes plagued by a multitude of serious social, economic, and technological conflicts, science alone cannot bail a society out of its dilemma. Thus, science becomes truly effective when employed in conjunction with cultural, social, and economic relationships.

National Environment Policy Act of 1969. America's nearly radical implementation of technology to achieve economic growth has led to complex socioeconomic and environmental "backlashes." The impact of technology has forced American society to adjust to accelerated changes, many of which have secondary consequences that disrupt communities, farms, and social patterns of living. In response to increased concerns over the lack of advanced studies on the possible affects of new technologies *prior* to introduction, Congress passed the National Environmental Policy Act of 1969. This act gives direction to the nation's *methods* for stimulating growth, hence complementing the Full Employment Act of 1946. In the National Environmental Policy Act of 1969, "The Congress, recognizing the profound impact of man's activity on the interrelations of all components of the natural environment, particularly the profound influences of population growth, high-density urbanization, industrial expansion, resource exploitation, and new and expanding technological advances, and recognizing further the critical importance of restoring and maintaining environmental quality . . . "[9]

Behavior Modification and Finite Resources. Ecology, raw materials, technology, and economic growth should be considered in the context of natural laws of science that govern the behavior of all forms of matter, including life. Here, cause-and-effect relationships evolve around the interfaces between life-supporting functions of global resources and mankind's demands on these resources. Natural laws support all life; science functions to serve mankind's struggle to achieve basic and commercial understanding of the natural laws. Hence, civilization is a part of the broader environment and, as such, is subject not only to natural laws, but also to the beneficiary or victim in the use of science to achieve economic, social, and political ends.

Advocates of the restricted-growth strategy consider the importance of behavior modification in resolving expansion-related problems. To them, the future is viewed in relationship with real choices relating to pollution control, responsibilities of technological progress, conservation of scarce resources, an economy that encourages a pricing mechanism that covers the total cost associated with discovering, extracting, processing, and distributing products.

THE EXPONENTIAL GROWTH THREAT

Exponential demand makes behavior modification associated with social change more difficult with time. "Briefly, exponential growth is geometric growth on a pattern of 1, 2, 4, 8, 16, etc., in contrast to arithmetic growth on a 1, 2, 3, 4, 5 pattern."[10] Mankind's requirements for metals, minerals, fibers, and foods are not only doubling, but doing so within shorter and shorter time spans. The lead time required to correct expo-

FIGURE 1-6

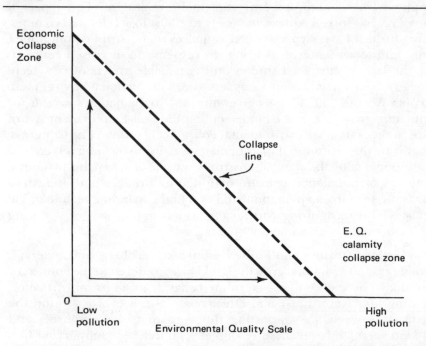

The figure reflects a relationship between economic expansion and environmental impairment. Using a simple proportional ratio, economic expansion along the GNP axis produces E.Q. impairment. If exponential growth rates push the economy to the point that the collapse line is reached, the nation faces the possibility of economic-environmental collapse. To avoid this possibility national policies must deal with both economic dislocations and environmental quality.

nential growth imbalances lengthens as a nation undergoes economic and environmental crises. Figure 1-6 illustrates a proportional relationship between economic growth and pollution build-up, showing environmental decay as a residual by-product of economic growth. In order to cope with pollution and resource shortages, and to adjust world trade patterns within a framework of peaceful international relations, major social, economic, technological, and scientific inputs are considered essential. Figure 1-7 shows how science and technology can utilize safe new processes for recovering formerly uneconomical resources.

FIGURE 1-7

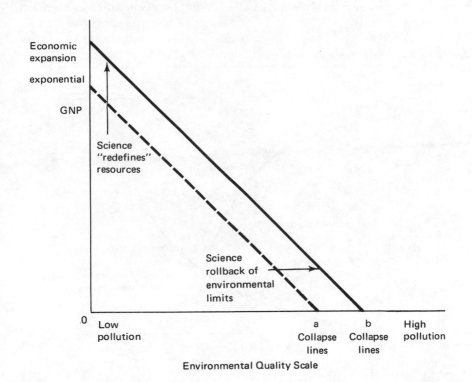

Under the no-limits-to-growth model, *science* has the responsibility to roll back environmental limits and economic resources. This approach establishes a new ceiling to growth at some higher figure. For example, as economic growth moves along the GNP axis toward collapse line (a), pollution and environmental impairment moves along the E.Q. axis, approaching collapse line (a). Unless the first ceiling is moved back, an economy would be threatened with calamity if either economic expansion or environmental impairment reached line (a). A new rollback ceiling allows an economy to grow until line (b) is reached. What economic-environmental factors are required as science rolls back each new crisis or collapse limit?

For example, assume that world oil reserves are estimated to be a little more than 2,100.00 billion barrels; and, assume further that world demand is increasing by 6.9 percent per year. Then, one may note from Figure 1-8 that demand will exceed available supply after the year 2000. But, well before this date would nations continue to share diminishing petroleum supplies?[11] Before the year 2000, political decisions making remaining oil fields inaccessible to other nations could provoke world energy crises much sooner. Unfortunately, exponential growth rates create illusions of ample reserves. Spectacular discoveries of fossil fuels or near-substitutes must be developed to offset exponential depletion rates of the world's petroleum reserves. The energy short-fall of 1973–75, caused by the combined forces of exponential demand and Arab boycotts, produced what might be the first sign that world trade patterns have moved into a new critical period in which both discovery and conservation are needed.

FIGURE 1-8   World Reserves of Crude Oil

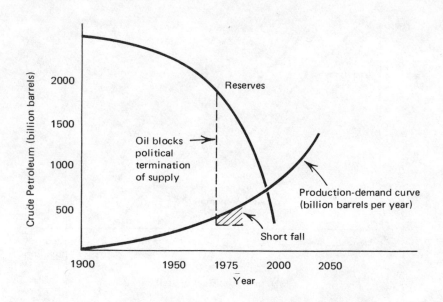

At exponential rate of demand with effects of political policies to create a world market shortage.

Mankind's future might be considered more optimistic if demands on finite world resources can be held within checks or limits that allow society time to make new discoveries and across-the-board adjustments in life styles, and economic and political policies.[12] Without this grace

period, social and environmental problems could easily overwhelm our
scientific capacity to find solutions to growth. Exponential growth rates
make behavior modification essential and support the limits-to-growth
strategy. Unless growth rates can be controlled through sound economic
policy, nations become dependent on high levels of imported raw materials to fuel their industrial systems. Figure 1-9 illustrates the increasing
dependancy of the U.S. on imported products. Figure 1-10 depicts the
increase of energy imports through the years 1946 to 1973. The Arab
Embargo in the Fall of 1973 caught the U.S. economy by surprise, and the
long-term effects of the resulting high energy cost era will be felt by the
economy for many more years.

FIGURE 1-9   Selected Measures of International Trade Performance

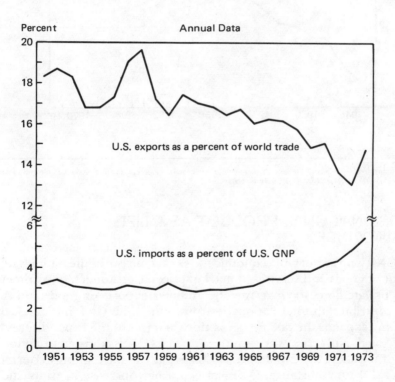

Source: Reprinted from Hans H. Helbing, "Recent and Prospective Developments in International Trade and Finance" *Review* Vol. 56, No. 5 (May 1974) Federal Reserve Bank of St. Louis.

FIGURE 1-10   U.S. Petroleum Supply and Demand

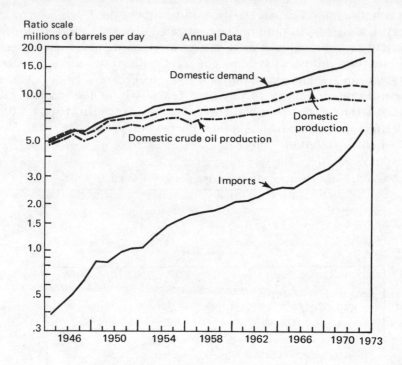

Source: Reprinted from Hans H. Helbing, "Recent and Prospective Developments in International Trade and Finance" *Review* Vol. 56, No. 5 (May 1974) Federal Reserve Bank of St. Louis.

GROSS NATIONAL PRODUCT AS A LIFE QUALITY INDEX

The GNP is an important economic index that measures the nation's total output of goods and services at market prices. Consumers, government, gross private domestic investments, and new exports of goods and services contribute to total national output. When the GNP increases, the economy expands the dollar transactions in terms of the expenditures by which goods and services are acquired. When GNP is adjusted to compensate for inflation, the expansion that takes place in the economy is termed as "real." In this instance, GNP reflects a new increase in transaction, investment, and productivity.

Technological Progress and New Business Enterprises

Productivity advances per man-hours of labor have risen steadily since the 1930s; the introduction of new machinery, techniques of manufacturing, methods of organization, scientific management principles, multiple-purpose equipment, larger-scale processing, and automation have resulted in net gains in efficiency, employment, income, and living standards for a broad segment of the American population. For example, in 1929 GNP of the United States was only $210.3 billion (according to 1960 prices). By 1950, the level of GNP had risen to $367.0 billion, an increase of 2.7 percent per year. As the rate of technological progress accelerated during the 1950s, GNP advanced 3.2 percent per year during the same period. From 1960 to 1974, scientific knowledge more than doubled and GNP soared above $1.3 trillion.

Technology has had a direct result in stimulating growth industries. New technologies have allowed these firms to expand at rates faster than the economy. Air transportation, data processing, synthetic materials, chemicals, instantaneous communications, and aerospace represent only a small number of the growth industries that have resulted from advancing technologies. Three industries—television, jet aircraft, and digital computers—have added more than $13 billion to the GNP and an estimated 900,000 jobs. All three of these important industries were commercially nonexistent in 1945. In the case of technology-based firms, such as Polaroid, 3M, IBM, Xerox, and Texas Instruments, combined annual sales growth has averaged nearly 16.8 percent per year. Within this group of companies, jobs have increased annually from about 7.5 percent in 1963 to almost 18 percent by 1969.[13]

Multi-industry corporations now compete with many business rivals in hundreds of different industrial classifications. For example, synthetic fibers came from the chemical industry, not from the textile industry. High-speed ground transportation is now as much the domain of the aerospace and electrical manufacturing industries as it is that of the automotive and railroad industries. Instant photography (the Polaroid camera) was not developed by the photographic industry. Electrostatic copying came from outside the conventional office equipment industry.

Large research and development divisions speed the flow of new innovations into industries, products, and consumers' living patterns. Technology is a powerful stimulant to economic growth. It has touched and altered the society it has served.

A Market Economy

In our market economy consumers play a central role in determining the size of GNP. Indeed, economic expansion is associated with improvements in the quality of life of or the standard of living enjoyed by consumers. This upward movement has resulted in more families enjoying the benefits of higher family income and in a general upgrading of standards of living. Consumer purchasing power, which expands along with an increasing GNP, determines the relative capability of a population to maintain health, safety, and the acquisition of a prerequisite life style.

Our affluent society has been made possible by a near tripling of family income between the years 1952 and 1972. During this period median money income for families increased from $3,890 to $11,120, reflecting an average annual rate of increase of 5.4 percent in current dollar terms. The gains at the higher income levels are also responsible for our affluent life style. In 1952, about 5 percent of all families had incomes of $15,000 or more; by 1972, the comparable percentage level had reached 30 percent.[14]

Personal consumption expenditures totaled $829 billion by the fourth quarter of 1973. The sales of expensive consumer products designed to express affluence in homes, furniture, transportation, entertainment, and clothing continued to grow in conjunction with the economy. As Figure 1-11 suggests, total spending climbed sharply between the years 1965 and 1973. Unfortunately, inflationary pressures were responsible for the growing gap between total spending and the real GNP. In relative terms, the consumer made measurable improvements in his living standard. In the opinion of many, the consumer improved his quality of life as he enjoyed higher income and more material goods. Robert Lampman's study revealed a real per capita consumption gain of 37 percent between the years 1947 and 1962. He concluded, ". . . the pattern of growth in the United States in the post war years yielded benefits to individuals far in excess of the costs it required of them. To that extent, our material progress had had humane content."[15]

DOES GNP MEASURE SOCIAL COSTS?

GNP is not accepted by everyone as an index of life quality. Social critics argue that GNP measures aggregate economic power, while many social problems are caused by relative distribution of America's wealth. Those persons lacking valuable job skills, those unable to work, those who are disadvantaged and unable to command a share in the total economic gains are locked out of the system. Urban ghettos, Indian reservations, migrant worker camps, and ravaged strip mine regions of Appalachia are reminders that affluence has not filtered through to the lowest income levels in the United States.

To the environmentalists GNP may be viewed as a symbol of myopic economic expansion; if pollution is to be eventually controlled, man-determined limits to the more destructive types of economic expansion are necessary even at the expense of some forms of commercial and consumer behavior. Legislation to establish pollution standards, methods for monitoring the system, and enforcement of existing standards represent self-determined limits on behavior. But pollution and conservation measures often add to the costs of doing business.

The more suddenly an imposed environmental control standard is

FIGURE 1-11   Demand and Production

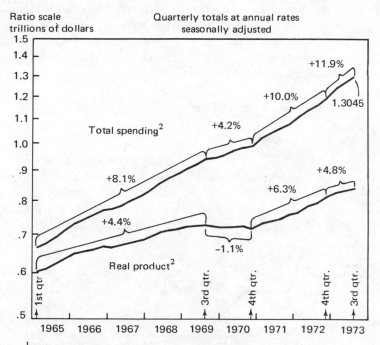

Ratio scale
trillions of dollars

Quarterly totals at annual rates
seasonally adjusted

[1]GNP in current dollars.
[2]GNP in 1958 dollars.
Percentages are annual rates of change between periods indicated.
Latest data plotted: 3rd quarter

Source: Reprinted from Gerald P. Dwyer, Jr. "Economic Slowdown: Demand or Supply Induced?" *Review* Vol. 56, No. 5 (May 1974) Federal Reserve Bank of St. Louis.

applied to industry, the more costly are the adjustments in technological techniques employed in factories and processing centers. Emission add-ons to existing processes and technological equipment are not final solutions to pollution control. While they are helpful as a first step toward bringing industrial processing in line with the environment standards, a more promising means of controlling pollution lies in the design and construction of production equipment that possesses built-in efficiencies that emit very low levels of pollutants. Here, such equipment not only becomes desirable in meeting pollution standards, but becomes even more productive than the last generation of technological techniques. But again, cost factors must be analyzed. From Figure 1-12, one may note that predetermined environmental pollution standards for automobile emissions become more costly as the air quality tolerances narrow. There are considerable differences of opinion about "safe" or "desirable" levels of air quality. Unless industry is challenged by emission standards, improvements in control techniques lag. On the other hand, as emission controls grow stricter and approach zero, industry costs rise sharply. It is becoming apparent that major reductions in automobile emissions will be developed from new improvements in engine function rather than from add-ons that compensate for "dirty" combustion characteristics of most motors used by today's motorists.

FIGURE 1-12   What It Costs to Approach Zero

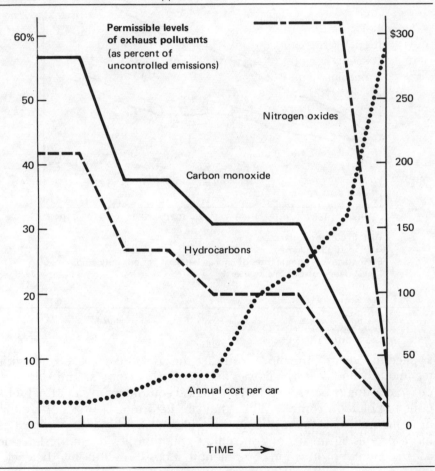

Federal standards for automotive emissions have grown stricter by stages since the first ones were put into effect back in 1968. Meanwhile, the costs of achieving them have risen more steeply for succeeding reductions in emissions levels. The first pollution-control measures achieved dramatic reductions for very little money.

  The costs charted here are derived from estimates by the industry and the National Academy of Sciences of total yearly operating expenses, plus amortized capital costs. Expenses include additional gas consumption—the costs of which are probably understated.

Source: Tom Cardamone for *Fortune Magazine, June, 1973*, pp. 120–21. Reprinted by permission.

Full-Cost Pricing Policies?

America's economic growth patterns following World War II were subsidized by abuses to the environment and by oversubscriptions of low-
priced raw materials. Products flowing into the nation's markets are
traditionally priced below their full costs. Artificially low prices fostered
careless exploitation of our air, water, and land. Dumping toxins, ash,
garbage, and solid wastes into these natural resources helped to intensify
the environmental problem.

Commercial deposits of ores, for example, occur in concentrated
veins. When treated, processed, shipped, consumed, and discarded, these
same metals and minerals become dispersed in minute quantities into the
environment. While the minute concentrations of the more toxic substances pose environmental hazards, these small dispersed elements have
little commercial value in relation to their recovery from the air, water,
and soil. G. Evelyn Hutchison comments on this relationship concerning
phosphorus.

> Among the numerous things that should be done to clean up our
> inland waters is a systematic attempt to prevent high concentrations
> (high here means over one part of phosphorous in 10 million of
> water) of phosphate or other assimilable phosphorus from entering
> our lakes and rivers, where it produces excessive algae growth and
> consequently unpleasant and unhealthy conditions. Ideally, trapping
> this phosphorus by at least one of two apparently feasible methods
> represents also the conservation of an essential resource. Unfortu-
> nately, with a considerable reserve of easily available phosphate in the
> United States, these recovery processes are not economically self-
> supporting, though highly desirable. They have to be subsidized if
> their ultimate benefits are to be enjoyed.
>
> The same sorts of difficulty will crop up whenever applied ecology
> is being directed to preserve for our use any large segment of our
> essentially continuous environment, be it air, inland waters, the ocean
> or the mantle of living beings.[16]

Extracting and processing ores, fibers, plastics, and wood damaged
the ecosystem in many regions. As a result, corrective work in these areas
is badly needed. In Appalachia and in the coal fields of Kentucky and
southern Illinois badly torn-up landscapes are common sights. Little
effective rehabilitation of these lands is evidenced.

Is Zero Growth Better?

If the prices paid for products covered all costs, including ecological, and
allowed for efficient recovery of discarded material, conservation practices would become an essential factor in our economic system. This
would allow for a growth rate that not only repairs the nation's infrastructure (maintenance services), but also prevents costly waste products from
polluting the environment as the economy expands. Combined with tax

incentives to improve productive techniques, this pay-as-you-go economy is pictured as progressive and growth-oriented. Economist point to the pricing mechanism as one way to obtain continued (through less rapid) economic growth and to reduce external diseconomy. (An external diseconomy occurs when a unit confers real costs upon other producers or consumers for which it is not charged.)

Economists argue that zero-growth economic systems leave little revenue and profit incentives to stimulate desirable social and environmental innovations. This suggests, too, that an economy with no growth would heighten social conflict between the wealthy and the impoverished. An economy that expands within the framework of external economies (i.e. controlled growth) offers the nation the best hope for avoiding an environmental crisis. This aproach is viewed as less disruptive to the economy, as long as prices are allowed to adjust to higher levels over long time periods.

Conservation practices and life-style adjustments to resource short-falls prevent runaway inflation. Environmentalists, while encouraged over the prospects of obtaining more responsive growth through full-cost pricing, are quick to point out that this method is slow and subject to political lobbying. Likewise, the pricing mechanism does not function well within the context of broad social-environmental issues. Our willingness to assign a price in conjunction with such issues as open space, wildlife habitat, wilderness preserves, clean air and water, and compatible social-economic developments within the private sector has customarily lagged behind traditional profit standards.

Case 1
Floods, Flood Plains, and Developments

Approximately 250 engineers, city planners, and environmentalists recently convened in Washington, D.C., at the National Conference on Flood Plain Management. Heralded as "a highly important event in the evolution of rational understanding of flood plains management problems," the conference sponsored by a group of private and national organizations provided a review of data and trends pertaining to flood plains management, policy, and legislative initiatives.

Flood plains play an especially important role in the ecosystem; along the long ribbons of waterways which cross our nation we find large areas of flat, fertile land which provides food and habitats for both wildlife and

Conservation News, Vol. 39, No. 17 (September 3, 1974) p. 7. An Educational Service of the National Wildlife Federation.

mankind. Flood plains are high-yield agricultural regions where climate and terrain permit farming. Marshes, swamps, lakes, and bayous give vital feeding and nesting grounds to numerous species of foul, fish, and fur-bearing animals. In cyclical fashion the streams flood across these adjacent lands, often causing substantial economic damage to crops and settlements.

Because of profitable agricultural operations, farmers living and working on flood plains have appealed to the government for protective levees. In addition, drainage projects lower the water tables in the fields and open up new acreage for cultivation. On the heels of drainage and flood control projects come suburbs, towns, factories, roads, and a host of facilitating investments. In many respects, builders fail to provide for special drainage requirements in these low-lying regions; sewers, storm drainage facilities, and dikes often malfunction, leaving homeowners in localized drainage nightmares.

Occasionally, devastating rain cycles force streams over the large protective levees built by the U.S. Army Corps of Engineers. These floods repeat themselves more often than most flood victims would care to remember. Late winter and spring rains are especially difficult to control because of the fast run-off conditions of exposed cultivated fields. In the natural state, the many varieties of vegetation, absorbant root systems, and myriads of small marshes and empoundments prevented flash flood conditions along many streams (especially in the midwest).

Since navigation represents one additional use of waterways, flood control is combined with channel improvements; in deepening and straightening navigable streams, further disruptions are noticed. When streams have been deepened to create a shipping channel, a surge of high water rushes downstream at much faster rates. This tends to force peak crests much sooner downstream. Flooding is held down when natural stream banks wander along, holding back great volumes of new flood water until streams downstream have the opportunity to empty out local watersheds.

At the National Conference on Flood Plains Management (Mid-year 1974) three major issues highlighted the symposium: (1) the need to consider flood plain management as a rational approach to land use; (2) the need to consider flood plain management as an economically and environmentally effective alternative to structural measures in flood control and water resource development programs; (3) the need for strengthened statutes and regulations to more clearly define and develop flood control programs. The symposium further called for strong state and local involvement in flood plain management. Structural control installations along our nation's streams cannot be expected to provide total protection against floods. The problem of minimizing flood losses involves zoning out developments and practices which are incompatible with high-risk flood plains and ecological balances. The most important idea coming out of the conference was the recognition that to effectively deal with the management of flood plains, we must come to recognize that flooding is a natural phenomenon, but that flood damage is not caused by an act of God but by acts of man.

Case 2
Boca Raton: Closing the Gate

During the November, 1972 elections, voters approved one of modern America's most revolutionary means to slow growth. But by measures commonly applied to urban change, this polished Florida east coast city of proud past and vibrant future has undergone a set of changes some say defies traditional timetables.

The reason, they say, is the city's pioneering growth cap itself. Never before has a city set an upper limit on the homes it would have. When Boca Raton set its limit at 40,000 homes, the decree was publicized nationwide and—as might have been expected, but wasn't—Boca Raton began growing like few cities have ever grown before.

"There seems to be a change in expressions when people come into the office or write," explains Chamber of Commerce Executive Vice President F. C. (Bud) Stewart. "They tell us they can't take it any longer where they are now, and that they want to come here before the door closes."

It's estimated that 32,000 persons lived in Palm Beach County's southern-most city in November 1972. The citizenry now numbers 45,000. And building permits during 1973, despite lengthy construction moratoriums, increased by roughly 50 percent from the year before.

"Normally, I think 20 percent is considered a high rate of growth. And even 15 percent is considered rather sporty," says City Manager William Law. "In a way, the community has suffered, growing at such an accelerated rate. We've compressed all the needs, all the pressures and all the politics into such a short period of time."

Law himself could be termed a growth cap result. Councilmen late in 1972 fired the old city manager of six years, saying he was too small-town and folksy. They hired Law in his place, paying the veteran administrator a $32,000 salary, seldom equaled by Florida public servants.

City fathers late in 1973 dedicated a multi-million dollar sewage treatment plant, a requirement for any burgeoning population, but better than any other in the area for treatment quality.

The plant was partly the result of the city's sweeping awareness of its own environment, evident also in the most energetic beachfront shopping spree by any city in history.

Conservation News, Vol. 39, No. 3 (February 1, 1974) pp. 8–130.

Voters overwhelmingly approved a $7 million bond issue for 32 acres of beachfront in April, upping their total tax bill for beaches to $13.5 million since 1966. Such expense would have satisfied most beachgoers for decades. But in Boca Raton, spurred by the same high-rise paranoia that prompted the growth cap, voters returned to the polls last December to okay another $19.4 million for 70 acres.

The purchase—totaling $400 over 10 years for the average homeowner—startled the country, sending park officials from Maine to California to their file drawers in search of a more expensive beach buy. Each returned with the same answer: no city, county, or state in history had ever spent more to assure access to the ocean.

"It takes my breath away," gasped California Park Acquisition Director Lester McCargo, who listed his state's major accomplishment as an $8 million buy underway at Huntington Beach. In Oregon, Park Land Supervisor Raymond Wilson said his beach buys collectively didn't even reach $19.4 million. And in Florida, the largest state purchase was $15.2 million for 243 acres last year in Broward County.

Again, Boca Raton had earned a national spotlight.

Probably the best example of how this city has matured beyond its years, however, can be learned from dozens of contented real estate brokers.

"It's hard to find a decent residential lot anymore for less than $15,000," said realtor Stephen Bodzo. "And as for houses, I built some for $19,000 in 1962 that are going now for $50,000."

The demand for homes has transformed the average $30,000 house into a $40,000 house almost overnight, realtors agree. The average house sale netted $47,000 for its owner during 1973, and the average lot doubled in price to at least $10,000.

"It's a seller's market in this city, not a buyer's market. A guy selling chicken coops make a killing," says Bob Hutsler, one of only a few builders who'll talk publicly of the growth cap's blessings upon the construction industry. Most others insist only that the cap has brought doom for their profit potential.

What prompted the growth cap and its resulting frenzy—setting Boca Raton as so exlusionary that even the planning board chairman sought cheaper housing elsewhere—was a small band of quite average citizens, adamant that the city wasn't moving fast enough to rezone Boca Raton against overpopulation.

Movement leaders listed membership in either the Citizens for Reasonable Growth, an organization of mostly retirees determined to keep Boca Raton's single-family character, or the conservation committee of the 450-member Royal Palm Audubon Society.

An initial victory had been scored in March 1972 when only one of five councilmen, Mayor Norman Wymbs, opposed rezoning to permit housing for 30,000 along the city's western limits. Residents easily collected 6,000 signatures, a city charter requirement to overturn council action.

It hadn't been uncommon in Florida communities for residents to talk about strict antidensity measures. The difference in Boca Raton, insuranceman Wymbs explained afterward, is the city's unique amalgam of well-heeled retirees, students, and professors at Florida Atlantic University, and engineers at the local IBM plant, the city's largest employer.

"The FAU people can spend time thinking. And the IBM people live and work in the community all 'day long, so they see the problems," Wymbs said.

"A high percentage of the others have fled from Fort Lauderdale, Miami, and other points south. After living here awhile, they discovered that the town they saw and bought in wouldn't be the same in 20 years. So they revolted."

Arvida Corp., the city's largest landholder, said after the rezoning defeat they'd return with a compromise request. But before they could, the council imposed a 60-day rezoning moratorium.

The conservationist forces anticipated tougher building restrictions during the interim, "but when we saw nothing happening, we went to the streets," explained Richard Mayo, a retired army general who leads Citizens for Reasonable Growth.

"We felt if we could get a charter referendum (the growth cap), then the lands would have to be rezoned."

Members of the Audubon Society, meeting over kitchen tables late into the evenings, pooled social and environmental data to agree that the growth cap should be set at 40,000 living units. Zoning at the time would have allowed about 62,000 homes for an ultimate population of about 160,000—compared to the 105,000 conservationists sought.

As expected, it was Wymbs who made the council motion for a charter growth cap. And also as expected, the motion didn't receive a second. "We agree with your goal, but . . . " came the refrain to be heard time and again in months ahead.

Clipboards in hand, the conservationists again flocked to the supermarkets in search of signatures. "If you want low density, sign here" was their pitch. And signatures came easy, prompting the November election in which 58 percent of the electorate voted their city into the land planning history books.

"You have to realize that every one of us is motivated by self-interest," Wymbs explained in another postelection analysis. "And everyone's self-interest starts with his home.

"Oh, we can cover up that self interest with all kinds of explanations. We talk about the environment, but what's that?" he asked.

"A man's environment is his home, or possibly his business. In this city, thank goodness, we've got more folks concerned about their homes."

In the months that followed, no resident of the city escaped the bitter polarization which pitted neighbor against neighbor.

So the growth cap could become reality, the city's planning board desperately started slashing away at densities. Half the city had already been developed, so planners had to cut densities allowed on vacant property by 55 percent. Private golfcourses were also rezoned for permanent recreational usage, and zoning classes on individual parcels of land were switched.

For some the result has been financially devastating.

The Ben Brace family, for example, moved to Florida six years ago to invest their life savings in a 12-unit apartment building. To help meet the growth cap, planners rezoned their property to allow only five units. As a result, the Braces can't remodel their building or replace it if it's destroyed by fire or hurricane.

Jack Willits, head of a major development firm, spent $8 million toward a 27-acre oceanfront condominium project. His investment was totally geared toward property allowing 810 housing units before the growth cap. Only 365 units were allowed after the new density ordinances.

"We have neither sought to contravene what we consider your good and sound density and zoning plan," Willits wrote the council, "nor have we threatened the city or individual members of the council with litigation. However, our patience and our pocketbook have worn thin."

Other developers were more poignant. Three court suits, including one by Arvida, have been filed to declare the growth cap as unconstitutional.

"People who voted for the cap were saying. 'I voted this way because I remember 12 years ago to when this was a tiny town.' " explained Jack Dimond, an angry Arvida vice president. "Well, that attitude is selfish, it's not morally supportable. I wonder how this can be squared with the U.S. Constitution, which provides people the right to live wherever they choose."

"The segment who can afford to buy here must be diminished. Are there that many fat cats left who can come down from Cleveland and live in this type of community?" he continued.

"The conservationist leadership is gaining results at the exclusionary end of the spectrum. They're appealing to a basic human motive—I've got my toehold in heaven, so close the gate."

Court hearing dates were postponed until 1974, giving the council desperately needed time to justify the 40,000 figure as something other than arbitrary. Councilmen gave the $100,000 job to a Califorina consulting firm—an action backed by, of all people, the Audubon members who decided on the figure in the first place.

"Now, as I think back to the formulation of the cap, the referendum movement, the democratic participation on the part of many people, one of the things we were accused of was being rank amateurs," Audubon member Roy Thompson confessed to councilmen the night in July when the growth study was ordered.

"We were told we were backyard barbecue people, that we were kitchen-table people," he continued.

"Well, we do reconize that we were amateurs. We were amateurs trying to set a community's designed policy. We were trying to get a handle on what the ultimate size and population of Boca Raton would be."

The planning board, since November 1972, has reshaped the city to about 44,000 housing units, or about 4,000 short of its required goal.

City officials, including the city attorney, say any more density cuts would certainly doom the growth cap to court defeat. The remaining units, they say, will be whittled away by attrition and future municipal park purchases. The $19.4 million bond issue, for example, eliminated 1,100 potential living units.

And while the experts deal with numbers and statistics, the residents of Boca Raton have struggled to stamp out the bitter feelings in their city.

Voters refused to return Wymbs to office, naming as their new mayor the soft-spoken and folksy city manager who'd been ousted several months before. Arvida also shipped Dimond out of town, replacing him with a seasoned executive who politely says "no comment" when reporters call.

A majority of the city's armchair judges have already ruled that the growth cap will be stricken from the city charter, primarily because it was placed there with more emotion than basis of fact.

But the density ordinances may still stand, they say, because property owners may have to sue, saying how the ordinances have hurt them individually.

"But even if Boca Raton loses the court suits tomorrow, it's been clearly established that we want a low-density, basically single-family community," says City Manager Law, pointing to development after development that's already been built under the new density limits.

"We're going to achieve the goal this city wants—what these folks in favor of the growth cap wanted is going to happen. There's no question about it."

TOPIC QUESTIONS

1. Why are exponential growth rates illusionary?
2. Is technology a substitute for diminishing finite resources?
3. What role does behavior modification play in avoiding an environmental crisis?
4. Is zero oconomic growth well suited for a society with a richly developed market economy?
5. Should convenience remain a primary market goal for our distribution system?
6. Is the Full Employment Act of 1946 incompatible with the Growth-within-limits proponents?

7. Why are many social issues not readily resolved by advancing scientific and technological innovations?
8. Has the "green revolution" completely discredited the Malthusian thesis?

Case 1

9. How do economic growth patterns crowd in on flood plains?
10. Should a community value a marshland as a resource or should the land be drained and a shopping center built in its place? What values should be considered in making the choice?
11. How does nature "backlash" against channel improvements and stream structures?
12. Should water resources be viewed in the context of long-range land use plans? Discuss.

Case 2

13. What are the major issues in the Boca Raton Case?
14. Do you agree with the "citizen movement" that was influential in getting a growth cap placed on the city? Why, or why not?
15. What is the environment in this case and how did it figure in the growth issues?
16. Has the growth cap doomed the city to zero growth in the future? Discuss.

RECOMMENDED READINGS

Robert Dorfman and Nancy S. Dorfman, eds., *Economics of the Environment* (New York: Norton, 1972).

Robert E. Will and Harold G. Vatter, *Poverty In Affluence,* 2nd ed. (New York: Harcourt Brace Jovanovich, 1970).

Mancur Olson and Hans H. Landsberg, eds., *The No Growth Society* (New York: Norton, 1973).

Richard T. Gill, *Economics,* 2nd ed. (Pacific Palisades, Calif.: Goodyear, 1975). Part 4.

Paul W. Barkley and David W. Seckler, *Economic Growth and Environmental Decay* (New York: Harcourt Brace Jovanovich, 1972).

FOOTNOTES

1. Jack E. Ravan, *The Challenge of Land Pollution* (Atlanta: Proceedings, Keep America Beautiful, Inc., Southern Regional Conference, Sept. 14, 1972), p. 1.
2. See Alvin Toffler, *Future Shock* (New York: Bantam Books, Inc., 1971).
3. *More? The Interfaces between Population, Economic Growth, and the Environment* (Washington, D.C.: League of Women's Voters Education Fund Publication, 1972), p. 18.

4. See Harrison Brown, James Bonner, and John Weir, *The Next Hundred Years* (New York: Viking Press, 1957). Also, Walter W. Heller, "Economic Growth and Ecology—An Economist's View," *Monthly Labor Review*, Reprint No. 2769 (November 1971). He points to the possible commercialization of fusion power: "One gallon of water would give us the energy we now get from seven gallons of crude oil."

5. *Toward Balanced Growth: Quantity with Quality* (Washington, D.C: National Goals Research Staff, 1970), p. 118.

6. Harry V. Warren and E. F. Wilks, *World Resource Production: 50 Years of Change* (Vancouver: Tantalus Research Limited, 1966). The authors conclude that per capita availability of corn and rice, for example, were less in 1945 (130 production pounds per person) than in 1910 (143 production pounds per person). The so-called green revolution, with its emphasis on plant research, chemical fertilizers, and high-capacity capital equipment, has more than out-stripped population growth in the post–World War II years. There are now growing concerns that continued world population growth has begun to reach present world production capabilities for raising food.

7. One of the more optimistic utopians, R. Buckminster Fuller, viewed the future in terms of a "one town world" without pollution or resource shortages before an audience at the fall seminar entitled "Shaping the Environment" on the Edwardsville campus of Southern Illinois University, 1973.

8. Norman N. Bowsher, "1973—A Year of Inflation," *Review* 55, 12, (December 1973): 2–11.

9. *Toward Balanced Growth: Quantity with Quality*, op. cit.

10. *More? The Interfaces between Population, Economic Growth, and the Environment*, op. cit., p. 7.

11. See Richard T. Gill, *Economics* (Pacific Palisades, Calif: Goodyear Publishing Company, 1973), pp. 729–44.

12. Donella H. Meadows, Dennis L. Meadows, Jorgen Randers, and William W. Behrens, III, *The Limits to Growth* (New York: Universe Books, 1972), p. 150.

13. Donald L. Perry, *A Survey of State Technical and Business Assistance Programs* (Springfield, Ill.: Illinois Commission on Technological Progress, 1969), pp. 10 –14.

14. Data for family income and GNP were derived from *Consumer Income* (Washington, D.C.: U.S. Department of Commerce, December 1973), and *Survey of Current Business*, Vol. 54, No. 1, (Washington, D.C.: U.S. Department of Commerce, January 1974).

15. Robert J. Lampman, "Recent U.S. Economic Growth and the Gains in Human Welfare," *Perspectives on Economic Growth*, (New York: Random House, Walter W. Heller, ed., 1968), pp. 143–62.

16. G. Evelyn Hutchinson, "Ecological Biology in Relation to the Maintenance and Improvement of the Human Environment," *Applied Science and Technological Progress* (Washington, D.C.: National Academy of Sciences, 1967), p. 176.

CHAPTER TWO

CONSUMERS

AND LIFE-STYLE

STRATEGIES

LIFE-STYLE INTERPRETATION

An abundance of natural resources, a vigorous market economy, advanced technology, and systems-oriented business skills sparked our nation's economic growth. To many persons and families who share the economic gains, the American dream of the good life and its material horn of plenty is largely fulfilled. In the wake of social-economic preoccupation with materialism and its role in life-style interpretation, values, self-esteem, and status, the American dream is questioned increasingly by an ever-widening circle of subcultures and professional groups. While most of the marketing projections into the 1980s view the future in terms of increased sophistication, income, leisure time, material plenty, education for all, and the hint that we have entered an era that promises opulence, a growing undercurrent of doubt and disillusionment with this view has crystallized.

Perhaps, in our preoccupation with materialism we have placed far too much emphasis on psychological life style imagery and fantasizing in marketing many categories of consumer goods and services. This tendency to relate success, happiness, status, sex appeal, youthful ways, acceptance of change, and peer group approval to products, brands, services and corporations has led us toward what may be termed as an "unreal world" filled with "unreal people".[1]

The advent of the environmental movement and the sudden impact of raw material shortfalls on consumer products have given us new impetus for reflection; we live in a finite world with mutually interacting forces that hold mankind, in the final analysis, fully responsible for resource depletion, waste, and pollution.

ARE WE DEPENDENT ON THE INTERNATIONAL MARKET?

Are we dependent on this worldwide system of trade for the minerals, metals, food, fibers, and rare earths to keep factories in operation? As the world's largest waste disposal unit, we share a great responsibility to sustain the planet's ecosystem. If the futures of the industrialized nations are interwoven into the political fabric of raw material producing, under-developed countries, it would be misleading to view natural resources, whether renewable or nonrenewable, in terms of absolute world reserves.[2]

A much more meaningful picture of raw materials for the remainder of this century is considered in terms of accessibility. An affluent society such as ours can deplete large concentrations of ores in the world resource inventories. On the world market the U.S. actively bids on large quantities of raw materials that eventually flow into industry and homes. Inflation and shortages are important symptoms of exponential growth strains on the world supply of accessible minerals, foods, fibers, and energy. We should be concerned with the supply dimensions of natural resources as well as with their end use and market side. A market economy establishes quantity and quality dimensions of resource and product use that, in turn, establish demand requirements for raw materials. Hence, marketing is at the forefront of societal trade-off decisions that determine not only our economic future, but the kind of world community that controls the flow of raw materials to international markets.

AFFLUENCE AND MARKETING MANAGEMENT

In an affluent society, consumer spending plays a vital role in the economy. Although our population increased by only 13 percent during the 1960s, demand for goods and services advanced by 60 percent for the same period. New homes, automobiles, furniture, appliances, recreation vehicles, college educations, and a variety of services reflected this strong increase in market demand.

To satisfy market demand business extracts, processes, fabricates, molds, and finishes raw materials into final products. A seemingly endless quantity and variety of product choices flow into consumer markets. Raw materials are the "grist for the mill" that feed industrial processes. Indeed, "raw materials are regarded as fuel for the full-employment machine".[3]

Affluent Society: A Definition

Affluence and life-style choices invariably shape the nation's inventory of goods and services that consumers purchase. To this extent marketing delivers the product-services mix in context with consumer-desired standards of living. Marketing's responsibility to provide society with prerequisite goods in the context of psychological, sociological, economic, and physiological requirements is both complex and difficult to carry out on a macro-marketing basis. The countless individual product decisions of firms, consumers, and society make up the total distribution mix; here, deficiencies within the system when viewed in broad perspective often appear to be glaring. That is why critics of advertising techniques, stylized product obsolescence, pricing strategies, and consumer wastes have found fertile fields within which to journalize about practices of individual firms, products, brands, and services.

In the process of satisfying individual markets, segments, and micro-segments, firms have often not considered the total result of specific product decisions. The affluent society has deepened and complicated the responsibilities of marketing; the rich scientific, technological, and specialized aspects of our industrial base have served to dramatically increase the costs and consequences of product mistakes. Hence, the rising potency for injury or death in the use of chemicals, electrical appliances, toys, automobiles, barbiturates, patent medicines by uninformed consumers has focused national attention on marketing practices. Because an affluent society measures success, satisfaction, self-esteem, values, and behavior by standards increasingly intangible and, thus, more difficult to define, the roles of both marketers and consumers have become more difficult.

The relationship between an affluent market demand and product choices is described by Philip Kotler:

> An affluent society can be said to exist when a substantial number of persons have a surplus of money over basic biological needs and they constitute a considerable market for goods and services that cater to psychological, social, and cultural needs and desires. While such a society may still contain pockets of poverty and therefore not qualify as an opulent society, a large number of its people have been freed from the need to spend all their waking hours in work and are able to engage in activities of self-expression and community service.[4]

Within the affluent society consumer behavior is influenced increasingly by psychologically derived utility or value. Here, buying motives may be viewed as segmented, ". . . in terms of behavioral variables rather than consumer use or consumer demographic characteristics."[5] In conjunction with these abstract purchase decision variables, branded products are linked through advertising with "images" and "symbols"; these, in turn, are interwoven with the very fabric of life-style situations, human recognition, and interactions. Belonging psychologically to peer groups may be expressed in terms of acquired products, brands, services or in the context of an atmosphere within which a purchase transaction takes place (such as in a prestigious restaurant). Trading up to higher quality and higher-priced brands has long been linked to human needs concerning belonging to groups that are emulated by others. Through advertising, scenarios of perceived characteristics and situations depict product enjoyment by youthful, gregarious, sophisticated, opulent, and synthetically admired trend setters.

Advertising has been accused by its critics of resorting to life-style interpretation and manipulation of consumer wants in order to exaggerate a product's importance in an individual (or group) assortment of prerequisite goods and services. Quite simply, marketing's cultivation of psychologically derived intangibles stimulates consumer purchase behavior, which in turn leads to questionable duplication and waste of natural resources. As marketers seek to incorporate societal aspects into marketing strategies, the need to modify the marketing mix to avoid blatant fantasizing and life-style fabrication will become more desirable. Unfortunately, where a great deal of confusion exists concerning values, satisfaction, life patterns, and self-esteem, the task of incorporating societal inputs into the marketing processes will be a difficult task.

Consumerism As a Way of Life
In the complex world of change and changing value interpretations, marketing functions within a growth environment need to provide for a systematic means of resolving consumer difficulties. Economic progress has consisted largely of finding more efficient ways of matching heterogeneous supply with heterogeneous demand. Within this framework of growth of heterogeneous wants and of psychological attributes associated with branded products, marketing holds not only an important economic role in American affluent society, but also is considered by many as having a manipulative capability to alter consumer behavior—indeed, perhaps altering or influencing life style.[6]

Consumer backlashes to marketing's implied manipulative role of taste counselors have sparked the consumerism movement, with Ralph Nader as its symbolic head. Consumer safety, product quality, service, and price and communication deficiencies are considered important concerns by the consumerism movement.[7] When products are so closely identified with life style and its manifestations—fads, fashions, and short-lived psychological attachments—their utilities are prematurely destroyed. In the case of paper disposal, the temporary life is mourned by no one, except perhaps the processors of solid wastes; but in the instances of durable goods—automobiles, appliances, lawn equipment, and miscellaneous motorized "gadgets"—shortened product life produces growing burdens on the nation's natural resources.

Environmentalists have expressed concern over the waste-making, obsolescence-prone philosophy of business. If marketing does not consider the implications of product design, material choices, and mix in conjunction with the ecology and natural resource utilization, the results may be a coalition of consumer and government forces versus industry, which could lead to expanded federal regulations for industry.[8] Whereas the 1960s produced an emphasis on managerial systems for improved marketing efficiency, the 1970s are important for the developing of societal emphases in our distribution ideologies. Kotler and Levy suggest that

> The resolution of the contemporary issues of consumerism, social responsibilities, and marketing ethics is probably the most crucial task facing marketing in the decades ahead. Progress in these areas is essential if the competitive marketing system is to survive at all.[9]

Our concern for marketing behavior should extend beyond sales volume, goals, profits, mix selections, and psychological sell. However efficient and complete our system may be, our distribution concepts have neglected long-term associations with the total environment. Consumers have often become the object of marketing plans rather than the source of product ideas, features, and viewpoints. We have become so preoccupied with individual product plans and strategies that we have tended to neglect the disturbing macroeconomic trends that environmentalists suggest are leading our nation into major resource shortages and into a continuing build-up of pollution levels. Figures 2-1 and 2-2 depict the effect this has had on the environment.

A Need: The Reverse Channel

Higher sales are also linked to higher discharges of gases, liquids, and solid wastes into the ecosphere. "At the same time that waste increases, resources shrink. About 25 tons of minerals were taken from the earth and processed [in 1969] to support each American."[10] The Environmental Protection Agency referred to our consumption habits as indicative of a ". . . use-it-once, throw-it-away society. . . ."[11] Products once destined for the market, later consumed, become solid wastes. Our annual throwaways total 71 billion cans, 38 billion bottles and jars, 4 million tons of plastics, 7.6 million television sets, 7 million cars and trucks, and 35

FIGURE 2-1

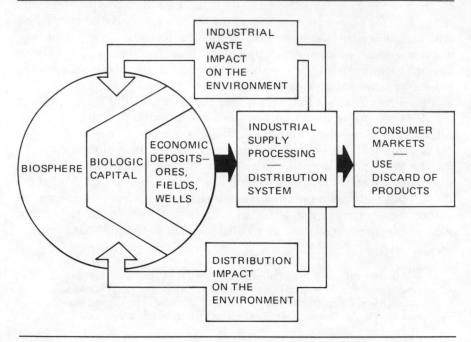

Wastes enter the environment from two primary sources. Industrial and distribution wastes are widespread pollution sources which threaten to disrupt the ecosystem and pollute the environment. Mankind has traditionally relied on natural filtration processes to dispose of economic wastes, but as the volume of wastes grow and their toxic properties become more dangerous, natural filtration processes are overwhelmed.

million tons of paper. To rid ourselves of these and an avalanche of other wastes, we spend more than $4 billion annually. Since most of the once glimmering products, packages, and other material end up in municipal dumps, their value as resources likewise end. While to some, the distribution processes are concluded once consumers purchase, consume, and discard products, others see the system eventually developing into a circular return mechanism. William G. Zikmund and William J. Stanton suggest that solid wastes are a "channels of distribution problem."

> The escalation of public concern over environmental issues has, to an increasing extent, led government officials, business leaders, and conservationalists to seek a solution to the problem of solid-waste pollution. One ecologically desirable technique for the disposal of trash is recycling. Simply stated, recycling consists of finding new ways of using previously discarded materials.
>
> The recycling of solid wastes is being recognized as a tenable solution to cleaning up the cluttered environment. Scientists view recycling as a substitute for the declining supply of natural resources. Technology has responded to the recent interest in recycling with

many new and sophisticated techniques capable of turning solid wastes into basic raw materials.

Although science and technological innovations are necessary aspects of recycling, the task of alleviating solid-waste pollution may be treated as a marketing activity; that is, the marketing of garbage and other waste materials.[12]

FIGURE 2-2 Cumulative Pollution Build-up in the Environment

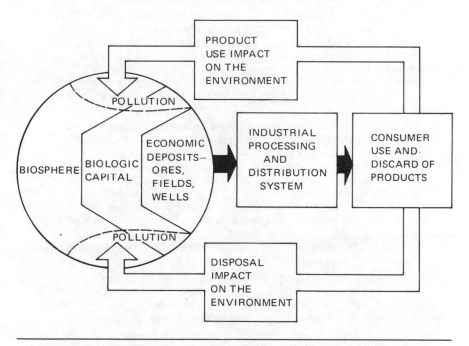

The shaded areas within the pollution zones illustrate local pockets of toxic build-up. Recycling and reclamation are two steps that can be taken to reduce industrial and distribution waste loads.

An affluent society, with life-style choices calling for heterogeneous consumption patterns with materialistic acquisitions as the focal point of self-esteem, has found that *material disposition* becomes a necessary prerequisite for basic maintenance and pollution control. Marketing's influence on the affluent society reaches from transactions involving the distribution of commodities, ores, fibers, and minerals to processors, fabricators, and millers. These basic resources become the raw material that constitutes the product and service mix that flows to the consumer markets. Marketing's choices of materials and ingredients determine the extent of demands made on our raw materials. The design, function, and perceived use of products within the context of life styles are reflected in marketing plans and strategies.

Collective Goods Are Private Goods?

Perhaps one of the major stumbling blocks on the road toward a more complete integration of broader societal issues with marketing is not the profit motive per se, but the confusion arising from evaluation processes of society and its individual sectors, in which values pertaining to collective "goods" and "bads" collide increasingly with private "goods" and "bads."

> Most consumer goods and services in any economy are, or eventually become, private goods. Such private goods may be used by only one person at a time. Their use is competitive—either you use them or I use them. Some goods, however, are not competitive in use. Two or more people can simultaneously use them. Indeed, some of these goods may be used simultaneously by a large number of people without diminishing the supply of the good. They are called collective goods.
>
> A common example of a collective good is a lighthouse. Once it is operating, a great many ships can use the service of the lighthouse without in any way affecting the quantity or quality of warning available to the others. Rare species of plants and animals are also collective goods. The same number of whooping cranes can simultaneously satisfy the demands of large numbers of people who want the cranes preserved. Reception of radio and TV signals is a collective good since any number of persons can tune in without forcing anyone else to tune out. A scenic view can be shared by a great many people without diminishing the supply to any one individual.
>
> There are also collective "bads." A noxious odor can simultaneously nauseate any number of people in its vicinity. Similarly, any number can become ill because of poisons and diseases borne by the environment. An ugly building can disgust innumerable people. When a species becomes extinct, thousands mourn.[13]

In our market economy, the enjoyment of private goods in ever higher numbers and varieties has long held a position of priority over collective goods, especially those related to natural resources. Economic growth has been stimulated by this priority rating; the increased use and popularization of the automobile, for example, have been encouraged by government, business, and society alike. Now, with over 250 million automobiles, and with their near strangulation hold on numerous metropolitan centers, we have begun to consider how adversely the automobile, the highways, and the automble's facilitating amenities have affected the environment through pollution, loss of open spaces, and suburban sprawls. National and state parks have become inundated with automobiles, campers, trailers, and motor bikes; their numbers are now controlled around many of our more fragile natural attractions in the nation's park system.

Collective goods require management and protection from exploitations; biological capital provides the natural wealth on which private goods are derived from economic processes. A collective good differs from biological wealth to the extent that a collective good can also be an economic creation (such as a lighthouse). Biological wealth can be extracted, harvested, concentrated, farmed, converted, and processed. But mankind can only impair or improve on it; biological capital is not a creation of the economic system or a product of science. Our society has learned to utilize biological capital for economic ends. As such, our emphasis tends to focus on the economic rather than on the biological aspect. As the most accessible and concentrated, stocks of natural wealth become exhausted, the economic system is affected by higher transportation and processing costs.

One way of avoiding resource depletion and excessive inflationary pressures is to voluntarily reduce demand. Voluntary cooperation in such areas as conservation, recycling, civil outdoor projects (such as general clean-ups and tree plantings), and restoration of spoiled landmarks is complicated by the presence of "free riders," those who enjoy collective benefits without contributing to the group's or community's actions. The benefits from constructive projects accrue as much to the bystanders as to the participators. Since free riders do not pay their share of the costs, legislation and mandatory requirements often become necessary if a collective bad is to be avoided.

SELLING THE AFFLUENCE DREAM

For many consumers, the nation's expansions in GNP and real income have meant an improvement in the quality of life. Few persons questioned their rising living standards or expressed alarm at social and economic conditions. Surprisingly, even the race riots failed to disrupt most affluent Americans in their quest for greater material acquisitions. Happiness comes in the form of three-bedroom suburban homes with attached garages for two new automobiles; greater mobility, more labor-saving appliances, and motorized gadgetry heightens the demand for convenience. Swimming pools, more lavish vacations, outdoor lawn furnishings, informal entertainment, richly appointed home interiors, and college education for the children round out the material acquisitive search.

Country homes in quiet, scenic agricultural and recreational areas have become much-sought-for status symbols for the more opulent members of our society. Not-quite-so-expensive country lots have become available to the middle class consumers who seek quiet vacation and recreation sites. Lake, river, and shore developments are bringing suburban-spawned civilization into remote areas. Entire communities spring up almost overnight, erasing rural living scenarios that provide important green belt, food-producing, and wildlife habitats. Less scrupulous real estate promoters use mail order advertisements to lure the unwary "land investor" into a distant "ranchette," retirement home-stead, or lake-shore lot. Affluence makes it easy for the more imaginative real estate promoters to convert large tracts of former agricultural lands into sprawling developments.

The Professional Sell

Promoting and influencing the growth dream became an obsession with many professional groups and organizations during the 1960s and early 1970s. Architects, engineers, chemists, industrial associations, economic planners, and executives lobbied, promoted, lectured for, and encour-aged statewide participation in economic growth programs. All manner of interpretations of intellectual projections, views, and futuristic living patterns helped to sell to the public the need to view technology, change, and growth as synchronous attributes to the good life. American drive to attain convenience and to extend mobility seemed to fit right into the modern view of life. Technology produced new change-inducing items, and change brought with it a sense of cultural excitement. New growth industries, in turn, brought with them more jobs, higher wages, and even more assurance that unrestrained growth was an essential feature of our philosophy.

Dream Making Moves from Hollywood to Madison Avenue

Before the breakup of Hollywood's movie empire soon after the Paramount Case, Hollywood was known as the dream-making capital of the world. Fantasies became the escape valve for millions of low-income workers in the dark days of the 1930s and in the perilous years of World War II. By the 1950s it was becoming obvious to informed observers that the opulence of the Hollywood dream could be merchandised to upper-middle and middle income families throughout the U.S. The dream-making apparatus shifted from Hollywood to Madison Avenue. With the refinement of the "psychological sell" and with steady increases in pur-chasing power of middle income families, industry moved in earnest to put status in the homes of millions of Americans. Objects of affluence, whether leveraged by heavy consumer debt or purchased with tidy sav-ings, marked the unique character of the American consumer within a world where basics were still being sought. To this extent, the American dream was unique and it, in turn, became the object for other nations to emulate.

ALTERNATIVES TO THE DREAM

Within less than three decades the U.S. economy zoomed from the depths of the Great Depression into the age of affluence of material wealth. Most of the population 40 years or older can remember the stark reality of scarcity in manufactured goods. The outdoor privies; hand pumps; pot-

FIGURE 2-3

The Belle Isle Bicycle Trail in Detroit is one of the 40 National Recreation Trails located throughout the United States.

Source: Courtesy of Bureau of Outdoor Recreation

bellied heating stoves standing in the center of living rooms and kitchens; coal, kerosene and wood-burning cooking "ranges"; feather beds; home-grown vegetables; home-cured meat; flour; seed-sack clothing made by hand-operated sewing machines; long, cold walks to rural one-room school houses; and customs that went back to two or more generations within many families were a few of the nostalgic memories of the life style of the 1930s. People far outnumbered automobiles, and mobility, socially as well as physically, was difficult.

To those persons living with these all-too-vivid memories of the Depression era, material acquisition was seen as the means to erase hardships associated with hard labor, scarcity, and, in some cases, isolation from neighbors, ideas, and trends in urban areas (or the world's international developments). Most conveniences were expensive and often beyond the purchasing capabilities of families living in rural areas.

The advent of the affluent age has largely erased the hardships, inconveniences, and immobility experienced during the Great Depression. Braced by the stark living requirements of those years, material acquisition became the means to fulfill dreams and wants that scarcity often spawns. Affluence as a philosophy of life, however, did not influence the American culture until the 1960s, when the first generations of young adults born in the post-Depression era made their way into the nation's economic stream as consumers and employees. These sophisticated, brand-conscious, and socially tuned young adults accelerated America's social and economic revolution. Figure 2-3 shows a bicycle trail near a congested metropolitan area. Bicycle riding is a fast growing recreation for affluent Americans seeking a quiet, relaxing outdoor activity. Figure 2-4 represents a cluster diagram showing an alternative life style where individuals group around a soil oriented interest.

FIGURE 2-4 Two Life-Style Alternatives Cluster Illustration

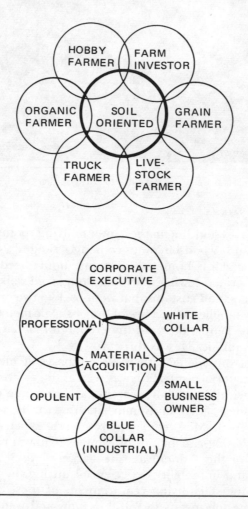

Homesteading: 1970s Style

By the end of the 1960s an antimaterialistic subculture began surfacing across the nation. Mostly visible in ghetto-like colonies, these subcultures lured the youth from wealthy and middle-class families to a different form of life—a life based on natural, simple relationships between persons. This anti-institutional movement spilled out into the colleges and universities; its proponents protested the injustices of the establishment, whether in the political system or in the materialistic-oriented values of the "over-30" adults. Various new experiments in life styles and living customs resulted.

Without question, many youths were rebelling, honestly, against suburban snobbery, sameness, parental conflicts, and were searching for a replacement for material acquisition as a measurement of self-esteem. These youths volunteered for the Peace Corps, Vista, Action; others became interested in various forms of communal living as a means to achieve collective, people-centered life styles. Within the ranks of those seeking to find an alternative to the living patterns of parents, many were turning to hand skills in labor markets and farming and many were starting "shoe string" businesses. The values of personal relationships; natural, old-fashioned customs; and environmentally held views were interwoven into alternative life styles. The underlying personal satisfactions associated with the rediscovery of now nearly forgotten crafts, arts, skills, and methods for providing self-sufficiency have turned many youths into a soil-oriented subculture. The migration of young people to rural farming communities to work and to own the land marked the beginning of a movement away from suburbia. In this new culture, collective goods are viewed with a value equal to private goods. Included below are selected letters to *The Mother Earth News* which illustrate a growing, back-to-soil movement in this nation.[14]

> We're a young couple (28 and 29) looking for 40 to 100 acres where we can work toward self-sufficiency and spiritual peace. Ideally, the property would include a livable dwelling, a good water supply, and a spot for our garden . . . with the balance in timber. We're presently considering Missouri, Arkansas, Tennessee, southern Colorado, New Mexico, Arizona, northern California, and southern Oregon.
>
> One of us is a former English and history teacher who would love to teach in a free school environment. The other is a dentist willing to trade services for food, shelter, a helping hand, etc. We'd like to hear from anybody out there who has some guidance to offer, or anyone who is on a similar path and would like to rap about it.
>
> Help! We're looking for a rural place to raise bees and mushrooms . . . in the Rockies or someplace out west where there's a decent growing season and trees. We've got cats, a little money, a desire to buy land—or whatever we can work out—and want to enjoy like-minded neighbors . . . peace-loving, back-to-the-earth folks. Would also like to help with conservation efforts . . . either paid or volunteer work.
>
> I'm looking for an opportunity to tune in on earth's life forces by living and working on a farm/homestead. I'm a single man (24) with bio-dynamic gardening and forestry experience and am capable in the fields of light carpentry, masonry, and plumbing. I work hard and can help with many aspects of a farm . . . even to creating a fully integrated and self-sufficient homestead.

I'm a male (21), with a strong back, interested in finding work on an organic farm or homestead where I can learn as much as possible about all aspects of a life close to Mother Nature. If I could live, learn, and work with you, all I'd ask in return is room and board and possibly a few dollars (but the last is not necessary). I've got one year of organic gardening experience behind me and am a hard worker . . . also know something about nutrition, cooking, and fruit science.

My wife and I are getting ready to flee the city and want to combine teaching (I have degrees in elementary and secondary education and she has a Ph.D. in English) with homesteading in the Alaska panhandle or coastal British Columbia. We very much like to hear from people who have gone the homesteading trip in these areas and would kindly share their hard-won knowledge with us about everything from land availability to job opportunities and weather.

Beyond the Basics

In very early times the earth's soils and natural resources were readily available to those cultures lucky enough to be located near large deposits of fertile loam, copper, gold, silver, and fibers. For example, written history begins with the great cultures of Egypt and Babylonia in the river valleys of the Nile and Tigres-Euphrates. In these two regions of the Near East the annual floods provided fertile soil, because the river waters overflowed their banks and left a deposit of silt on the land. The needs of drainage and irrigation required cooperation under strong and unified control. The rewards of labor, however, were very great and men were able to accumulate wealth and to develop culture. Labor and animal power provided the economies of these very early civilizations with the productive means to advance beyond subsistence. Wealth was the end-product of unified systems of government and abundant natural resources close to the earth's surface; public works allowed for the channeling of water into productive fields.

Paradoxically, in our age of science, technology, mass education, and space achievements, nearly one-third of the world's population lacks basic essentials—food, clothing, shelter, and the means to acquire desperately needed cash incomes. While the so-called less developed nations have turned to industrialization to break the poverty cycle, population gains and marginal farmlands (subject to frequent droughts and famines) have largely negated economic gains.

The United States owes its wealth to an abundance of natural resources, skilled labor and technological capital, unified government, an abundance of the world's most fertile farm lands, and management and financial capabilities. Like the great early civilizations of Babylonia and Egypt, America achieved remarkable economic gains. The United States accomplished this by combining a tremendous natural bounty with the productivity of technology. In turn, an ever increasing flow of convenience products and services reaches consumers in even the lower income levels. Except in some important cases, Americans enjoy an assortment of goods and services that go beyond providing the minimum essentials of life.

DRIVE TO SUSTAIN GROWTH

The study of marketing history reflects the trend from subsistence to affluence. In its infancy, marketing of commodities and bulk items occupied the attention of economists, agricultural specialists, and others. As the economy continued to expand following World War II, the emphasis in marketing shifted to functions and managerial-organizational systems. We moved from a position of manufacturing scarce goods in the 1940s to having an abundance of ever widening heterogeneous offerings of products. Marketers were challenged to increase product demand in the face of apparent market saturation conditions, especially for durable goods.

The psychological sell represented one means of extending market demand to ever higher levels. An intangible world of options, views, endorsements, symbols, peers, admirers, followers, brands, and status was interwoven into advertising and promotion plans, strategies, and techniques. This intangible world, representing for the consumer self-esteem and security, is depicted in nearly endless scenarios of models, actors, endorsers, sports heroes, situations, locations, and scripts—each defining that slice of life most centrally linked with the product brand and its strategic place in lives of consumers. Consumers are viewed as being manipulated not only in choosing brands, but also in the psychological associations derived from using or being seen using a particular brand. Hence, a consumer becomes a part of something—a group, a feeling, an atmosphere in which enjoyment, even for simple basic products, widened his association with sexual potency, masculinity, peer acceptance, success, and culture. Consumer satisfaction becomes a fragile, intangible thing, subject to sudden change and manipulation by others sometimes far from the scene.

CONCLUSIONS

In several respects, image making and the intangible world of socio-psychosomatic marketing is like the hybrid plant-growing experiments involving vegetables, flowers, and trees. The process of hybridization can be continued only so long over a short period of time before generic deficiencies begin to appear. Disease susceptibility causes crop destruction. Agronomists must then reintroduce wild strains into the generic line. This once more establishes vitality, vigor, and increased resistance to insects and blight. In our world, where suggestive life-style patterns evolve around psychological brand images, we can, like a hybrid plant, suffer from continued hybridization of what we are. Perhaps the movements back to nostalia, folk music, or homesteading suggest deep felt needs to re-establish life values with guideposts of the past. In our frantic rush to be young at heart, successful, modern, and ahead of the Joneses, we may have become materialistic and more insecure about the role of human beings within a technologically dominated society. Living better has been associated with product choices limited only by purchasing power and consumption trade-offs, which encouraged trading up to products with brand portraying quality, larger size, more horsepower, and accessories.

In our drive to maximize convenience, an entire disposable-oriented industry has arisen in paper and metal products ranging all the way from surgical gowns to wedding gowns—all designed to be used only once and then disposed of. While the needs relating to convenience foods, paper products, and other items are introduced into our modern life style, we as a nation must balance resource use as we make important market decisions. In the final analysis, life-style decisions determine product choice; in a democracy, consumer willingness to make progressive strides in resolving ecological conflicts strongly influences industry's behavior in many supply-and-demand relationships. As environmental conflicts mount and force industrialized nations to strictly regulate pollution to avoid serious collective bads, consumers who once refused to cooperate voluntarily, will through mandatory restrictions alter traditional behavior.[15]

Case 3
Cleaning Up High Mountain Ecosystems

Whenever the state parks, wilderness areas, and other lowland retreats started feeling the pangs of too many careless people, the mountaineer could always escape to the mountains. They offered a remote avenue for only a few hardy souls—mountain nuts, wilderness freaks, and the like—who were willing to trade the whole crunch down below and all its industrial amenities, litter, pollution, etc., for the physical challenges and the wild, clean air of the heights.

Because most of the mass remained scrambling below and only a few could ever make it to the aloof, high areas, the mountains were where it was . . . where the mountain nut could really put it all together and get into the wild oneness of nature, earth, stars, flowers, animals, and unlimited horizons.

Conservation News, Vol. 38, No. 11, (June 1, 1973) pp. 8–10.

At least, that's what the mountain nuts thought!

Gary Grimm thought so too, but he was apprehensive. Grimm, a Pacific Northwest mountaineer, altitude freak, and head of the University of Oregon Outdoor Program, was feeling that same cold oneness with the mountain world one day at 16,000 ft on Mt. McKinley. He was a McKinley veteran though and knew that he would probably be jolted back into reality just 1,000 ft higher by the sight of a 100-sq ft garbage dump, a disgusting composite of cans, plastic bags, aluminum foil, paper bottles, new and broken equipment, underwear, half-burned parachutes, and even some lightweight plywood doors.

Besides their principal intention to try to clean up the debris-littered mountain, the mid-1971 expedition of seven men, organized and led by the 33-year-old Grimm, had cross-country, skied up to 11,000 ft and planned to climb the 20,320-ft McKinley.

Though vicious winds and snowstorms kept them pinned down most of the time and denied them a chance for the summit, Grimm and the six others were able to do a remarkable job of cleaning up. They burned what junk they could, buried what couldn't be burned or moved, and carried out the rest, tying much of the junk in stuff sacks around their waists and methodically dragging them behind. Even the incinerated wastes were carried off the mountain.

After 27 grueling days on the mountain, the seven men left, hauling with them about 380 pounds of unsightly junk.

Grimm puts much of the blame for the widespread McKinely litter on some of the commercial guide outfits "who seem to be more interested in profits than environmental quality. They won't bother to bring it back because their clients don't pay to carry garbage."

In recent years, Alaskan outfitters have guided several hundred climbers on the massive peak, the highest in North America. The physical and mental strains of high-altitude climbing on McKinley have too often tempted exhausted climbers to dump unneeded (at the time!) baggage anywhere handy. To be fair, expedition mountaineering the world over doesn't have a very well-established tradition of picking up after oneself. Even the pile of trash on the "highest junkyard in the world," the 26,000 ft South Col of Mt. Everest, continues to get deeper with each assault. A certain inherent wastefulness seems to come naturally as breathing becomes more difficult and pitches grow steeper. And, in years past, it could easily be justified—because "nobody will ever be around here again."

But the population crunch has now even hit the mountains. And, of all the world's diverse ecosystems, mountains can probably stand the pressure the least. Despite their rugged grandeur, mountainous environments are quite fragile, easily susceptible to damage, slow to recover. Even basic organic waste takes hundreds, sometimes thousands of times longer to break down in the high, cold mountain terrain than in lowland reaches.

PLANS TO RETURN

Grimm had no sooner returned to the thawing comforts of home in Eugene, Oregon, when he determined to return to McKinley again, this time for a thorough clean-up. Through a scheme called the Denali Arctic Environmental Program (Denali is the native term for McKinley meaning "The Great One"), Grimm proposed that 20 climbers from the University of Oregon and other Pacific Northwest schools make two trips to McKinley in the spring and summer of 1973 for climbing and a massive refuse pick-up.

Enthusiastic outside support for the ambitious DAEP project poured in, though mostly in the form of goodwill endorsements rather than funding help. Some financial support, as well as the use of four Bishop tents and communications equipment, was given the project by the American Alpine Club, and $450 was donated by various advocates. The biggest share of the costs, however, was to be borne by each of the 10 climbers in each trip.

In order to prepare for the rigors of an extended stay on the flanks of the Alaskan arctic, a series of tough preliminary climbs were planned, including ascents on Mt. Rainier in Washington, the Wyoming Tetons, and 12,078-ft Hyndman Peak in Idaho's Sawtooth Range. During the climb of Hyndman Peak, four climbers, including a 13-year-old youth, reached the summit in what was probably a first winter ascent.

DAEP NOW ON MOUNTAIN

The first DAEP team, led by Grimm and composed of nine other mountaineers from five Pacific Northwest universities, are preparing to descend after spending over a month on the massive McKinley. A second group, under the leadership of Australian Jeff Elphinston, plans to spend another month on the mountain.

Both groups plan to spend time collecting refuse on the West Buttress and Muldrow routes of McKinley. Large plastic bags full of garbage will be hauled to a storage area where, with the assistance of the National Park Service, they can be picked up by aircraft. The National Park Service has reportedly "guaranteed" that it will get all of the collected garbage off the mountain by either helicopters or planes. Reports on the extent of cooperation by the Park Service have not yet been made available.

The preparation on paper for the McKinley clean-up and the acclimatization climbs "really solidified our environmental senses", according to Elphinston, a graduate fellow at the University of Oregon. Elphinston emphasized that the future of climbing and all other forms of wilderness experience depends on consideration of "the continuing quality of the recreational environment as well as the quality of the experience."

Case 4
A Case for Pesticide 2,4,5-T?

When a threat to public health is seriously suspected but the evidence isn't complete, who bears the final burden of proof? Too often the unsuspecting public itself—that's the opinion of many environmentalists and public interest advocates. This ongoing dilemma in environmental decision making once again has come to national attention in recent Senate hearings which uncovered strong disagreement within the Environmental Protection Agency about the safety of the continued herbicidal use of the most toxic synthetic chemical known to man.

The chemical in question is dioxin, an unavoidable manufacturing by-product contained in the herbicide 2,4,5-T, which was widely used as a defoiliant in South Vietnam during the late 1960s. Proven to cause birth defects in laboratory animals and considered toxic in doses so minute that they can't be measured, 2,4,5-T was banned by the Department of Agriculture in 1970 for all uses in the United States except on forest lands, pastures, rangelands, rice lands, and highway rights-of-way.

Environmentalists have cited the laboratory evidence on dioxin's extreme toxicity plus research which indicates that it may be persistent in the environment and build up in the food chain while urging EPA to ban even the remaining uses of 2,4,5-T for the sake of public safety. But after promising for almost a year to hold public hearings on the matter, EPA in June reversed itself and decided against hearings. The explanation: There isn't enough data available to suggest a substantial question of safety exists. Therefore, 2,4,5-T continues to be used.

In congressional hearings in late August, however, one of EPA's own top scientists disputed the agency's decision. Dr. Diane Courtney, a pharmacologist specializing in toxic effects research at EPA's National Environmental Research Center in North Carolina, told the Senate Commerce Committee, "I think it (2,4,5-T) should not be used. We are using a chemical we can barely handle." Asked if she had been consulted by EPA's policy makers before the agency made its decision on 2,4,5-T, Dr. Courtney said "No."

Some research indicates that dioxin is so toxic that only six parts of it in 10 billion (bodyweight) can be lethal to laboratory animals. In 1973, the Science Policy Division of the Library of Congress extrapolated from animal studies that one medicine drop of dioxin could kill 1,200 people. A Federal Drug Administration scientist reports that in chick and mammalian studies, dioxin is "some 100,000 to a million times more potent" than the

Conservation News, Vol. 39, No. 4, (December 15, 1974) pp. 5–7.

tranquilizer thalidomide which caused a large number of birth defects in Europe.

With information like that and more, you might wonder how there can be any dispute at all about banning the remaining uses of 2,4,5-T with its deadly companion dioxin, let alone allowing them to continue. The issue is not the toxicity of dioxin as studied in the laboratory. Rather, it is the persistence of its toxicity in the environment—how long does it remain toxic when introduced into the out of doors. EPA's Deputy General Counsel Robert Zener attempted to make the distinction to the Committee when he explained that Dr. Courtney's work does not deal with persistence. According to Zener, 2,4,5-T breaks down rapidly in the presence of sunlight and therefore the risks of exposure are minimized.

But the main reason for EPA's decision not to hold hearings on 2,4,5-T was the lack of either data or techniques to gather relevant data on the effects of dioxin in the environment and on humans in the U.S. The extreme toxicity of dioxin at parts per billion and perhaps even parts per trillion only exacerbates the data problem.

During the months it had planned on holding hearings, EPA counted on a method of detecting dioxin which had been developed in Vietnam. But when tried out in the U.S. under different circumstances (for one thing, the 2,4,5-T used in the U.S. has a lower dioxin level than that used in Vietnam), it proved inadequate. Consequently, there is no comprehensive monitoring of 2,4,5-T and inadequate health data, according to EPA. The agency is pushing ahead with additional research, but until new methods for detection can be devised and the necessary data collected, 2,4,5-T can continue to be used.

There may be inadequate environmental monitoring of 2,4,5-T in EPA's view, but there has been some in the U.S. and especially in Vietnam where more than five million acres were defoliated with the herbicide Agent Orange—of which 90 million tons of 2,4,5-T were an ingredient. In fact, an EPA document on the use of 2,4,5-T in national forests, the agency reported: ". . . 2,4,5-T-related tetra-dioxin is persistent and it bioconcentrates (accumulates in the food chain). It is quite capable of penetrating the environment and contaminating the human food supply."

Furthermore, the document says, "Monitoring wildlife collected along rights-of-way in the U.S. demonstrates as does the Vietnamese aquatic residue data, that 2,4,5-T-related TCDD (dioxin) can enter the food chain from 'nonfood uses.' " Dr. Courtney told the committee that dioxin could be in the steak purchased in stores since cattle can graze on 2,4,5-T-treated fields. But because of the inadequacy of existing detection systems, the food chain in the U.S. is not monitored for dioxin.

TOPIC QUESTIONS

1. What is the "American dream" and how has it sometimes conflicted with sound environmental policies?
2. Is material acquisition a sound long-range life-style philosophy in today's world?
3. What are alternative life-style choices that some groups are following?
4. What is the intangible world of psychological appeals employed by many firms to stimulate demand for their products?
5. How has the influence of Hollywood affected life-style choices for consumers?
6. When does consumer responsibility begin in the waste disposal problem?
7. Are companies responsible for litter that people carelessly leave on the grounds of public and private property?
8. In the final analysis, do life-style decisions determine product choice?

Case 3

9. Discuss life-style choices and their relationships to the problem of littering.
10. Are future wilderness activities threatened by careless actions of hikers, campers, and tourists? If so, how might the federal government restrict entry into wilderness regions?
11. How does the mountain ecosystem differ from low-altitude regions?

Case 4

12. In the case of pesticide 2,4,5-T, who is responsible for any latent health hazard that may evolve from its use?
13. How is a material acquisitive culture especially vulnerable to potentially toxic substances that flow from research and development labs?
14. What are the options that consumers may exercise to toxic substances [some of which may trigger health problems from 5 to 10 years after initial contact(s)]?
15. Why do opinions of various groups differ so strongly on the potential harmful effects of toxic substances?

RECOMMENDED READINGS

Ralph Nader, ed. *The Consumer and Corporate Accountability* (New York: Harcourt Brace Jovanovich, 1973).

Barbara B. Murray, ed., *Consumerism* (Pacific Palisades, Calif.: Goodyear, 1973).

John S. Wright and John E. Mertes, *Advertising's Role in Society* (New York: West, 1974).

Harold H. Kassarjian and Thomas S. Robertson, rev. ed., *Perspectives in Consumer Behavior* (Glenview, Ill.: Scott, Foresman, and Company, 1973).

FOOTNOTES

1. In those instances where advertisers create a characteristically unique "generation" or peer group that exhibits supportive psychological reactions to product enjoyment, they often do not relate to the consumers' realistic routine of everyday life and acquaintances. In real life, consumers are seldom thrilled or burst into song when buying, using, or associating needs with convenience goods.

2. The world's natural resources are unevenly distributed. Moreover, political strategies of governments have incorporated natural resources into economic, military, and national alignment policies. World reserves that are developed and constitute supply sources for international trade are subject to political power plays. Many of the world's reserves are underdeveloped and lie in the more geographically inaccessible regions of the earth. It is not an easy matter to shift dependency from a major developed source of natural resources to these speculative remote reserves on short notice without severe damage.

3. Louis O. Kelso and Patricia Hetter, "The Energy Crunch: A Crisis That Did Not Have to Be," *Business and Society* 7, 3 (February 5, 1974): 1.

4. Philip Kotler, *Marketing Management* (Englewood Cliffs, N.J.: Prentice-Hall, Inc. 1972), p. 9.

5. Joseph C. Seibert, *Concepts of Marketing Management* (New York: Harper and Row, 1973), p. 41.

6. The question of consumer manipulation is subject to a great deal of debate. While studies suggest that consumers throw up a defensive barrier against manipulative advertisements to protect them from brand images, suggestions, life-style interpretation, and value determination, critics have been quick to argue that consumer defensive mechanisms fail to stem producer influences on consumers. This point is stressed vigorously where children are the objects of psychological sell campaigns involving toys and, especially, cereals. In the case of cereals, the product is more than a form of food, a package of nutrition and vitamins, and a brand name. The product is a complete scenario involving animations, characterizations, excitement, taste appeal, and complimentary "free" enclosures.

7. See Ralph Nader, ed. *The Consumer and Corporate Accountability* (New York: Harcourt Brace Jovanovich, 1973).

8. Richard H. Buskirk and James T. Rothe, "Consumerism—An Interpretation," *Journal of Marketing* 34 (October 1970): 61–65.

9. Philip Kotler and Sidney J. Levy, "Broadening the Concept of Marketing," *Journal of Marketing* 33 (January 1969): 10–15. Reprinted from the *Journal of Marketing* published by the American Marketing Association.

10. "Turning Junk and Trash into a Resource," *Business Week* (October 10, 1970): 66–75.

11. *Mission 5000* (Washington, D.C.: United States Protection Agency Publication, 1972).

12. William G. Zikmund and William J. Stanton, "Recycling Solid Wastes: A Channels-of-Distribution Problem," *Journal of Marketing* 35 (July 1971): 34–39. Reprinted from the *Journal of Marketing* published by the American Marketing Association.

13. From *Economic Growth and Environmental Decay* by Paul W. Barkley and David W. Seckler, pp. 125, 126, © 1972 by Harcourt Brace Jovanovich, Inc. and reprinted with their permission.

14. Material from *The Mother Earth News*, Nos. 25 and 26 (January and February 1974). Published by Mother Earth News, Inc., P.O. Box 70, Hendersonville, N.C.

15. William H. Peters concluded in his study on voluntary recycling programs that ". . . it is reasonable to assume that the can and bottle recycling program in Madison [Wisconsin] never got much beyond the early adopters to the large bulk of the people (later adopters). There was some promotion of the center during the first six months of the program. But then it died down to virtually nothing. In the opinion of the local Coca-Cola Bottling Company manager, only a small fraction of the families in Madison had regularly taken part in the program." The study concluded further that voluntary cooperation was limited to the upper and upper-middle classes of persons in the Madison area.

William H. Peters, "Who Cooperates in Voluntary Recycling Efforts?" *Increasing Marketing Productivity and Conceptual and Methodological Foundations of Marketing*, Reprinted from *Proceedings*, published by the American Marketing Association, 1973, p. 508.

CHAPTER THREE

UTOPIAN INFLUENCES

ON THE

MODEL SOCIETY

DEFINING THE MODEL SOCIETY

Mankind's conceptualization of the future in the form of an ideal time or epoch in which the earth's material greatness becomes fully realized is deeply rooted in his religious, cultural, economic, and scientific thought. To the technocrat, the future utopia is expressed in terms of a civilization served by wonderous technological marvels that free the human race from famines, diseases, work, boredom, poverty, and global immobility. In this view the ideal state of human existence parallels the full fruition of science and technology in nearly every aspect of human life. But to the moralist, utopia is not a function of science or technology, but a state or condition in which social justice, freedom, and peace exist in a civilization that has cast off prejudice, ignorance, and greed. Views on the utopian state are as diverse as the present divisions within our international community.[1] Indeed, while the concept of a model society differs as to its features, the dream of utopia is consistent with human history.

Under contemporary thought we view the march of progress in terms of economic growth and innovations in science and technology; additionally, we have experimented with programs designed to advance social justice. Our educational system is without equal in embracing all segments of society. To many persons living in underdeveloped nations experiencing poverty and static living conditions, America represents an ideal state or utopia. While this ideal view of society is not shared by critics, the U.S. is one of the most affluent nations.

BASIC ROOTS OF UTOPIA

Technology and science have presented mankind with new tools for accelerating productivity and stimulating economic growth. We embrace new products openly, accepting them as visible signs of progress and well-being. Marketing processes respond to the consumer need for excitement and innovation with new products and services. Economic wealth and purchasing power are widely distributed in the U.S. today and thus make new product marketing a highly visual social process. The role of marketing in the innovation process is illustrated in Figure 3-1. Market

FIGURE 3-1   Marketing's Role in the Innovation Process

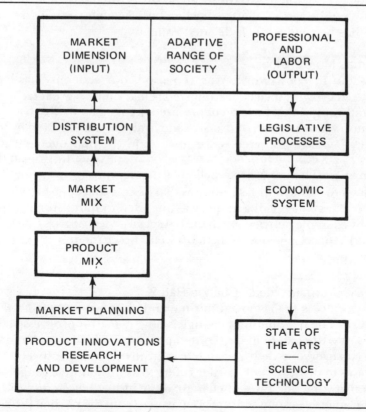

research measures society's tastes and determines the product mix. Purchasing patterns and technological advances are considered in making product decisions. The flow of products, ideas, values, and institutional policies are all parts of the innovation process.

American consumers today can see more evidence of an approaching opulence or utopian-like future than previous generations. In short, once-obscure and far-off visions of utopia are becoming formulated as national goals; utopia has, therefore, implications to present-day social and economic thought. For example, many market forecasts project opulent life styles by the 1980s. This visionary view of the approaching decade depicts society as attaining cultural goals, sophistication, technological marvels, and an end to poverty as we know it today.[2]

Faith in the future helps to build up optimistic views concerning the future. This, in turn, fuels the capital markets, consumer spending, and business expansions. The ability of a society to change with the times, that is, to accept new scientific and technological breakthroughs, is considered essential for stimulating continued economic expansion. Indeed, the question of change is becoming an important *social* matter. We have the technological capabilities to drastically reorder the landscape and living patterns, but the rate of change in which social stability retains a sense of balance has become a much debated issue.

Sir Thomas More's Utopia

Throughout the post-World War II period, our economy has experienced rapid growth; society has adjusted remarkably to great technological breakthroughs that have revolutionized the American life style. In the 16th century, however, an oppressive and drab life was endured by mankind. Then, change occurred more slowly and the improvement factor, whether it was economic or social, was all but nonexistent. Utopian thinkers such as Sir Thomas More rebelled by presenting a contrasting society within a set of values and assumptions that he considered to be "ideal" for mankind. This concept of a utopia was intended to spur reform by pointing out by example deficiencies in the old social order. More's *Utopia*, published in 1516, became one of the most well-known models promoting social change.

Do We Differ on the "Ideal" Change Rate?

Today's society is far removed in time and circumstances from that of More's era. The pendulum of change is now swinging progressively faster. The rate of change in our contemporary society has had a marked impact. Not everyone views social change from the same perspective; each of us seems to possess what Toffler refers to as an adaptive range, which relates environmental rates of change to the individual. Figure 3-2 illustrates the adaptive range concept. Departure from the normal range may

FIGURE 3-2   An Adaptive Range Scale

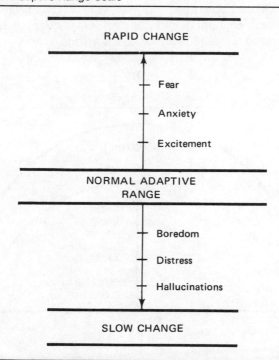

RAPID CHANGE

Fear

Anxiety

Excitement

NORMAL ADAPTIVE
RANGE

Boredom

Distress

Hallucinations

SLOW CHANGE

Note: An adaptation of incongruity and arousal relationship.

produce unwanted psychological reactions. The farther one departs from his adaptive zone, the more likely adjustment problems will increase.

> When the level of environmental stimulation or change falls below a certain point, the individual is forced below his adaptive range, he suffers distinct distress and takes action to increase the level of stimulation. When the level of environmental stimulation forces him above his adaptive range, he exhibits many of the same symptoms—anxiety, confusion, irritability, and eventual apathy. In short, all of us, from before the instant of birth to our very deathbed, wage a continuing, sometimes desparate, sometimes quite creative, struggle to keep the level of stimulation from pushing us above or below our adaptive range.[3]

Many of the current debates over the environment and mankind's future are centered around our interpretation of change and how change relates to individuals, groups, and nations. A utopia painted in glowing splendor, showing a future civilization enjoying opulence, peace, and scientific wonders is not simply a technocrat's pipe dream, but an expression and interpretation of one's adaptive range concerning contemporary society and the relative optimism which one assigns to the future. Without doubt, the affluence that America possesses is directly related to the ability of our political, economic, and cultural sectors to adapt to new situations, institutions, roles, behavior, and scientific advances. Figure 3-3 illustrates and discusses the adaptive range for a society.

FIGURE 3-3 The Change Factor and Social Adjustment Limits

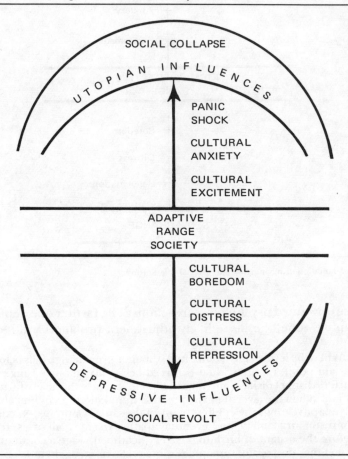

When the adaptive range concept is applied to a macro social structure, utopian and depressive influences may be considered in terms of contrasting polar magnets. Groups, cultures, regions, and life style patterns attempt to balance the opposing utopian–depressive influences. Nations may rise above the adaptive range in "good times" and fall below it during "bad times" (such as during depressions and wars).

Economic progress, business expansions, and market growth are linked to the change factor; it has been good economics and good business to promote change. Given a near-universal taste for money and the good life, we have shaken off the security of community, the comforts of old beliefs, the close web of family circles, the peace of a rural life, and the simple familiarity of one's locality in preference to the often bewildering pecuniary relationships among unknown persons within the social formlessness of sprawling urban centers. This abandonment of familiar guideposts for new life styles has opened up vast new markets, leveraged high finance, expanded bureaucratic organization, and sharpened technical specialization. Combined with the excitement that arises when personality has become intimately a part of a cultural adventure, the pace or rate of change which contemporary society experiences becomes synonymous with affluence and the better life. Utopian thinking in our modern society is directly linked to accelerating the pace of social, technological, and economic changes; here, the most adaptive citizens of these pro forma cultures of the future emerge as the new elite. The adaptive range of utopian societies will require higher adaptive levels, which in turn force greater psychological stresses and shocks on those unable to adjust to quickening living paces.

Marketing Technological Innovations
The current worldwide mobilization for change culminated more than 6,000 years of isolated thrusts toward civilization and some four centuries of applying the scientific method to achieve that end. Only in the historic instant of the past few decades has there arisen a general recognition that international development is even possible in our time.

For one-third of mankind, largely in Europe and North America, the gathering momentum of development in the past century and a half brought about a massive urban industrialism through the perfection of technology (the organizing of specific properties of materials and machines) and bureaucracy (the organizing of specific capacities of persons and institutions).

The mobilization of resources to provide society with new products and services is made possible by technological innovation. Innovation introduces new facets, adaptations, and adjustments to life. Whether we praise or condemn technology, one fact about it remains clear: technology is the driving force behind economic growth in the U.S. In this context innovation means that process by which a new idea is successfully translated into economic impact within our society by providing better products and simultaneously creating new jobs in the manufacturing and application of those products. The innovation process in the factory can result in plant efficiency. New technology has played a major role in lowering per unit labor costs in the industrialized nations. Figure 3-4 reflects the downward trend in unit labor costs that occurred during the years 1960 to 1973. An idea or invention is a necessary but not a sufficient prerequisite for innovation. Only after an invention is put into sufficient use to have an economic effect is it to be termed an innovation.

FIGURE 3-4 Ratio of United States Labor Costs to Selected Foreign Countries

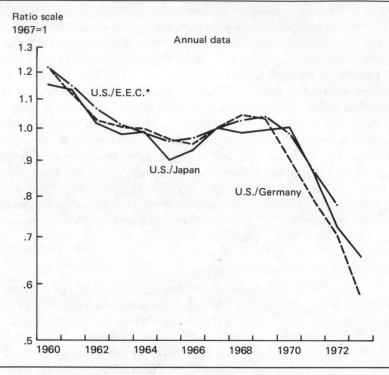

Note: Data represents the ratio of the indexes of unit labor costs for the designated countries. Foreign unit labor cost indexes are calculated from cost data expressed in U.S. dollars.

The European Economic Community includes Belgium, France, Germany, Italy, Luxemburg, and Netherlands.

Source: Reprinted from Hans H. Helbing, "Recent and Prospective Developments in International Trade and Finance", *Review* Vol. 56, No. 5 (May 1974) Federal Reserve Bank of St. Louis.

Innovation takes many forms. For example, the supermarket is a marketing innovation, as are the personal credit cards that many of us use for instant identification and credit at service stations, restaurants, and airline ticket counters throughout the country. Although such innovations have had consequential economic impact, they do not provide an increase in the technical content of the product involved, but merely serve as a novel means of providing a conventional result.

Advances in Communications and Productivity

Computers represent an innovation that not only increased technological content for the communications industry, but also revolutionized the technological content of all major business operations. The great scientific successes of the National Space Administration programs were possible primarily because of computers. The influence of computers goes far beyond their technological impact; they have become the subject of much debate concerning mankind's cultural association with these information, communication, and decision tools. These tools have the potential to advance the social goals of a progressive society or, as many writers have suggested, computers could become the instruments of oppressive autocratic governments.

During the past 25 years, whole new industries have developed on an across-the-board application of technological innovations. Besides computers, such innovations as television, synthetic fibers, and jet engines have given stimulus to the dramatic growth of many successful new enterprises. Such technically based advances as semiconductors, electrostatic copying, and instant photography have filtered into the marketplace in the form of new products. Chemicals, plastics, and electronics are examples of three industries whose dependencies on new technologies for new products, services, expanded marketing distribution, and organization growth are well known.

Economists estimate that 50 to 80 percent of the constant dollar (real) growth in the GNP is attributable to gains in productivity, nearly all of which flows directly from new technology. For example, the chemical industry is producing twice as much per man-hour now as it did 10 years ago. Thus, technological innovation is truly the cutting edge of the economic vitality of the nation.

Just as the economic well being of a nation is a proper concern of the federal government, so should be the innovative processes that stimulate economy. The dissemination of new technologies to business makes possible new techniques, processes, products, and services that provide important growth incentives to innovative industries. Thus, technology, innovation, and processes that commercialize new advances from research and development labs to business operations and products are important to our economic growth policies. To this extent, our growth policies have become national guidelines for achieving affluence. The synchronous participation of the federal government, the states, communities, industries, institutions, civic groups, and trade and professional associations have so cemented our future promise of opulence with technology that the average citizen is often willing to undergo major changes in his life just to be a part of the "team." Moreover, the future will require even more rapid life-style accommodations to technological renovations of our nation and environment.

SKETCHES OF THE MODEL SOCIETY

Technocrats are promising to completely renovate our landscape with a virtual blitz of new technological conveniences. Many of these plans would have been considered science fiction just 15 years ago:

Domed cities with environmentally controlled atmospheres.

Fast, efficient, and fully integrated pedestrian transit modes such as moving sidewalks, computer-controlled monorails, and shuttle car service will wisk persons in the domed cities of tomorrow into completely harmonious living, working, recreation, and shopping areas.

Push-button conveniences will allow consumers to dispatch mechanical servants to perform routine tasks.

Direct lines to merchandisers will allow consumers to make shopping decisions from home.

Rocketships will move passengers and cargo from one world location to another in a matter of minutes.

Weather systems will control the earth's climate for crops.

Monoculture will blanket the earth with scientifically managed agribusiness systems using space technology to monitor, control, and harvest crops.

Genetic manipulation will allow science to increase physical and mental powers of human beings.

Family life as we know it will all but disappear. Individuals living in loosely knit relationships will seek to maximize options in leisure, education, and travel.

Childbirth will be conducted in laboratories, completely outside the uterus. Child-rearing and education will be professionally handled, freeing parents from these confining domestic duties.

Oceans will be processed for food, minerals, fuel, and fibers by giant commercial ventures.

Matter conversion processes will transform ordinary substances into valuable minerals and fuels.

Farming in 2076 A.D.[4]

It's a scientifically managed, computerized, push-buttoned, virtually self-contained farm. Its livestock are in a high-rise building and its crops are indoors "under glass."

It's a farm that helps maintain natural resources as it produces enough food for 50,000 people year around. All the while it has ample surrounding land for recreation, wildlife, and natural beauty.

The hired man gets the imposing new title of "manager."

A dream farm?

Sure. Dreamed up as a farm of the year 2076 A.D. It's constructed in a model by agricultural engineering students at South Dakota State University, many now graduated and on their first job. Late last year the students selected as an agricultural engineering club activity the idea of looking to the agricultural future. It's a project for the American Revolution Bicentennial "Horizons" years.

Here are some of the future farm's features projected by this university's student branch of the American Society of Agricultural Engineers:

The farm of 9 square miles will use only about 1800 acres, less than one-fourth of which is for production. The remainder will be a buffer of "relaxed" zone for recreation, wildlife, and living under the "blending with human values" aspect of the overall planning.

Livestock will be housed (and products processed) in a 15-story 150' X 200' building. It will also contain certain power facilities, administrative headquarters, veterinary facilities, repair shops, refrigeration and packaging units, storage, research labs, water and waste treatment facilities. At capacity, the high-rise building will house 2,500 feeder cattle, 600 cow-calf units, 500 dairy cattle, 2,500 sheep, 6,750 finishing hogs, space for 150 sows and litters, 1,000 turkeys, and 15,000 chickens.

Crops will be grown year around under plastic covers that provide precise climate control in three circular fields each a mile in diameter. At any given time, regardless of weather, one field or crop will be in the planting stage, another in the growing stage, and the third in the harvesting stage. Exceptionally high yields mean that only a fourth of the total 5,760-acre farm area would be needed for agricultural production.

Only a half-inch of water will be needed for each crop. That's because evapotranspiration from growing plants would be recycled under massive, permanent plastic enclosures. The huge plastic field covers are considered an engineering problem to be solved over the next 100 years; smaller areas under plastic are currently being used successfully for intensive crop production.

Underground magnetic patterns, arranged to fit crop or machine, will attract specially treated seed blasted from overhead tubes in the enclosures.

If tillage is needed, it will be done by electromagnetic waves. Air-supported, remotely controlled machines will harvest entire plants because by 2076 A.D., the students believe, multiple uses will be needed and found for most crops.

"Trickle" irrigation is to be electronically monitored to provide subsurface moisture automatically whenever needed.

Recycling human, animal, and crop wastes will be a key to the operation of the farm. Carbon dioxide from the respiration of livestock is to be piped into the circular enclosures for use by crops in exchange for the oxygen transpired by crops.

Weed control is not anticipated as a problem because weeds would be eradicated under the field covers.

HOW CERTAIN IS THE MODEL SOCIETY?

Economic growth, social acceptance of change, technological innovation, pollution control, and international cooperation are necessary requirements for building a utopian-like economic system. In the process of building a science-based opulence, we should consider the necessity of greatly expanding economic activities on a global systems basis. This means that science will become an essential tool of mankind for gathering and transporting natural resources from all corners of the earth. A global trading order will determine the context of this worldwide endeavor to discover, process, transport, and distribute natural resources. Science will be forced to resolve serious global shortages and economic crises resulting from raw material shortages. The more rapid the economic expansion, the more responsive will science have to be to substitute for dwindling stockpiles of minerals, foods, energy, and so forth. Mankind's dependence on science alone (in the absence of conservation, pollution controls) may well be the biggest gamble in all history.

Inflation is another economic problem that world-wide trading systems must consider. Figure 3-5 shows the growing inflationary threat. Hyperinflation can wreck economics, throw nations into political turmoil, and disrupt living patterns. The U.S. has managed to avoid inflationary threats to a large extent, but other nations may be nearing the crisis phase. Unless inlfation can be checked the model society becomes even more remote.

Technological Optimists

Science is singularly responsible for making the subject of utopia a contemporary issue. Since the advent of the Atomic Age, mankind began acquiring the means to potentially reshape civilization. Our society has absorbed great quantities of new products, ideas, concepts, processes, and techniques. We have altered our living patterns to accommodate these new advances. No previous generation has seen its landscape and life style remodeled within such short periods of time.

To technological optimists, technology is the hope of tomorrow, the means for achieving continued increases in productivity, for developing natural resources, and for raising our standard of living ever higher. Utopia has begun to take shape in the form of new research breakthroughs unfolding from advanced research and development centers, labs, and institutions. This task of delivering an opulence which former civilizations only dreamed of in vague abstract dimensions is an enormous assignment, even for science. Remodeling society in order to make science truly effective in promoting economic growth is not without its side effects, faults, problems, and concerns.

FIGURE 3-5   Comparative Rates of Inflation

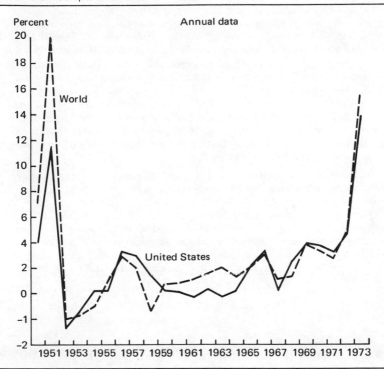

Note: The world inflation rate is measured by changes in Wholesale Price Indexes for eleven major foreign countries weighted by their trade shares with the United States. The United States inflation rate is measured by changes in the Wholesale Price Index.

Source: Reprinted from Hans H. Helbing, "Recent and Prospective Developments in International Trade and Finance," *Review* Vol. 56, No. 5 (May 1974) Federal Reserve Bank of St. Louis.

No Technical Solutions?

The stress factors listed above have become a serious limitation to the effectiveness of scientific progress in resolving social problems. This condition is discussed by Meadows et al. in *The Limits to Growth:*

> When the cities of America were new, they grew rapidly. Land was abundant and cheap, new buildings rose continuously, and the population and economic output of urban regions increased. Eventually, however, all the land in the city center was filled. A physical limit had been reached, threatening to stop population and economic growth in that section of the city. The technological answer was the development of skyscrapers and elevators, which essentially removed the constraint of land area as a factor in suppressing growth. The central city added more people and more businesses. Then a new constraint appeared. Goods and workers could not move in and out of the dense center city quickly enough. Again the solution was technological. A network of expressways, mass transit systems, and helicopter ports on

the tops of the tallest buildings was constructed. The transportation limit was overcome, the buildings grew taller, the population increased. Now most of the larger U.S. cities have stopped growing. (Of the ten largest, five—New York, Chicago, Philadelphia, Detroit and Baltimore—decreased in population from 1960 to 1970. Washington, D.C. showed no change. Los Angeles, Houston, Dallas, and Indianapolis continued to grow, at least in part by annexing additional land.) The wealthier people, who have an economic choice, are moving to the ever-expanding ring of suburbs around the cities. The central areas are characterized by noise, pollution, crime, drug addiction, poverty, labor strikes, and breakdown of social services. The quality of life in the city has declined. Growth has been stopped in part by problems with no technical solutions.

A technical solution may be defined as "one that requires a change only in the techniques of the natural sciences, demanding little or nothing in the way of change in human values or ideas of morality." Numerous problems today have no technical solutions. Examples are the nuclear arms race, racial tensions, and unemployment. Even if society's technological progress fulfills all expectations, it may very well be a problem with no technical solution, or the interaction of several such problems, that finally brings an end to population and capital growth.[5]

A Shift of Emphasis?

While technological optimists have experienced more resistance from the environmental movement in promoting such technological plans such as the supersonic transport, deep-port facilities for super tankers, and atomic power plants, their faith in science remains firmly entrenched. The role of science can be altered to include infrastructure and resource development roles. In the book *In The Environment: A Human Crisis*, Piburn discusses this new direction for advanced technology:

> Technological optimists like Athelston Spilhaus and Buckminster Fuller argue that science and technology have the potential to cure the problems of mankind and the world. Fuller is perhaps the boldest of this group of creative thinkers, and he has recently announced his decision to create a nonprofit organization, the Design Science Institute, dedicated to "reforming" the "environment of man."[6]

The technologist is generally a specialist who views the functioning of innovation with expandable social limits. When the technocrat is confronted with faulty or defective technology, he seeks to correct the problem through further improvements with still more new research and development. He is the chief architect and promoter for the technologically oriented utopian dream.

PROMOTING THE UTOPIAN DREAM

Scientific progress has already shaped our contemporary society, and as the march increases its tempo, the future has become focused. This focus centers around the strong technological emphasis as applied to nearly every aspect of our society. While the future utopia envisioned by optimistic technologists is expressed in glowing terms, its promise is at best speculative and by no means certain. The link to the future is rooted in today's science, technology, products, services, and economic systems. For scientific projects to be funded, for new technological advances to become commercially accepted, and for new products and innovations to become entrenched in emerging growth markets, they must be promoted extensively. This widespread lobbying for new innovations has become an essential part of government, organizational, and corporate growth strategies.

New technology and scientific advances are considered just as much a product to be promoted for military, industrial, and consumer uses as, for example, a brand name convenience product. Utopia is not only a projected composite of scientific wonders, but it is also a concept, a philosophy, an attitude. Moreover, the more important science becomes to our present, contemporary society, the more positively the technologists view their roles in reshaping the future.

In a U.S. House of Representatives report by the National Academy of Sciences, the concensus on the meaning of technological progress was interpreted as embracing "more than engineering." It also includes medicine, agriculture, scientific management, and educational psychology. The report further concludes that the most important invention in the pursuit of modern applied science is the big mission-oriented industrial or government laboratory. In fact, the Academy of Sciences suggests that modern applied science can hardly be discussed without reference to these "homes" of applied science. These institutions derive their power from three sources: (1) their interdisciplinarity and the close interaction between basic research and application; (2) their methodology for precipitating and organizing coherent efforts around large problems; (3) their ability to adapt their goals to the requirements of their sponsors. The industrial laboratories in particular have been remarkably successful in adapting the requirements for scientific innovations to the profit motivations of business enterprise.[7]

Scientists who promote the highly opimistic view of the future see humanity as the beneficiary of new discoveries from pure scientific experimentation as well as from rapid, innovative, and widespread adaptation of the applications of advancing science to new generations of products, techniques, and services. In the process of accelerating scientific progress, it is often difficult to divorce the discoverer of the new breakthrough from the one who commercially exploits the invention. New advances must somehow become useful, wanted, needed, and added to our society. This is true whether we consider societal discoveries or basically commercial ones. The enthusiasm with which new discoveries are sponsored is both the stimulant for rapid innovations at the applied level and the source of difficulty in moving new concepts into the arena of more widespread uses. Since sponsors of new discoveries tend to adopt and protect them in the funding game, basic flaws or faults go unstated or merely underplayed.

Incompatible Systems?

A flaw in the utopian dream evolved around the view that vast new technologies systematically blend into compatible systems; we have discovered that this basic aspect of technology, however, has thus far eluded us. Faults, conflicts, defects, and latent side effects are felt in our society as major new technological advances are introduced. The utopian dream of a bright new world basking in scientific splendor may elude mankind because our own impatience prevents us from applying safeguards and sound managerial controls to technology. For example, the need for new sources of energy has stimulated the Atomic Energy Commission to step up its campaign to promote more energy-oriented research and experimentation. One of these projects is entitled Liquid Metal Fast Breeder Program (LMFBP). The Atomic Energy Commission did not plan on writing an environmental impact statement until forced to do so in court. A careful study of LMFBP at the study stage is necessary because of plutonium, the fuel used in the process. Plutonium has widely known carcinogenic effects: (1) one-millionth of a gram injected into the blood system of a dog has caused a substantial incidence of bone cancer; (2) a few hundred thousandths of a gram injected in the lungs of 29 beagle dogs resulted in lung cancer in every dog.

In a report by Dr. Thomas Cochran and Dr. Art Tamplin of the Natural Resources Defense Council, the researchers claim that the present plutonium standards should be lowered by a factor of 1,000. In conjunction with the new technologies of LMFBP, the nation still has no long-range storage plan for highly lethal radioactive wastes. As of now, wastes are held in storage tanks. Ninety-three million gallons of wastes are stored at sites near Richland, Washington and near Aiken, South Carolina. According to the General Accounting Office, more than 277,400 gallons of plutonium leaked straight into the ground. This procedure has been repeatedly condemned by the General Accounting Office and the National Academy of Sciences' National Research Council Committee on Radioactive Waste Disposal. This committee maintains that when safety to the public is concerned, cost should be secondary; the AEC, however, spends less than 1 percent of its funds on a permanent solution. The introduction of a permanent storage solution is considered more than 10 years away. Environmentalists question what will happen if 10 years from now the AEC's solution is not sufficient and if the country has made even deeper commitments to nuclear energy.

To offset the public's concern over large-scale expansions of atomic power facilities, the electric power industry and the AEC launched publicity campaigns that projected nuclear energy as safe and efficient, and they called it the fuel of the future (replacing petroleum). Despite the promise that this advanced technology shows, the technical control problems remain as major operating flaws. While catastrophic reactor accidents have been avoided, problems with control techniques are responsible for radiation leaks into the environment. The growing list of atomic plant mishaps warrants caution. A few examples from across the country include the following:

1) The San Onofre nuclear plant was closed on October 22, 1973, after a turbine blade broke, causing alarmed operators to turn the reactor off too fast. A back-up cooling system (which should have been off) was activated. A plant spokesman simply explained, "Someone forgot." The additional water cooled the reactor too quickly which caused the pressure to drop which, in turn, simulated a pipe break. The emergency core cooling system water flooded the reactor, but since no water had been lost, the water hit the valves with immense force. The resulting vibrations damaged the plant and the emergency core cooling system. The plant was shut down for months. 2) Consolidated Edison's Indian Point I in New York has been inoperable for over a year. Since start-up in 1962, it has functioned less than 50 percent of the time. 3) Indian Point II, plagued with a $10 million fire in 1971 and recommendations against licensing by a Westinghouse subcontractor, was granted an operating license by the AEC in September, 1973. Seven weeks later the plant was closed when an 18-inch cooling water pipe cracked. Weeks later, Con Ed admitted that the liner of the reactor dome had buckled. The dome, which officials had earlier boasted could withstand a crash of a B-52 bomber, is designed to contain radioactivity in the event of an accident. It will not be working for months. 4) The R. E. Gina Plant was shut down on January 1, 1974, for excessive vibration. 5) Peach Bottom II facility in Pennsylvania was closed during the middle of November, 1973, for problems with its heat exchanger. 6) Five of New England area's six nuclear power plants are currently operating below full capacity. Vermont Yankee has been on and off since it was licensed. The Milestone Plant in Connecticut was closed for seven months when seawater entered the reactor. 7) The Palisades plant in Michigan was shut down with serious vibrations problems and leaks in March 1974. This facility has operated only one-half of its first two-year time span.[8]

These examples show that significant technological risks exist in operating atomic power facilities. The more rapid the expansion of nuclear power, the more numerous thc leaks and accidents; minor flaws in atomic power installations can produce dangerous levels of radiation to the environment (especially if the size of the industry greatly expands).

In a world where complex systems must function together to produce private goods and opulance, new technologies such as nuclear power must be integrated into society as conservatively as state-of-the-arts improvements in control techniques permit. Those who sponsor new innovations need to balance their vested interests in the promotion phase with evaluations from broad segments of the nation's scientific community (including those in the social sciences). As our total demands for raw materials grow, we are less likely to find a single technological innovation that can fill a void or gap. Rather, if some model society awaits mankind in the future, it will be possible only if man's *appetite* and *means* for creating economic wealth are controlled in harmony with both social and environmental limits.

GROWING CONSUMER APPREHENSIONS— A CASE ISSUE

In one instance of strong, consumer protest, opponents of a new nuclear power facility presented a well-organized argument for rejecting the project, despite the energy short-fall that plagued the nation. The views they presented were as follows:

> Opponents of the Union Electric Company's proposed nuclear power plant in Callaway County have told the Missouri Public Commission that the facility would be:
>
> (1) Liable to breakdowns that could cause a major nuclear catastrophe.
>
> (2) Unreliable and therefore unsuitable to carry out its intended purpose of providing continuous "base-load" generating capacity for the utility's electric customers.
>
> (3) Dependent upon an uncertain supply of atomic fuel—a supply so uncertain, in fact, that the United States may be forced to purchase enriched uranium from the Soviet Union.
>
> (4) Susceptible to sabotage or theft of nuclear material by terrorists.
>
> (5) Probably unnecessary to meet Union Electric's future customer demands.
>
> (6) The least safe source available to the utility.
>
> (7) So costly that the only way Union Electric will be able to pay for it will be through huge increases in electric rates.
>
> These are some of the arguments advanced today in prepared statements by four witnesses for opponents of the propoosed installation.
>
> They were filed jointly by the Utility Consumers Council of Missouri and the St. Louis Coalition for the Environment with the commission in Jefferson City.
>
> The two groups have intervened in the case of Union Electric's formal application to the commission for a permit to build the plant.

The witnesses are Sheldon Novick, editor of Environment magazine in St. Louis; James J. MacKenzie, chairman of the Union Concerned Scientists Fund of Massachusetts; Henry K. Kendall, a physicist at the Massachusetts Institute of Technology; and Robert L. Sorensen, a St. Louis economist.

Quoting from a recent study on the probability of nuclear accidents prepared for the Atomic Energy Commission, Novick said the chance that the cooling system would fail and the reactor would melt would be one in 17,000 each year.

But because Union Electric plans two reactors side by side, the chance that one of them would melt down sometime in their 30-years of expected life would be one in 280, Novick reasoned.

Because the AEC estimates, by its own admission, could be off by a factor of 10, the probability could be a high as one in 28, he said.

Novick, Kendall, and MacKenzie all said there was a crisis in the availability of nuclear fuel.

Nuclear power plants use an enriched mixture of two isotopes of uranium, only one of which—uranium 235—is actually involved in the power-producing process.

Currently, the one enrichment plant that produces commercial fuel is overtaxed and the cost of building new ones is so high that private corporations have refused to undertake it, they said.

Furthermore, spent fuel from reactors must be reprocessed so that it can be reused and there are no reprocessing plants currently in operation, they said.

The one reprocessing plant in the country is closed for repairs. A second was to have been built by General Electric Co. at Morris, Ill., but construction plans have been canceled because of design problems.

"Union Electric has not presented any details of its uranium supply contract," Novick said.

Novick, MacKenzie, and Kendall all said that the shortage of enriched uranium had forced the AEC to consider substituting plutonium, an artificial element actually created out of uranium in the course of a nuclear reaction in the reactor core of a power plant.

Plutonium is so toxic that a particle of it the size of a grain of pollen can cause cancer and a few pounds of it can be fashioned into a Hiroshima-scale bomb in a garage machine shop, they said.[9]

CONCLUSIONS

Utopian thinkers are encouraged to roll back natural limits to mankind's industrial expansion by promoting growth economics requiring strong reliance on science and technology. Economic growth exceeded population gains for many of the post-World War II years. A growing optimism among planners encouraged the view that the postwar boom could bring long-lasting prosperity to any number of people. Because technology could substitute scarce resources for more abundant raw materials, conservation practices and pollution controls were unnecessary. Secondly, as certain resources become scarce, price increases would provide profit incentives to discover and utilize substitutes. Technology became thought of as an all-purpose growth tool and problem solver as economic expansion brought us within the reach of affluence and the much discussed "good life."

However, exponential growth within the confines of finite resources and space must, invariably, reach a ceiling or limit. Scientists now using science and technology to resolve resource shortages and pollution difficulties know that these tasks will require much time, effort, and expense. Technological solutions become increasingly difficult as time requirements reach emergency stages. Because environmental problems are rooted in cultural, social, economic, and business factors that are synchronously interwoven, technical solutions become less able to resolve mankind's growing survival dilemmas. The concept of a model society must embrace more responsible views about the role of science in a world beset by serious environmental problems.

Case 5
A Case for Solar Energy Development

Chairman Mike McCormack (Wash.) expressed the feelings of several members of the committee when he told Dr. Betsy Ancker-Johnson, Assistant Secretary for Science and Technology of the Department of Commerce, that "I cannot help but observe that the situation that this country is facing with respect to energy is far more serious than the public recognizes and that most members of Congress recognize and that obviously it is worse than even the President recognizes. It is far worse than he stated last week, I am sure you know that . . . my question is, can we afford to delay legislation which is practical, which shows that the Congress and the President, the Executive Branch, is willing to move on programs? Can we afford to sit around and hold up these programs in order to defend an organizational name which has been established by the President, or must we not go ahead and show the people of this country that the Congress is moving on these programs even though we know that they are not going to substantially relieve the immediate problem?"

Commenting on the substantive issues, Dr. Ancker-Johnson observed that ". . . technology for developing a solar heating system is in an advanced developmental stage and sufficiently close to commercial application that three years is a reasonable estimate of the time required to develop and demonstrate the practical use of solar heating technology. However, at the outset it should be specified clearly what will be concidered an acceptable level of performance of the solar heating system."

Conservation News, Vol. 38, No. 40 (November 30, 1973) pp 547–50.

She also observed that ". . . solar heating systems should be reasonably priced in the near future." Dr. Ancker-Johnson also felt that provisions of building codes as currently drawn may not be consistent with the realization of optimum solar heating performance, that open competition should be held to encourage the building industry to submit imaginative and original designs, and that there should be a long-range evaluation of the performance of any solar heating and solar heating and cooling systems developed. Asked by Chairman McCormack whether the five-year provision in the bill was a reasonable deadline for developing and demonstrating a system using solar energy for both heating and cooling she said, "That is more difficult to predict because we are not as far advanced in our ability to produce chilling or refrigeration, but I think that it is not impossible by any means. Five years is a little on the short side, but fundamentally it is a reasonable target to shoot for."

Dr. Michel, commenting on the state of development of solar technology, said that "at this time it is technologically possible, and may even be economically feasible for solar energy to provide as much as one-half the energy needs for buildings. Thus, solar heating and cooling, including solar heating of domestic water, has the greatest potential for technological accomplishments in the shortest period of time."

Dr. Peter Glaser, Vice President of Engineering and Sciences for Arthur D. Little Company, told the subcommittee that his firm was coordinating the efforts of several dozen corporations in this country to bring solar heating and cooling into being as soon as possible. "Basically, the way we see it the question is not 'if solar energy for heating and cooling,' but when?" He pointed to a number of demonstration projects which are currently under construction and suggested that the demonstration phase of solar energy will be developed within the next year or so anyway, and suggested that the most important thing Congress could do would be to create the conditions where industry will provide its own research and development funds. It has been estimated by the major industrial organizations which his firm represents that "a plant can be built within three to five years to produce 500,000 units per year," which will partially utilize solar energy.

Rep. Charles Vanik (Ohio) urged the committee to include a Solar Energy Data Bank. Such a centralized energy data facility "not only would provide specifics on solar equipment but also would assess important information on other factors which affect the overall energy efficiency of buildings—its orientation, design, insulation quality, and the like. Utilizing the sun's energy to warm and cool a building is one element in a total effort to make a building as energy efficient as possible."

Mr. Wilson Clark, energy consultant to the Environmental Policy Center, urged the subcommittee to include the adaptive architectural aspects of solar heating and cooling and a "low technology use of solar energy, i.e., we can save as much as 30 to 50 percent of the energy needs of a building by simply orientation, siting, the use of overhangs, and other architectural techniques, none of which are practiced on a large scale today." He also pointed out that the basic materials like copper needed to develop solar devices may be in short supply, and he felt that the bill should be also expanded to allow expenditures for the development of decentralized wind power systems to be used in conjunction with solar energy equipment. Speaking for the National Wildlife Federation, Mr. Sheldon Kinsel said, "There is no question in our mind that the development of clean alternative energy sources is the key to solving the energy crisis in an environmentally responsible manner. Solar energy is clearly one of the most promising of these alternative sources and we agree that solar heating and solar heating and cooling systems are technologically feasible now." He encouraged the subcommittee to include a requirement that the federal research and development effort be coordinated insofar as possible with private efforts like that being undertaken by Arthur D. Little Company, and suggested that the solar heating demonstration homes could also demonstrate other energy conservation technologies, like improved lighting and insulation.

Most of the other witnesses appearing before the subcommittee were scientists from universities and industry or representatives of private industry. They were, in large majority, optimistic about both the potential for the use of solar energy in space conditioning and the mechanism which the subcommittee is suggesting be established. Professor Raymond D. Reed, Dean of the College of Architecture and Environment Design at Texas A&M University, said "in my judgment solar heating and, to a lesser extent, solar cooling of buildings, is well within existing feasibilities and has been for years. Refinements of the technologies of these systems are discrete, highly defined, emission-oriented problems, well within and particularly suited to the management balance of NASA."

Mr. William F. Rusk, Manager, Systems Application Research, of the Institute of Gas Technology, outlined the development of a gas fuel device which is "capable of heating, cooling, ventilating and controlling humidity in the home with high efficiency." He said that since the device uses heat, it is readily convertible to use available solar collectors. He concluded that "with a proper hardware development program units suitable for field testing could be built within two years." Mr. Ralph J. Johnson, Staff Vice President of the National Association of Homebuilders, said that "the technological feasibility of solar heating and water heating for housing and related buildings has been demonstrated, and we are well on our way to demonstrating the technological feasibility of solar cooling, although this subject requires more technological research." He suggested that what was now needed was a demonstration of the practical use of solar energy including a determination of costs, market acceptability, and reliability. Dr. Ian R. Jones, Manager of the Solar Energy Programs for TRW Systems Group said, "Solar energy is one of the most attractive supplemental energy sources because it is essentially inexhaustible and pollution free . . . I concur with the assessment of this committee on the near-term readiness of the technology and your commitment to achieve the early commercial application of solar energy to the heating and cooling of buildings." He outlined what TRW has been doing in the field and made suggestions on areas which may cause problems and ways to meet those problems. "However," he said, "there is certainly no question in our minds as to the near-term practicability of the commercialization of solar heating and cooling."

Case 6
Mona—Island in the Sun in Trouble

From the air, it really doesn't look like much. The island of Mona is just a small strip of land anchored in the Caribbean about 45 miles midway between the shores of Puerto Rico and the Dominican Republic. Together with its sister island, tiny Monito and Desecheo, 22-square-mile Mona has never been seen as being worth much to its mother island, Puerto Rico.

To get to the tiny isle, one either has to brave 10-ft. waves through the turbulent Mona Channel or fly a small plane into the short strip hacked out of the thick jungle mat. And once there, there isn't much attraction for the Palm Beach set—no towering luxurious beach hotels and neoned night spots, and there isn't even a single burger stand on Mona. In fact, there are only two permanent inhabitants on the island and, with a scarcity of fresh water, they have to depend on precious rain. Even the U.S. Coast Guard has deserted it, leaving its traces behind in a few ramshackle huts and mounds of garbage.

All in all, Mona doesn't come across as anything of much use. But the rich treasures that it shelters have sparked a tremendous controversy in the Caribbean.

Despite its shortcomings for humans, the island possesses a magnificent wealth of life. Havened within the strangely pristine world of the island are over 700 species of plants and land animals. Of those, at least 58 species are found nowhere else in the world and another 75 species exist elsewhere, but not in Puerto Rico. Twenty-nine of the island species are considered endangered, including the shy, giant iguana lizards that survive here up to five feet in length, rugged remnants of a long-ago age.

The island also thrives with wild doves, goats, and boars, and legal hunting is considered excellent. Endangered sea-turtles use the solitary

Conservation News, Vol. 39, No. 1 (January 1, 1974) pp 2–5.

beaches to lay their eggs unmolested. And, with no natural predators, millions of birds nest in rookeries along the elevated sea-facing cliffs and in the thick undergrowth of the island.

Life also abounds in the seas around Mona. The 1973 Environmental Quality Board of Puerto Rico stated that "Mona Passage is one of the main passageways for fish traveling from the Atlantic to the Caribbean, including the white and blue marlin, the humpback and pilot whales and the dolphins." It continues, saying that the "waters surrounding Mona are extraordinarily clear with a visibility of up to 200 feet. The fishing is excellent: large fish are very abundant, as well as lobsters and edible sea snails."

For years, isolated Mona has existed as a Wilderness and Wildlife Management Area of the Puerto Rican Department of Agriculture. The area has been managed in cooperation with the U.S. Department of the Interior and, in fact, both of the residents of the island are wildlife advisors.

The seemingly inexorable pressures of time, however, which have thus far eluded Mona are now threatening to unglue its remarkably intact ecosystem. The quiet little island with its abundant wildlife has suddenly burst its way into the headlines of the Caribbean. Over the loud protests of the Environmental Quality Board, the Puerto Rican Bar Association, other countries, and local conservationists, Gov. Rafael Hernandez Colon has decided to develop a major deepwater port and petrochemical complex on Mona Island. The development would include:

- an industrial complex of petroleum refineries and petrochemical industries;
- a superport for supertankers bringing now questionable supplies of oil and petroleum from the Middle East;
- a trans-shipping process to the U.S. mainland and to Puerto Rico;
- a desalination plant;
- a power plant with an underwater power coaxial cable crossing the Mona Channel;
- a huge breakwater complex;
- an instant community of 2,500 families complete with schools, housing, etc.

The decision to develop Mona Island was made by the governor partly on the basis of a whirlwind stop by Colon and two helicopterloads of cabinet members and aids. According to Tom Wiewandt, a Cornell University ecologist who was on the island during the August 18 incident, Governor Colon spent "only 4 minutes and 17 seconds" inspecting the resources of the island. The governor and his entourage breezed through part of the island's lighthouse, touring two rooms. The governor's only comment, according to a Department of Natural Resources staffer who was present, was to observe how large the regulation-sized billiard table in one of the rooms was.

Besides the Puerto Rican environmentalists who have vigorously opposed the project, Governor Colon is finding other detractors. Neighboring Dominican Republic, downwind and downcurrent from Mona, is also strongly opposed to the construction of a superport and refinery on the tiny island and has promised to fight the project to the end. One means of pressure the Dominican Republic has hinted it might bring to bear is withholding the massive amount of food stuffs it exports to heavily dependent Puerto Rico.

To complicate matters, the feasibility of the project may ultimately depend on Navy plans to switch its weapons range from distant Culebra to nearby Desecheo and Monito. The Navy, however, has never been anxious to leave Culebra, and having the superport built on Mona could provide it with a good excuse for abandoning the move plans because of Mona's proximity to its proposed new weapons range. The U.S. House Armed Services Committee recently confirmed its hesitancy to prompt a move when it announced that it favors maintaining Navy target practice on Culebera until 1985. It stated that it will not approve funds this fiscal year to transfer the weapons site to Desecheo and Monito Islands, apparently clearing the way for Governor Colon's superport visions.

So there it sits, tiny green Mona alone in the water with all her giant iguana and other wildlife passengers wondering if and when the heavy hand of progress is going to come down. Though a timetable on the superport has not apparently been made public yet and the current Arab oil embargo might affect plans, the Governor is reportedly anxious to move ahead with what one Puerto Rican conservationist called a "mortgage for present short-term economic gains against future long-term losses."

In a letter to President Nixon expressing opposition to the proposed development, a Puerto Rican M.D., Ada T. Capo de Colley, compared Mona to California's Channel Islands: "How would you feel if you placed your superport and your shelling range in the Channel Islands off the coast of California if you knew this was the last place where seals bred and lived? Our three tiny islands are the last place where our native species of giant iguana breeds and lives . . . and we like our iguanas just as much as you like your seals."

"For us who live in western Puerto Rico," Dr. Colley continued, "this is the only place we can turn to where we do not see people and people and more people, but nature as God intended it to be: balanced, silent, peaceful, and beautiful. When we go there we have to brave 10-ft. waves in a turbulent channel, yet we do it just to see this priceless treasure. You have many virgin areas in your spacious country. Please do not take away the only one we have."

TOPIC QUESTIONS

1. What is the "model society" and is this concept a reality or basically a long-term dream?
2. What is the role of technology in the context of the utopian view of the future?
3. Has the utopian concept influenced social planning and professional contributions by scientists, economists, technocrats, government officials, architects, and business leaders?
4. What is the ideal rate of change that a given culture should experience?
5. How severely could exponential demands on diminishing supplies of natural resources disrupt utopian influences in our society?
6. Are behavior modifications (pollution controls, resource conservation, responsible consumption) incompatible with model society concepts?
7. What is a technocracy and who determines resource allocations within it?
8. What is cultural lag and how does it influence marketing innovations?

Case 5

9. What makes solar energy such an attractive energy source for the nation?
10. How does solar energy compare with atomic energy as a long-term energy source for the nation?
11. What accounted for the long neglect that solar energy received from scientists and business firms?

Case 6

12. In your opinion is Mona Island a kind of utopia in its undeveloped and natural state? Why or why not?
13. Does the Puerto Rican governor have a different concept of a utopia in the case of Mona Island? How will his petrochemical project change the island?
14. How would you compare the economic benefits with the ecological costs of developing Mona Island?
15. What international aspects are involved in the proposed development of Mona Island?

RECOMMENDED READINGS

Alvin Toffler, *Future Shock* (New York: Bantam, 1971).

Donella H. Meadows, Dennis L. Meadows, Jorgen Randers, and William W. Behrens III, *The Limits to Growth* (New York: Universe, 1972).

William H. Whyte, Jr., *The Last Landscape* (Garden City, N.Y.: Doubleday, 1968).

Michael Piburn, *The Environment: A Human Crisis* (Rochelle Park, N.J.: Hayden Book Company, 1974).

Richard D. Steade, *Business and Society in Transition: Issues and Concepts* (San Francisco: Canfield Press, 1975).

FOOTNOTES

1. Webster defines utopia as "any visionary scheme or system for an ideally perfect social order." *Websters New World Dictionary* (Cleveland and New York: The World Publishing Co., College Edition, 1958) p. 1605. In our contemporary society utopia has become more than a vague, abstract dream world. It has taken on structure and it has been subjected to systematic model building processes. Science and technology have given mankind the means to design model societies and to organize the resources required to progress to a higher standard of excellence or a "better way of life." In a sense, our planning and resource utilization patterns are being determined by a "technocracy" of increasingly influential importance. A technocracy represents a doctrine and system of government suitable for a technological age, in which all economic resources, and hence the entire social system, would be controlled by scientists and engineers. The sometimes sharp disagreements concerning a proposed project that erupt at public hearings originate between moralists and social scientists on the one hand and technological specialists on the other. Moralists are typically concerned with how the pieces fit together in social cohesion; the technological specialists are evaluating new technical plans on the premise that they will contribute to the benefit of society.

2. See E. B. Weiss, "New Life Styles of 1975–1980 Will Throw Switch on Admen," *Advertising Age.* Vol. 43, No. 38 (September 18, 1972) pp. 61–67.

3. Alvin Toffler, *Future Shock* (New York: Bantam, 1971), p. 516.

4. Reprinted with special permission from *The American Farmer* (October 1974).

5. From *The Limits to Growth: A Report for THE CLUB OF ROME'S Project on the Predicament of Mankind,* by Donella H. Meadows, Dennis L. Meadows, Jorgen Randers, William W. Behrens, III, pp. 149, 150. A Potomac Associates book published by Universe Books, New York, 1972.

6. Michael Piburn, *The Environment: A Human Crisis* (Rochelle Park, N.J.: Hayden, 1974), p. 118.

7. *Applied Science and Technological Progress* (Washington, D.C.: National Academy of Sciences, 1967), pp. 4, 5.

8. *Conservation News* (May 1, 1974). National Wildlife Federation, Washington, D.C., p. 10.

9. As reported in the *St. Louis Post-Dispatch* (Thursday, September 26, 1974).

PART TWO

THE

ENVIRONMENTAL

RESTRAINTS

CHAPTER FOUR

ENVIRONMENTAL

MYOPIA

DEFINING THE PROBLEM

In man's impatience to convert natural resources into material affluence, he lost sight of the ecosystem; indeed, he evolved a myopic view of his place in the environment. Mankind disrupted long-established, life-giving processes that are governed by physical laws. In advancing rapid economic growth, technological innovations, and industrial productivity mankind enjoyed the fruits of economic efforts; but in the process, the human race greatly discounted damage incurred to stockpiles of natural wealth (or biological capital). Man is not unique in the earth's ecosystem, but an integral part of it. The integral relationship between exponential economic growth and environmental quality is depicted visually in Figure 4-1. Carried to an extreme, exponential growth can destroy a nation's economic system. At the same time, extreme ecological stresses bring environmental quality to crisis or collapse conditions.

Man's own biological life structure belongs in the intricate web of the ecology. Continued disruptions to the ecosystem and its resultant deterioration in natural wealth stocks threaten his survival. Only a determined resolve to correct ecological abuses can enhance man's long-term survival.

FIGURE 4-1 Exponential Growth, Economic and Ecosystems Impairment shown by Progressive Stages

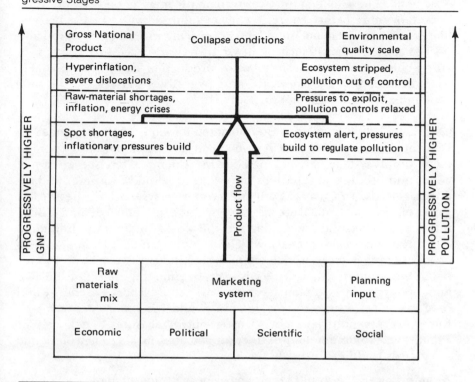

The relationship between the human factor and the natural order is described by Rachel Carson in her classic book *Silent Spring:*

> The balance of nature is not the same today as in Pleistocene times but it is still there; a complex, precise, and highly integrated system of relationships between living things which cannot be defied with impunity by a man perched on the edge of a cliff. The balance of nature is not a status quo; it is fluid, ever shifting, in a constant stage of adjustment. Man, too, is part of this balance. Sometimes, the balance is in his favor; sometimes—and all to often through his own activities—it is shifted to his disadvantage.[1]

In many respects the human race is more susceptible to adverse biological disruptions than are many other species. Man is situated at the top of the food chain; toxic substances have a way of becoming increasingly concentrated in the body tissues of animal life. Since man claims many species of higher animal life as food, he reaps toxic chemicals and minerals that were originally dumped hundreds (if not thousands) of miles away. In this respect, the human body eventually receives the stiffest dose of all. These toxic substances remain dormant in body tissues for a decade or more before triggering serious illnesses. Cancer has become increasingly linked to pollution levels occurring in both background and pocket concentrations (such as in or near lead-processing centers, in vinyyl-chloride work areas, in asbestos-production sections, by pesticide users in orchards and vineyards, and from food sources that become contaminated by local pollution sources).

Can Raw Material Shortages Be Alleviated through Crash Programs?

Demands for more of the earth's raw materials are expanding exponentially. Supply systems have not matched these demand levels; even capital goods and production capacities have lagged behind consumer and industrial needs. In essence, both the economic system and the world's stocks of biological capital are affected by this exponential demand. Both inflation and recession have plagued the world community simultaneously. Raw material shortages, which developed in part from abuses to biological capital stocks, stimulated many key industries to lobby for lower pollution standards. Raw materials even became the subject of international power politics, diplomacy, and world conferences for energy and food. Strong pressures to resolve energy and food shortages may well force governments to take more drastic control measures. A new wave of exhaustive exploration and extraction activities lacking environmental safeguards could easily break out.

Atomic Power. It would be an act of desperation to allow short-term expediency to further undermine biological capital. The time lags between cause and effect might well produce serious health problems at some future time. Robert and Leona Rienow discuss this health aspect, regarding efforts to expand atomic energy power sources to replace fossil fuels:

> The atomic energy people dwell on the fact that the dribbling from one plant is very minute. They fail to note that we aren't planning on building one plant. What we are building is a vast industry, gulping more water from our streams than any other industry in the nation.
> What is more, however much man dilutes radioactive wastes, nature, as with DDT, goes right on concentrating them. Take the case of zinc-65, a by-product of an atomic plant. Once the radioactive zinc-65 is let loose in the waste water it begins working its way toward man as if he were a magnet.[2]

The very presence of atomic energy plants represents a continuing health and safety hazard to mankind; until our management control systems can employ scientific means to neutralize radioactive wastes and prevent reactor accidents (which are blamed for radioactive leaks in water sources), many communities will be apprehensive about proposed atomic installations located in their regions.

Safety and health risks are not the only obstacles to the creation of a great atomic energy power industry. During 1974, nearly 40 atomic power projects representing an estimated cost of $10 billion were cancelled by U.S. electric utilities. The principal reasons cited by these utilities for cancellations were economic rather than environmental. While environmentalists opposed sudden expansions of atomic energy power installations primarily for health and safety reasons, customers citing projected higher costs and rate increases provided the final *coup de grace* to many proposed atomic power plants.

Oil Shale. If we should decide to quickly exploit our huge oil shale reserves in Colorado and other western states to increase energy production, what problems would be associated with this power source? If we were to extract as many as a million barrels of oil a day from shale deposits, we would have to move as much dirt in that day as we did in building the entire Panama Canal.[3] If we wanted to boost that output to 2 million barrels daily, which would equal the output of the Alaska pipeline, we would have to build a dam every 21 miles on the Colorado River just to get the water to cool the oil shale extraction plants. The interaction between economic capital and biological capital gives us a sense of perspective as we consider shale as an immediate oil source to alleviate energy shortages.

Major oil shale projects would further impair the environment of the western states. The Colorado River is a strategically important source of water for the rich agricultural industries in the southwestern states of California and Arizona. The Colorado River is extensively employed in irrigating American and Mexican crops. This long, narrow, winding river is already polluted. A major shale oil project on the Colorado River would threaten this valuable watershed as an agricultural resource.

Cultivate More Land? While energy shortages have disrupted the world community, food shortages have emerged as a potentially more dangerous threat to mankind's survival. The much acclaimed "green revolution," which employs chemical fertilizers, herbicides, plant hybrids, and heavy capital equipment promised to provide adequate supplies of food for the earth's billions. The energy crises disrupted both the supply of fertilizers and the energy to run the expensive farming equipment. In addition, unfavorable weather conditions made the problem even more serious.

How easily can we resolve the food gap? Are both economic and biological problems inherent in massive, new, food-growing projects? During 1974, the nation's farmers converted grasslands and set-aside (conservation) acreage to cropland. This conversion totaled an estimated 9,500,000 acres of grasslands and set-aside (conservation) acreage to cropland. Much of this land is marginal as cropland; thus, it requires heavy applications of costly fertilizers as well as favorable weather. (Unfortunately, in many of the western and Great Plains states droughts occur frequently.) Since the dust bowl years of the 1930s, greenbelts, tree line windbreaks, and conservation-minded farming practices have prevented the reoccurrence of wind-blown catastrophes. Figure 4-2 depicts a scene showing wind erosion.

FIGURE 4-2   Massive Soil Losses Predicted in Crop Conversion

Soil losses this year could exceed such 1957 losses as this severely wind-eroded field in Nebraska.

Source: Courtesy of USDA Soil Conservation Service.

The Great Plains "soil-bank" and "set-aside" programs, which removed millions of acres from crop production, have protected millions of acres of topsoil from the elements. The principle aim of set-aside legislation was the encouragement of conservation practices, which in turn limited huge grain surpluses that plagued the nation's agricultural industry during the 1950s and the 1960s. Idle acreage planted to legumes and grasses restored organic matter to the topsoil; moisture was retained better because of the dense cover of vegetation. These acres were in turn rotated to good grains, thus providing favorable soil conditions for increasing crop yields; the fields that had been in grain production were eventually rotated into the soil bank for revitalization. Soils protected by forestlands and grasslands experience a loss of less than a single ton of topsoil per acre; conversely, exposed land in cultivation has lost from 5 to 300 tons per acre of topsoil.

During 1973, growing concerns over inadequate world supplies of wheat, feed grains, and cotton spurred the U.S. Department of Agriculture to suspend set-aside programs for the next planting cycle. In an effort to encourage food production many conservation tracts were converted to croplands. Less than one-sixth of these 9.5 million "new acres" of farmland are considered ideally suited for crop production (U.S. Department of Agriculture Soil Conservation Service Criteria). In striving to fill a growing world food gap by dismantling sound conservation practices, we undermine the biological wealth that has made the nation's agriculture a great industry. Ironically, as soil conditions deteriorate, higher doses of fertilizers, pesticides, herbicides, and expenditures are required to produce crops of adequate yields. The combination of higher economic costs, unfavorable weather trends, shortages of vital items, and increased cultivation of marginal and drought-plagued farmland has given the agriculture industry disquieting moments. From nearly every aspect, the crash food grain drive of 1974 fell far short of its original production goals.

A Trade-off Dilemma: Food for Energy?   In our increasingly complex world, few answers to major problems are easily found. In the vast semi-arid regions of Montana a major environmental battle has emerged. In this spacious "big sky" land major deposits of low-sulfur coal are located near the surface of the earth. Low-sulfur coal has suddenly developed as an alternative to high-sulfur bituminous coal found in great abundance in such states as Illinois, Kentucky, Indiana, and Iowa. Air pollution standards discriminate against high-sulfur coal; under the original standards, industrial users of coal could not comply unless sulfur emissions were reduced by switching to coal with low-sulfur content. Montana is one of the nation's most scenic states, and it also has a vigorous cattle-ranching industry. Since many coal seams are found in river valleys, strip mining these areas would make cattle ranching most difficult, because the irrigated river valleys produce the winter hay and feed grains. Without these winter feed producing fields, ranches could not put away enough forage from the semi-arid hills to sustain cattle herds through the long, harsh winter months. An ecosystem uniquely adapted to the semi-arid climate of Montana and one that supports such diverse economic activities as tourism, cattle ranching, slope mining, and timbering can be easily destroyed by massive strip-mining projects. The dry climate discourages the return of vegetation at excavation sites.

In this case, biological capital is either wisely managed for long-term (ecologically sound) reasons, or it may be destroyed through highly disruptive means for short-term gain. To this extent, the reluctance of Montana ranchers to see their lands threatened by strip mining differs little from the reluctance of Floridians to see off-shore oil wells; tourism in Florida generates more than $7 billion per year income, much of which enhances small businesses, communities, and regions. The ecological disruptions and the ensuing losses in food production are severe in strip-mined regions. The impact of strip mining could be reduced drastically by thorough reclamation projects. Retention of topsoils in the black prairie soil belt is a necessary conservation practice if agricultural production is not to be sacrificed for short-term energy demands.

BIOLOGICAL CAPITAL: THE CRADLE OF LIFE

At the dawning of human history, mankind struggled against the perils of wilderness living. The human race was locked into a desperate fight to win a secure niche in the earth's ecosystem. The strong and the alert survived these perils. With senses sharpened and with determination to exist honed from encounters with marauding beasts, natural elements, and warfare, man became the top predator for food, fibers, and shelter in the wilderness.

Early civilizations were largely nomadic—skilled hunters and gatherers of fruits, vegetables, and berries. Despite all the perils of wilderness life, survival skills provided natural bounties that met the needs of entire villages or tribes.[4] This natural abundance could be harvested without capital goods; only simple tools and implements marked the staple items used by early wilderness civilizations. When a region's food or water supplies were exhausted, the inhabitants would simply move into a new, unspoiled area.

In North America, colonial settlers from Europe found the wilderness full of wild game; great forests yielded an abundance of wood, nuts, herbs, and tubulars. Rivers, lakes, and coastal estuaries contained a rich variety of fish, lobsters, oysters, shrimp, fowl, etc. The fertile soil, which nature nurtured through many centuries in grasslands and forests, became the cornerstone of a flourishing agricultural industry (especially in Virginia). An abundance of mineral deposits that could be harvested by simple hand tools from the earth's surface provided early settlers with the expanded assortment of items needed to establish permanent communities—first along the Atlantic coast, and later into the vast interior of the United States. To this extent, our nation quickly rose from the wilderness to become a great world power. Indeed, throughout human history the abundance of biological capital has given impetus for the forging of powerful civilizations.

Throughout the world as mankind destroyed the wilderness and, simultaneously, reduced by primitive means the availability of biological capital, the ecological balance of nature became disrupted. Deserts, diseases, dust bowls, barren hillsides, stagnant waterholes, dried river beds, eroded soil, and famines brought once-powerful civilizations to decay and oblivion.[5] Acts that deteriorate the earth's biological capital have accelerated greatly since the Industrial Age. Within just the past three decades, science and technology have combined to assault the environment with pollutants, earth-alteration projects, and resource-acquisition schemes that threaten to disrupt the environment so seriously that our own survival has become threatened. The incompatible relationship between our conventional employment of economic capital and its effect on biological capital is underscored by Barry Commoner.

> The course of environmental deterioration shows that as conventional capital has accumulated, for example in the United States since 1946, the value of the biological capital has *declined*. Indeed, if the process continues, the biological capital may eventually be driven to the point of total destruction. Since the usefulness of conventional capital in turn depends on the existence of the biological capital—the ecosystem—when the latter is destroyed, the usefulness of the former is also destroyed. Thus despite its apparent prosperity, in reality the system is being driven into bankruptcy.[6]

Inflation, shortages, pollution, international tensions, famines, poverty are symptoms of our contemporary world. If most of the earth's economically accessible raw materials are consumed by a single generation, can science fill this tremendous resource void?

Biological capital can become impaired by economic activities in two primary ways. From Figure 4-3, one may note that biological capital can be extracted from its original state, whether the source is in a wilderness condition, in an estuary, in a mountainous region, on a flat prairie, or in populated regions. Indirect activities related to extractive work, including explorations, road building, immigration of workmen and families, and processing installations can often do more ecological damage than the primary extraction work itself. Biological capital is also impaired as economic products of all kinds begin returning to the earth as solid wastes, liquids, and gaseous pollutants.

THE CASE OF STARSHIP 0011[7]

The initial fiery rocket launch was executed as programmed, sending the gleaming spaceship into the stratosphere. Recovering from the first anxious moments of blast-off, the crew became confident that the mission

FIGURE 4-3

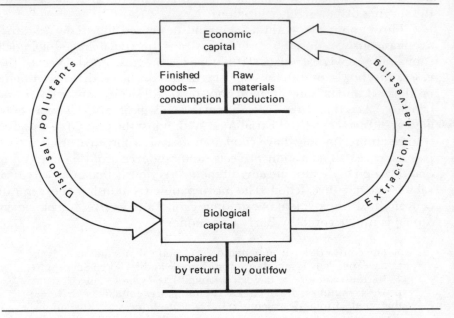

would be successful. Targeted for Mars, the ship slipped through the earth's gravitational field into the void of deep space. For the next eleven months, the crew of Starship 0011 would journey to the mysterious red planet and would chart, map, photograph, and conduct scientific experiments. Two scientists aboard the ship would use special photographic equipment to search for large deposits of natural wealth. The planet would be closely analyzed to determine if any form of life exists or if any life ever manifested itself on the bleak surface.

Spaceship 0011 was a self-contained vessel, being able to sustain life during the mission. Although the crew was completely freed of earth's gravity, it retained the fullness of the earth's life-supporting resources—an atmosphere, food, energy (except solar), protective gear, water, etc. The mission's success in deep space depended on items borrowed from our world, which would nurture human life even in the vast void of deep space. Without these provisions, the crew would quickly expire; the great space technology as evidenced in Spaceship 0011 would drift lifeless for countless ages—eventually leaving the solar system entirely.

During their journey to Mars, the astronauts would carefully ration their demands on the provisions stored away in the space vessel. Initial satellite reports indicated that Mars has neither a life-supporting atmosphere nor the water or food stocks that could replenish depleted supplies in a mother ship. The entire eleven-month journey would be supported entirely by the initial inventory provided by ground control on earth. If the crew wasted its allocated stores, they would die in space, long before reaching the earth on the return flight. If the crew damaged the engineering system on board Starship 0011, the journey would end in some tragedy—such as loss of oxygen, directional controls, cabin heat, or power to the main rockets.

The severity of the abject harshness of space requires careful husbanding of all life-supporting elements to the travelers to distant celestial bodies. Scientific and biological requirements must be harmonized carefully.

OUR LIFE-SUPPORT SYSTEM

The Atmosphere

"Spaceship earth" is a self-contained, self-supporting home for countless forms of life. Despite the earth's long orbit around the sun through the barren hostility of outer space, a highly protective but thin strata of life-giving atmospheric gasses remains trapped on this globe.

Nearer the earth's surface atmospheric gasses are more concentrated. The 20 percent oxygen content in this rich layer of gasses makes it possible for higher forms of life to exist. Carbon dioxide supports plant life, while nitrogen, hydrogen, and other gasses assist in their growth and development. Through the process called photosynthesis water and carbon dioxide, stimulated by sunlight on chlorophyll, give off oxygen into the atmosphere. This process results in a delicate exchange system between plants and the atmosphere, thus keeping oxygen and carbon dioxide levels stabilized.

Our atmosphere further facilitates life-support functions by being the agent for inducing weather changes. Winds, temperature, water vapor, lightning, and precipitation help regulate water levels, climate, and other conditions conducive to life. Where rainfall is abundant and temperatures are warm, insect, plant, and animal life exists in lush proportions. Near the equator in the vast tropical rain forests of the mighty Amazon River Basin the vegetation literally engulfs the landscape; these forests shelter a rich variety of wildlife, insects, plants, and reptiles.

The Water Kingdom

Water and oxygen combine to produce the earth's most extensive kingdom, the sea. This vast ecosystem thrives despite the ocean's salt content. In fact, the shallow estuaries along the coasts are among the most abundant producers of life found anywhere on earth. Annually one acre of this water may produce more than 10 tons of fish life![8] An estuary is all or part of the tidal portion of the navigable waters up to the mean high water line, including—but not limited to—any bay, sound, lagoon, or channels. Here fresh water ends its long journey to the sea and mingles with salt water. Nutrients flowing into the sea from the land provide food for the diverse sea life that breeds, spawns, and grows along the coasts. Shore birds, wading birds, and water foul patrol the shallows; shrimp, clams, crabs, oysters, and various other forms of sea life swim around in the oxygen-rich waters of these coastal areas. Plant life abounds, providing habitat and food for the small frey that hatch in the warm coastal waters of estuaries. It is unfortunate that these wonderous sea nursuries are being systematically destroyed along the coasts from pollution, dredging, shell fishing, dumping, and chemical poisons.

In deeper water along the continental shelf an abundance of larger sea life abounds. Oxygen is produced by plankton, a floating mass of minute species of plant and animal life. In fact, this prolific life produces oxygen not only for use by sea life, but it also provides the earth with approximately 70 percent of its oxygen! Plankton is also a valuable food for schools of fish. Larger sea life follow the plankton as it moves along the ocean currents. Sharks, whales, salmon, porpoises, and tuna feed on smaller fish. Even within the depths of the ocean where fish life have become specially adapted to living in total darkness, oxygen filters down to their levels. Currents moved by winds and by the earth's rotation agitate and mix the ocean's waters, sending oxygen and nutrients to lower depths. Cold water from the poles flows toward the equator, cooling coastlines and islands in hot areas of the world. Warm water from the equator flows toward the poles, touching in its circular path the coastlines of cold countries, thus influencing the climate toward milder temperatures. These differences in temperature in ocean currents add substantially to the amount of precipitation that falls to the earth.

ACCUMULATION OF BIOLOGICAL CAPITAL

Life does not take from nature. Except for modern man, there is no net drain on earth's resources because life exists here. All forms of life have for countless ages left more than they extracted. Even the deaths of plants and animals enrich the soil and provide food, shelter, and sustenance for the living. Henry David Thoreau, one of America's greatest naturalist-philosophers, observed the relationship of life and death. "Every part of nature teaches that the passing away of one life is the making of room for another. The oak dies down to the ground, leaving within its rind a virgin mould, which will impart a vigorous life to an infant forest."[9] Decaying vegetation releases quantities of free nitrogen, which remains in the humus. Seedlings and young plants find this organic nursery ideal for growth. Water, nitrogen, air, and nutrients are easily attainable by vegetation living in the rich humus topsoil of forests and grasslands. Where forests and prairie grasses have existed for thousands of years free from man's exploitation, the humus and topsoil may have accumulated to depths of several feet.

The vast American midwestern corn belt with its rich, black soil was made through the processes of life, death, and decomposition of vegetation. Fall prairie grasses, which grew profusely for centures, fell to the ground every winter and deposited thick mats of decaying vegetation. In the spring new grasses from roots and seeds utilized the previous year's grasses for food, water, and protection. All forms of life especially adapted to this prairie land lived in abundance. The large, shaggy buffalo was an undisputed king in this flat domain. Strong, courageous, hearty, and uniquely adapted to this prairie land, he lived in abundance in Illinois. An unsuccessful French voyager, Sieur d'Iberville, hoped to skin between 60,000 to 80,000 buffaloes in Illinois country during the early 1700s.[10] How many of these shaggy animals once roamed the tall grass country in Illinois before the European fur traders decimated them is not known.

Although numerous, the buffaloes gave to the prairie grasses more than they took. Their droppings fertilized the soil. Their meat provided food for bears, wolves, lynx, and other alert predators that killed young, wounded, or weak buffaloes. The vigorous prairie grasses nourished all prairie life either directly or indirectly. Water was held in grassy marshes, swamps, and slow-moving streams. Beavers built reservoirs behind massive dams. The prairie grasses and the humus sheltered the soil from the hot summer sun, preventing the land from drying out. Underground water reserves were easily attainable by long-rooted big bluestems, switchgrass, Indian grass, and prairie cordgrass. So balanced was the vegetation in the original prairie that few, if any, noxious weeds grew.

So rich and deep was the prairie's topsoil that decades of specilized agricultural practices have failed to exhaust the humus and fertility of this valuable biological resource. This valuable biological capital is becoming increasingly important as a world resource for food. Unfortunately, our farming practices have deteriorated this valuable natural resource; reliance on chemical fertilizers and double-cropping practices has increased soil erosion and lowered organic content. As pressures for higher food production mount to meet growing feed requirements in the United States and in world markets, the age-old practices of crop rotation and planting green manure crops (both of which revitalize the soil and maintain its biological wealth) will continue to decline.

The vast grain-producing region known as the corn belt is an essential world resource. The unique combinations of organic matter, soil depth, rainfall, fertility, and temperatures in the midsection of our nation can not be duplicated in any other region in the world. In this temperate-zone ecosystem, energy derived from the sun by plant life is stored in the ground.

In the immense tropical rain forests, however, nutrients are stored primarily in the vegetation instead of in the soil. These plants retain 70 percent of the total mineral nutrient supply of the system. The remaining soil nutrients are quickly leached from the topsoil once the underbrush is cleared and exposed to the torrential rains. Intensive agricultural practices usually must be abandoned on cleared sites after only the third harvest. Only along the ribbons of flood plains and lakes do rich soil and silt deposits exist. In a comprehensive study of the two largest wilderness areas remaining on earth, 28 scientists and anthropologists concluded that jungle lands could never be opened up to support large populations.[11] Thus, these last tractless wilderness lands cannot be considered as a future soil bank to eventually replace our own corn belt.

Does Nature Recycle?

We normally associate recycling with a human experience. Because man has the power to alter the environment, he may overload the ecosystem with pollutants and reap the consequences of toxic substances. The natural forces of the ecosystem are much more important in recycling these wastes than we may first realize. Natural recycling systems are continuously at work purifying the air, water, and soil.

The interactions of wind, air, water currents, sunlight, chemical reactions, and lifeforms are capable of processing vast quantities of waste materials. Unfortunately, contemporary culture considers natural recycling to be a free resource. As continued cumulative build-ups overload the natural recycling processes, visible pollution occurs. There is a limit to the waste burden that natural systems can process without endangering the ecosystem and the lifeforms within it. Pollution can literally saturate the cleansing processes. Waste becomes recirculated in the biosphere rather than removed from it. Small quantities of highly toxic chemicals and nuclear substances can be especially destructive to the ecosystem. Since mankind is at the top in the life chain, he either reaps the benefit of the natural cleansing (a clean environment) or he suffers the consequences of absorbing the impurities that nature could not filter out. Either way, mankind participates in the drama of natural filtration and recycling processes.

An enlightened view of natural recycling processes is to consider how we might assist the ecosystem in waste material disposition. Reducing the flow of poisons into the natural arena and developing new technologies that more rapidly neutralize wastes represent two approaches.

EARTH DAY 1970— AN HISTORIC TURNING POINT

Americans inherited an abundance of biological capital from a continental land mass that remained virtually unsettled until the 17th century.

Early settlers struggled against natural elements to forge a frontier civilization. The great abundance of wildlife, wood, seafood, waterways, and favorable climates brought this wilderness colony to the formative years, where a national identity and purpose emerged; the struggle for indepence created a new nation which soon assumed the status of a world power. This early wilderness experience created the spirit of self-sufficiency, which in turn became possible because of our natural wealth. Although the early Americans lacked manufactured goods, they managed to maintain a viable economy despite coastal blockades imposed by the British Naval Fleet during the Revolutionary War and the War of 1812. They wrestled food, clothing, fibers, and fuel from biological stocks provided by nature.

The traditions of exploitation—impairing and depleting natural resources—are so ingrained in this nation's character that little social thought was given to the subject of environmental quality until 1970; more than 300 years elapsed between the early Pilgrim days and Earth Day!

The Awakening

Environmental awareness literally sprang from college campuses all across the nation. In seminars, rap sessions, protest marches, and sit-ins, young people speculated about the terrifying consequences of man's myopic abuses of his environment. One sobering thesis caught the attention of affluent America: we were heading for a colossal collision with nature—a collision that could literally eradicate the human specie, or at least make it an endangered specie. At these university gatherings speakers projected when such natural backlashes might occur, if we were to remain on the collision course. Such dates as 1984 (more symbolic perhaps than realistic), 1990, 2000, and 2020 were cited as critical years during which American society would be confronted with complex combinations of natural calamities. While too much of our attention was focused on the possible biological catastrophies during Earth Day, the many pronouncements of impending doom served to startle an affluent society from other matters.

One of the most frustrating aspects of the early environmental activities was the lack of data, cases, studies, integration, and conceptualization of man's conflict with the environment. Conservationists, wildlife experts, and dedicated scientists such as Rachel Carson provided valuable fundamental knowledge to the environmental question.

The author conducted a marketing seminar on marketing and the ecological issues during the spring quarter of 1970. The reading materials then available to the class are listed here:

1. Boughey, Arthur S., *Ecology of Populations* (New York: Macmillan, 1968).

2. Carson, Rachel Louise, *The Sea Around Us,* rev. ed. (New York: Oxford University Press, 1961).
3. Carson, Rachel Louise, *Silent Spring* (Boston: Houghton Mifflin, 1962).
4. Coyle, David Cushman, *Conservation, An American Story of Conflict and Accomplishment* (New Brunswick, N.J.: Rutgers University Press, 1957).
5. Darling, Frank Fraser, *Future Environments of North America* (Garden City, N.Y.: Natural History Press, 1966).
6. Darling, Frank Fraser, *Men and Nature in the National Parks* (Washington, D.C.: Conservation Foundation, 1967).
7. Day, James Wentworth, *Poison on the Land* (New York: Philosophical Library, 1957).
8. George, John L., *The Pesticide Problem* (New York: New York Zoological Society, 1957).
9. Goldman, Marshall I., *Controlling Pollution* (Englewood Cliffs, N.J.: Prentice-Hall, 1967).
10. Jennings, Burgess Hill, *Interaction of Man and His Environment.* ed. B. H. Jennings and J. E. Murphy (New York: Plenum Press, 1966).
11. Committee on Pest Control and Wildlife Relationships, *Pest Control and Wildlife Relationships* (Washington, D.C.: National Research Council, 1962).
12. Netboy, Anthony, *The Atlantic Salmon: A Vanishing Species* (Boston: Houghton Mifflin, 1968).
13. Rudd, Robert L., *Pesticides and the Living Landscape* (Madison, Wis.: University of Wisconsin Press, 1964).
14. Whitten, Jamie L., *That We May Live* (Princeton, N.J.: Van Nostrand, 1966).
15. Ziswiler, Vinzenz, *Extinct and Vanishing Animals* (New York: Springer-Verlag, 1967).

The seminar was hampered by obvious omissions of integrative references in the business field. The class prepared detailed outlines of marketing topics most closely related to the ecology issue. Packaging, recycling, product planning, transportation, the marketing mix, and technological innovations headed the list. Vance Packard's *The Hidden Persuaders* and John Kenneth Galbraith's *The Affluent Society* provided added discussion stimuli. Unfortunately, this seminar became a casualty of still another crisis—student protests over the Vietnam war, during which the university was closed. Ironically, the tensions that originally gave impetus to the ecology movement also contributed greatly to much of the confusion that swirled around Earth Day 1970. The enormous task of providing clarification, data, and integrative studies that could give the movement direction remained to be done.

The Issues
Geologic ages tick off nature's timepiece by the millions of years. Human beings operate in much shorter time dimensions; speed, action, and

dynamic growth are factors of human experience that often ignore environmental laws. We often fail to detect the triggering mechanisms that move the natural world into a new phase or cycle. Climatic changes, for example, occur within shorter time frames than do the geologic ages, but exist well beyond man's time concepts. In the earth's rhythm climate has greatly influenced both the geologic features of land surfaces, as well as life itself. Scientists are expressing increasing concern that the earth has passed through a highly favorable weather cycle that may not reoccur for another 100,000 years.[12] If we are experiencing a climate change that is heading toward cooler temperatures, what influences will this have on global winds and moisture patterns? Is food production to be adversely affected? Has the world's population of 4 billion persons expanded well beyond the earth's carrying capacity? Have exponential demands for natural resources brought the human race to an impending economic crisis? In carving up the world for economic gain, has civilization reached the threshold of ecological survival?

These questions suggest the magnitude and complexities of the environmental problem. Solving these worldwide issues will call for patience, reasoning, restraint, resolve, and international cooperation. Unfortunately, expediency often dictates national policies, which in turn introduce military intervention. It seems clear that the restraint of the earth's most powerful nations in the face of possible worldwide famines, shortages, and political-economic blackmail will be severely tested. The temptation to overreach militarily to gain access to strategic raw materials invites nuclear war. While the world is approaching exponential growth limits in respect to many resources, the really dangerous period begins well before all raw materials are completely exhausted and the biosphere is choked with pollution. Power politics played by a single nation or by blocks of nations could easily disrupt world trading patterns and standards of living.

The environmental problem, based on human experience and options, is summed up by the *Club of Rome* into three categories:

1. If the present growth trends in world population, industrialization, pollution, food production, and resource depletion continue unchanged, the limits to growth on this planet will be reached sometime within the next 100 years. The most probable result will be a rather sudden and uncontrollable decline in both population and industrial capacity.

2. It is possible to alter these growth trends and to establish a condition of ecological and economic stability that is sustainable far into the future. The state of global equilibrium could be designed so that the basic material needs of each person on earth are satisfied and each person has an equal opportunity to realize his individual human potential.

3. If the world's people decide to strive for this second outcome rather than the first, the sooner they begin working to attain it, the greater will be their chances of success.[13]

The cultural and economic interests within our world community of nations are highly resistant to modifications. Shifting economic priorities, controlling pollution, shifting life-style choices, and limiting population growth to achieve an equilibrium on a worldwide basis are issues that seem remote. During the First World Population Conference, which took place in Bucharest in August 1974, representatives of underdeveloped countries were quick to point out that massive resource waste of the industrialized world accounts for far more resource depletion than does the underdeveloped world's population. The underdeveloped countries emphasized economic development as the prime means of solving population problems. From the industrialized nations, authorities contended that overpopulation of the world may overtax food and other resources and eventually decrease the quality of life. The famines of 1974 struck hardest of all in the underdeveloped countries of India, Pakistan, Bangladesh, the sub-Sahara, Indonesia, and parts of Latin American. Nearly 20 percent of the population of these countries starved to death during the famine. Malnutrition would account for disease-related deaths and for widespread mental retardation in the hunger zones. The lack of vitality and productivity of those deficient in nutrients contribute significantly to restoration difficulties.

Although food production is one-third greater than 10 years ago, demand for food has increased faster, principally because of world population growth and feed-grain programs for the livestock industry in the industrialized nations. The promise of the green revolution has diminished because of cooling trends in polar and temperate regions, droughts in subtropical regions, and fertilizer shortages. As a result, food production in underdeveloped countries has not only failed to keep up with population increases but has declined as well. The poor nations are struggling to maintain their largely cereal-based diet.

The growing food crisis continues to divide the world community in other ways. Depending on his relationship to the sea, man has been captivated by, challenged by, attracted to, and repelled by the oceans. But whatever the personal psychic relationship of man to the diverse riches of the oceans, the seas have always been there like time eternal—untouched, limitless, and nearly always profitable. Most people thought that the world's oceans were too huge to ever deplete, and the human dreams of never-ending ocean bounty continued unchallenged. That has all changed! Fishing has become more essential to underdeveloped nations both as a cash item and as food. The presence of large deposits of off-shore oil and minerals near coastal waters has sparked international squabbles over jurisdiction or ownership. In 1973, Peru unilaterally proclaimed a 200-mile tuna fishing limit; this act nearly touched off a military confrontation. More recently, the so-called cod war precipitated dangerous encounters between Icelandic patrol vessels and British frigates in disputed fishing areas off Iceland. Foreign fishing activities off the U.S. east coast provoked political confrontations.

Prompted by a burgeoning world population, diminishing agricultural production, pollution, and over-fishing decimating popular species, countries everywhere, including Iceland, Peru, and Equador, are becoming jealously possessive about their adjacent waters. While current international law limits territorial fishing water to 12 miles off shore, the growing food crisis and the dwindling supplies of the most popular species will motivate other countries to likewise extend sea limits to the 200-mile mark. Pollution can destroy the remaining fishing grounds on the earth. Figure 4-4 depicts two alternatives systems (or loops). Loop *A* illustrates the flow of pollutants from the economic system to the environment. Loop *B* illustrates the reuse concept.

FIGURE 4-4

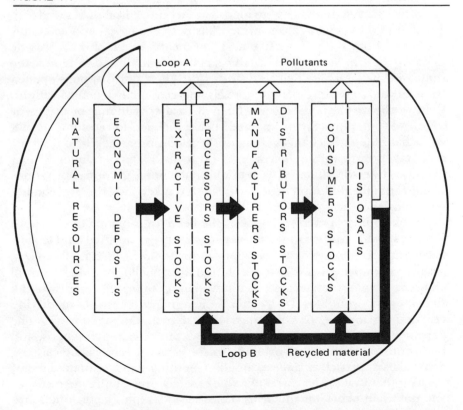

The basic conditions leading to a worldwide accommodation of or equilibrium between economic demands and environmental limits are not being met. The example of the food crisis suggests that the biological capital base that spawns an ecosystem, which in turn accounts for the relative yields of food-producing activities by man, will continue to erode.

CONCLUSIONS

Economic exploitation, technological splendor, and political rivalry by competing international systems are in many ways extensions of earlier civilizations; but our contemporary society is unique in history in three respects. (1) The current generation is recognizing that the earth is finite and that our economic appetites are pushing against the limits of our finite natural resources. (2) This generation is recognizing that high levels of worldwide pollution are a threat to mankind's own survival. (3) We are looking to science and technology to resolve our resource difficulties by creating economic wealth from oceans and from common matter such as rocks, soil, sands, etc.

The first two points serve to identify that our civilization is faced with a real environmental problem which has both ecological and economic segments. Both the way we live and the means we employ to provide private goods threaten to disrupt the earth's web of life and to deplete the finite raw material base that feeds industry. The painful options opened for mankind to balance pollution levels and economic demands with his finite world are to change the way he lives, to alter economic priorities, or to control pollution. Environmentalists are inclined to recommend that we initiate life-style changes that conserve consumer goods and adjust economic growth within the context of our raw material budget. Strong pressures by environmentalists to establish meaningful control programs suggest that the pollution issue is considered a key factor in any equilibrium model.

While our generation recognizes the need for initiating one or more solutions, much confusion exists over specific programs. We tend to view science and technology as an "eleventh-hour" savior from critical ecological and economic crisis. If science should bring pollution under control and relieve resource shortage, as many believe, then adjustments with a finite world would evolve without changing life styles, modifying economic priorities, or initiating restrictive pollution controls. The danger with this approach rests with flaws, defects, imperfections, and limitations of scientific innovations to solve broad ecosociological conflicts. This approach is, at best, an all or nothing gamble on the lives of future generations. The corrective role of science in eliminating resource and pollution problems should be considered within longer time spans and within narrow, specialized tasks. Environmentalists suggest that pollution regulation and conservation actions taken today will give mankind a better chance to cope with ecological and resource crises in future times. Science can better assist us if we do not place back to back cumulative crises that threaten within a single decade. Society requires lead time to adjust to individual problem areas. Thus limitations are not only scientific, but also require economic accomodations, political direction, and cultural cooperation. The environmental issues are complex and require coordinated programs from all sectors of society.

Case 7
The Backyard Wildlife Refuge

THE WILDERNESS ECOSYSTEM

The wilderness represents the ideal habitat for the earth's wildlife. Within their shrinking boundaries, wilderness regions offer sanctuary for a wide variety of animals, birds, fish, insects, and plant life. The ecosystem functions in harmony with the life-supporting processes; vegetation provides food and shelter for wildlife and protects the soil from erosion by laying down thick mantles of organic materials. Water flowing from underground springs and primeval watersheds is often pure enough to drink by man.

The wilderness is not the ideal habitat for contemporary civilization. The growth of our nation has historically been linked to subjugating or conquering the wilderness to accommodate cities, roads, industrial sites, recreation areas, farmland, and so forth. In many instances the wilderness is viewed as a hostile foe—to be eradicated to the last symbol.

Fortunately, the environmental movement is giving recognition to the value of wilderness areas in respect to the world's climate, ecosystem, water resources, and as a sanctuary to a growing list of endangered wildlife species. Man himself is viewing the wilderness as a necessary collective good which rekindles the human spirit and restores the physical vitality of bodies fatigued by routine suburban living. The wilderness is a unique ecosystem which deserves to have its value analyzed as a total entity rather than as a reservoir of singular items—minerals, furs, recreation, farming, rare earths, etc. The wilderness is a priceless resource simply because it exists, and its value grows as more of our world is converted into urban and industrial developments. The wilderness is a resource which requires both management and protection. Steele discusses this aspect of the wilderness in "The Marketing of the Wilderness Cause."

Of current social issues, one of the most broadly discussed is environment and ecology. While most attention focuses on pollution and energy, there is another irreparable loss soon to occur if current trends continue—namely, our wilderness resources. Albeit man could scrub clean his atmosphere and water resources, collect and recyle his rubble, and mine the seas for food, he cannot restore virgin wilderness. At best, he can struggle to retain what little remains.

The United States has only a finite amount of outdoor area from which to extract raw materials, on which to produce food, in which to reside, and with which people can amuse themselves. This fixed supply of land is being gobbled up at a ferocious rate for a host of uses. Our burgeoning population and high consumption orientation are placing unprecedented pressure on land area along many dimensions. Outdoor resources of all types are certainly feeling this pressure but perhaps recreational lands most of all.

Nationwide there is ample evidence of a distinct trend of Americans back to the out of doors. Sales of camper vehicles and camping equipment are booming. All-terrain vehicles, trail bikes, and snowmobiles are everywhere. According to Merrill Lynch et al., backpacking alone has evolved into a $25 million/year industry. Further, the U.S. licenses 15,000,000 to 17,000,000 hunters annually, and in 1970 Americans spent $3.4 billion at the retail level for boats and accessories alone.

Fortunately there have been some very legitimate and responsible organizations involved in conservation work. Some of the more widely known include the Audubon Society, the National Rifle Association, the National Wildlife Federation, the Sierra Club, and the Wilderness Society. Less fortunately, however, the battles these organizations wage are too frequently of a fire-fighting nature. Although they are in a sense very forward looking, they seem to lack the skills to accomplish that which is in their very best interests—namely, identifications and recruitment to membership of those sympathetic to their cause. All of these organizations have at least one common goal—specifically, wilderness preservation for wildlife habitat, natural beauty, and American heritage.[14]

Most Americans have little contact with the wilderness. Time pressures, distances, costs, and physical exertion prevent many persons from experiencing the solitude and challenges of remote regions. By their very nature wilderness regions are easily destroyed by economic and recreational activities.

BACKYARD HABITAT

Wilderness habitat is lost to wildlife in most developed areas in the U.S. Fortunately, many varieties of wildlife tolerate man and his living patterns. Suburbs, for example, can be made accommodating to a wide variety of animal and bird life. Homeowners can convert a backyard into a mini wildlife refuge by planting trees, shrubs, and vines, which supply both food and shelter. The attractiveness of these refuges can be greatly enhanced with the addition of small ponds and nesting boxes. Natural areas which contain hedges, long grasses, and bushes further enhance the backyard for wildlife. In one of the most popular articles published in *National Wildlife,* Thomas, Brush, and DeGraaf describe a step-by-step plan to create valuable wildlife habitat around the home. The plan consists of three basic stages.*

Stage I. If the homeowner starts with only a sodded yard an if trees, shrubs, and herbs suitable for the region are planted, some sparse, but usable wildlife habitat takes form. Artificial feeders and bird baths are usually required to augment food and water resources. Nesting boxes supplement nesting sites around the yard. Early residents of the backyard refuge should include robins, ground-feeding sparrows, finches, and an occasional cottontail rabbit. Besides the basic tree and shrub stock, additional decorative and food-bearing varieties may be provided as the homeowner evolves a specific habitat plan. Crowding of plants must be avoided, and where necessary relocate plants; those which will soon outgrow their growing spaces. Leave enough open space in the yard so that one can observe the visitors without disturbing them. The eventual heights of plantings should be considered early. The taller ones should be planted in the rear or edges of the yard. Visually pleasing growth can be accentuated by varying the heights of plants.

Stage II. Within about 5 to 10 years shrubs are fairly mature and the trees are about 25 feet tall. If the yard was originally thickly planted, dense wooded pockets of young trees and shrubs need thinning. This is necessary to achieve both balanced sun-grass-shade habitat and to give young growing plants sufficient room to acquire adequate water and soil nutrients.

In Stage II there will be enough flowers and fruits to attract a variety of birds and insects, which in turn attract reptiles and amphibians. A small pond will replace the bird bath. Robins will raise broods in the trees. Catbirds, cardinals, and song sparrows will nest in the denser shrubbing. Dusk will bring rabbits to browse in the security of your yard. Mornings will find chipmunks emerging from holes in stone walls to scurry up trees.

Stage III. Starting from scratch, one can expect Stage III to evolve some 30 to 40 years after initial planting. The Stage III yard consists of varied mature trees, with hardwoods in full fruit production, plus mature shrubs and sufficient open areas. If a homeowner purchases a yard with a reasonable number of mature trees (producing fruits and nuts) and a little shrubbery, Stage III can be achieved in 5 to 10 years. Additional plantings of shrubbery and low vegetation would provide such a yard sufficient habitat to qualify for this third phase.

This stage attracts the maximum number of wildlife species. Orioles and tanagers will nest in the higher branches. Rabbits will feed on the lawn and low shrubs and may even raise their young in well-hidden nests.

*Jack Ward Thomas, Robert O. Bush, and Richard M. DeGraaf, "Invite Wilderness to Your Backyard," *National Wildlife,* Vol. 11, No. 3 (April–May 1973), pp. 5–16.

Squirrels will live in tree hollows or nest boxes, if available. Chipmunks, field mice, garter snakes, toads, butterflies, and other insects make the backyard their home.

As darkness falls, bats and night hawks may swing through the sky on feeding flights. Deeper into the night, whippoorwills and owls will mingle their calls with croaks of frogs and the chirps and trills of katydids.

Four Wildlife Needs. All wildlife, indeed all life, requires four basic elements to survive: food, water, cover as protection from natural enemies and the elements, and areas where they can reproduce their young. Combinations of these four elements are unique for each species, but a well-planned habitat can offer enough combinations to attract the greatest number and variety of wildlife to an area, neighborhood, or backyard.

In urban apartment houses, window boxes and feeders give hardy birds the opportunity to find resting and feeding spots in an otherwise scenario of concrete and steel. On rooftops of downtown buildings small gardens and decorative arrangements of flowers and small, slow-growing shrubs provide at least some link with the natural world. In one high school conservation program, for example, urban students from apartments became enthusiastic about applying small touches of the natural world to their otherwise barren environment through window boxes, potted plants, rooftop gardens, vegetable gardens in small plots provided by a nearby landowner, and the use of park facilities to study natural systems.

Unfortunately, the tendency to crowd housing developments into bulldozed plots containing practically no vegetation (with the exception of sod) makes the job of habitat rehabilitation more difficult. Numerous other facilitating services such as large paved areas, streets, utility poles, insect spraying, industrial pollution, dense traffic, and so forth hampers the homeowner's search for links with the natural world through wildlife and its supporting habitat. Clean farming practices and drainage projects that rob areas of surface water and habitat further contribute to wildlife difficulties. The problem of environmental quality often begins and ends right at home, in a neighborhood, around a city, and in a region. We do not have to look thousands of miles away toward some exotic wilderness retreat for an issue or controversy.

Case 8
A Salt Marsh Ecosystem—Its Life, and Death

Along the eastern coast of North America—from the north where ice packs grate upon the shore, to the tropical mangrove swamps tenaciously hold-

John Teal and Mildred Teal, "Ribbon of Green—The Epic of a Salt Marsh," *Audobon*, the magazine of the National Audobon Society, Vol. 71, No. 6 (November 1969), p.4.

ing the land together with a tangle of roots—lies a green ribbon of soft, salty, wet, low-lying land, the salt marshes.

The ribbon of green marshes, part solid land, part mobile water, has a definite but elusive border, now hidden, now exposed, as the tides of the Atlantic fluctuate. At one place and tide there is a line at which you can say, "here begins the marsh." At another tide, the line, the "beginning of the marsh," is completely inundated and looks as though it had become part of the sea. The marsh reaches as far inland as the tides can creep and as far into the sea as marsh plants can find a root hold and live in saline waters.

The undisturbed salt marshes offer the inland visitor a series of unusual perceptions. At low tide, the wind blowing across spartina grass sounds like wind on the prairie. When the tide is in, the gentle music of moving water is added to the prairie rustle. There are sounds of birds living in the marshes. The marsh wren advertises his presence with a reedy call, even at night, when most birds are still. The marsh hen, or clapper rail, calls in a loud, carrying cackle. You can hear the tiny, high-pitched, rustling thunder of the herds of crabs moving through the grass as they flee before advancing feet, or the more leisurely sound of movement they make on their daily migrations in search of food. At night, when the air is still and other sounds are quieted, an attentive listener can hear the bubbling of air from the sandy soil as a high tide floods the marsh.

The wetlands are filled with smells. They smell of the sea and salt water and of the edge of the sea, the sea with a little iodine and trace of dead life. The marshes smell of spartina, a fairly strong odor mixed from the elements of the sea and the smells of grasses. These are clean, fresh smells—smells that are pleasing to one who lives by the sea but strange and not altogether pleasant to one who has always live inland.

Unfortunately, in marshes which have been disturbed, dug up, suffocated with loads of trash and fill, poisoned and eroded with the wastes from large cities, there is another smell. Sick salt marshes smell of hydrogen sulfide, an odor of rotten egg, which is only very faint in a healthy salt marsh.

As the sound and smell of the salt marsh are its own, so is its feel. Some of the marshes can be walked on, especially the landward parts. In the north, the *Spartina patens* marsh is covered with dense grass that may be cut for salt hay. Its roots bind the wet mud into a firm surface. But the footing is spongy on an unused hay marsh as the mat of other years' grass, hidden under the green growth, resists the walker's weight and springs back as he moves along.

In the southern marshes, only one grass covers the entire marsh area, *Spartina alterniflora*. On the higher parts of the marsh, near the land, the roots have developed into a mass that provides firm footing even though the plants are much more separated than in the northern hay marshes, and you squish gently on mud rather than grass. It is like walking on a huge trampoline. The ground is stiff. It is squishy and wet, to be sure, but still solid as you walk about. Jump, however, and you can feel the ground give under the impact, and waves will spread out in all directions. The ground is a mat of plant roots and mud on top of a more liquid layer which gives slightly by flowing to all sides.

As you walk toward the edge of the marsh, the seaward edge, each step closer to open water brings a change in footing. The mud has less root material in it and is less firmly bound together. It begins to ooze around your shoes. On the edges of the creeks, especially the larger ones, there may be natural levees where the ground is higher. Here the rising tide meets its first real resistance as it spills over the creek banks and has to flow between the close-set plants. Here it is slowed and drops the mud it may be carrying. Here, too, especially after a series of tides that are lower than usual, the ground is firm and even dry and hard.

Down toward the creek, where the mud is watered at each tide, the soil is as muddy as you can find anywhere. When you try to walk across to the water at low tide, across the exposed mud where the marsh grass does not yet grow, hip boots are not high enough to keep you from getting muddy. The boots are pulled off on the first or second step when they have sunk deep into the clutching ooze. There are no roots to give solidarity, nothing but the mud and water fighting a shifting battle to hold the area.

At low tide the salt marsh is a vast field, with slightly higher grasses sticking up along the creeks and uniformly tall grass elsewhere. The effect is like that of a great flat meadow. At high tide the look is the same, a wide flat sea of grass, but with a great deal of water showing. The marsh is still marsh, but spears of grass are sticking up through water, a world of water where land was before, each blade of grass a little island, each island a refuge for the marsh animals which do not like or cannot stand submersion in salt water.

This case is about one marsh on the East Coast of North America, and the effect of that influential animal, man.

DISMANTLING AN ECOSYSTEM

World War II brought with it prosperity. Mobility was decreased during the war years but increased tremendously just after. People had money to spend and more time in which to spend it. The city expanded rapidly around the marsh. Low-priced housing grew quickly and with it came demands for dealing with the mosquito problem. The cheapest and easiest method of ridding the area of the biting flies was to spray with a new miracle called DDT. The treatment was effective. The flies were killed—and so were crabs and other crustaceans. DDT began to accumulate in the flesh of fish—and in the flesh of herons at the top of the salt marsh food chain. The heronry on the island in the marsh had steadily decreased in numbers for a hundred years. But now, with pesticides affecting their nervous systems, the herons became jumpy and frequently destroyed half-completed nests. Often the eggs were thin-shelled, even spongy, from a lack of calcium carbonate, and they easily broke under the weight of the brooding adults. Finally the heronry disappeared altogether.

The marsh was dying. A marina built at the head of a creek hurried its death. The creek was dredged to increase the size of the basin so that large pleasure boats could anchor. Dredging spoils were dumped on the marsh as fill for an access road and parking. Boats dumped their wastes, without treatment, directly into the water. The water became so polluted that the creeks had to be closed to shellfish taking because they were a manace to public health.

Tidal flooding was restricted by a highway bridge across the bay which reduced the opening to the sea. The water could not flow fast enough to fully flood the marsh, especially at the upper levels. Marsh elder and weeds began to invade the high areas. Large areas of grass along the creeks were killed when oil slicks from powerboats settled on the mud. And there was not time to rejuvenate before another slick settled.

The Deacon house by the marsh was in final decay. The land was put up for sale and quickly bought by a contractor as a site for an industrial park. There was some localized objection from the summer colony, but it was quickly put down with the argument of new jobs and new taxes. The filling of the marsh began.

The land was first leased to a trash collector from the metropolitan area, who began dumping the day the agreement was signed. Trash collecting in the city had become a million dollar business with the great increase in the quantities of disposable packaging, much of which could not be burned and was highly resistant to decay.

Trucks brought trash in a steady stream. Permission to fill stopped short of the creeks and the marsh immediately on their banks, as these were to be preserved for drainage, boat passage, and shellfish production. When the entire area had received one covering of trash, another layer was added.

The filling took considerable time, but the marsh was breathing its last. Herring gulls were attracted to the dump in numbers, although there was little domestic garbage in the fill. They did find enough edible items to keep a large flock busy picking over the rubble. A number of rats moved into the dump but not as many as there would have been without the constant rumble of heavy trucks and the difficulty of finding hiding places in the compact fill.

Gone from the marsh were the alewives and minnows from the streams, the migrating ducks, the yellowlegs, sandpipers, dowitchers, bald eagles, ospreys, marsh hawks, sharp-tailed sparrows, short-eared owls, black-crowned night herons, white-footed mice, and the occasional bear, deer, or wolf, the muskrats, foxes, weasels, bobcats, skunks, raccoons, and mink. Gone were the bitterns, clapper rails, meadowlarks, doughbirds, golden plover, sickle-bills, grass birds, marbled godwits, Canada geese, and others.

Of the old marsh inhabitants, only the killdeers, never plentiful, made an attempt to stay. They used the edge of the fill where there was no active dumping. They even managed to raise a few young, although most of the chicks fell victim to rats and semiwild city cats.

There was no marsh elder or even weeds. Salicornia no longer grew. *Spartina patens,* the salt hay, was destroyed. Only the *Spartina alterniflora* marsh along the creeks was left. And it was not healthy and much of it died when oil was accidentally spilled onto the edge of the fill.

Filling was finally completed. Construction of the industrial buildings began with the driving of pilings into the soft substrate. The noise drove the last of the few remaining birds away.

The history of the marsh was over. From birth, after the retreating glacier, to death, under the laws of progress, the marsh had meant much to many. To scores of animal species it meant life. To the Indians it meant food. To the first colonist, John Deacon, it meant open space, a grassland in the wilderness, and sweet ground on which to found a dynasty. To his distant descendant it meant money.

TOPIC QUESTIONS

1. Has contemporary society elevated mankind above the world of ecological checks and balances?
2. How has marketing contributed to environmental myopia?
3. What are the trade-offs involved with increasing energy and food production levels?
4. Is biological capital an economic resource?
5. Do natural forces contribute to an enrichment of biological capital?
6. How did Earth Day 1970 influence social thought concerning the environment and mankind's role on "spaceship earth"?
7. What are the *Club of Rome's* three options for resource and environmental problems for mankind to consider?
8. What have stocks and flows to do with resource allocation problems?

Case 7

9. How do zoning laws affect wildlife habitat in urban regions?
10. If you represented a real estate firm with a listing in the Stage III category, what sort of a client would find this residence attractive?
11. Do wildlife creatures play an important part in the urban ecosystem? If so, how?

12. What firms market products that enhance wildlife survival chances in the urban environment?

Case 8

13. The saltwater marsh represents an amazingly complex ecosystem. What makes the salt marsh unique as a natural resource?
14. What are the signs of a dying marsh? What do living patterns have to do with how we value marshlands?
15. How does waste material from our contemporary society disrupt and even destroy a unique resource such as a saltwater marsh?
16. How can land use planning be employed to protect coastal marshes?

RECOMMENDED READINGS

Jerry B. Marion, *Energy In Perspective* (New York: Academic Press, 1974).

Leonard L. Berry and James S. Hensel, eds., *Marketing and the Social Environment* (New York: Petrocelli Books, 1973).

George Fisk, *Marketing and the Ecological Crises* (New York: Harper and Row, 1974).

Rachel Carson, *Silent Spring* (Greenwich, N.Y.: Fawcett Publications, 1962).

Robert Rienow and Leona Train Rienow, *Man Against His Environment* (San Francisco: Ballantine Books, 1970).

FOOTNOTES

1. Rachel Carson, *Silent Spring* (Boston, Mass.: Houghton Mifflin Company, 1962), p. 218.
2. Robert Rienow and Leona Train Rienow, *Man Against His Environment* (San Francisco: Ballantine Books, a division of Random House, Inc., 1970), p. 158.
3. *Conservation News* 39, 6 (March 15, 1974), p. 10.
4. Throughout mankind's history natural calamities have disrupted the march of progress. While primitive and wilderness life styles are not regarded by our contemporary society as ideal, the diversities associated with varied natural ecosystems throughout the earth greatly protected man from extinction. In the natural world biological specialization is subject to sudden extinction when the climate or geological system undergoes change. Conversely, diversity and adaptability insures survival even in the face of great natural calamities in one or more parts of the world. Many in the scientific community are concerned that specialized mono-culture is pushing the human race into a position that makes it more vulnerable to extinction. For a detailed account of early cultures see Peter Farb, *Man's Rise to Civilization As Shown by the Indians of North America from Primieval Times to the Coming of the Industrial State* (New York: E.P. Dutton & Co., Inc., 1968).
5. Historians often trace civilizations, their roots, their development, and their decline and fall in context with environmental abuses and impairment. While ecosystem disruptions rarely directly accounted for a nation's collapse, the

wasteful use of natural resources made such a society less able to resist military and economic pressures from rival powers. Babylonia, for example, once flourished in an environment that contained ample water, vegetation, and climate to spawn a rich and powerful civilization. The cutting of once-great forests, drainage projects, soil erosion—all contributed to the desolate desert environment which eventually engulfed ancient archaeological ruins of a great Babylonian empire.

6. Barry Commoner, "A Businessman's Primer on Ecology," *Marketing and the Social Environment,* ed. Leonard L. Berry and James S. Hensel (New York: Petrocelli Books, a division of Alfred A. Knopf, Inc., 1973), p. 95.

7. Starship 0011 is a simulated space mission illustrating the concept of "spaceship earth" as well as the absolute dependency of mankind on the world's resources in sustaining life aboard space vessels that travel into deep space.

8. Those readers interested in ocean ecosystems should read *The Ocean World of Jacques Cousteau,* Volumes 1, 2, and 3 (New York: World Publishing Company, 1972); also see Rachel Carson, *The Sea Around Us,* rev. ed. (New York: Oxford Press, 1961).

9. Henry D. Thoreau, *Thoreau on Man and Nature* (Mt. Vernon, N.Y.: Peter Pauper Press, 1960), p. 52.

10. Historic material describing the early wilderness ecosystem of the Illinois prairie was researched from the *Outdoor Illinois Magazine,* a publication of the Benton Evening News, Benton, Illinois.

11. See Betty J. Meggers et. al., *Tropical Forest Ecosystems in Africa and South America: A Comparative Review* (Washington, D.C.: Smithsonian Institution Press, 1974).

12. See Tom Alexander, "Ominous Changes in the World's Weather," *Fortune* (February 1974), p. 90.

13. *The Limits to Growth: A Report for The Club of Rome's Project on the Predicament of Mankind,* by Donella H. Meadows, Dennis L. Meadows, Jorgen Randers, William W. Behrens III, pp. 23–24. A Potomac Associates book published by Universe Books, New York, 1972.

14. Thomas J. Steele, "The Marketing of the Wilderness Cause," *Proceedings, American Marketing Association, 1973,* p. 411.

CHAPTER FIVE

WHY ARE THERE

RESOURCE

SHORTAGES?

THE UNDERDEVELOPED NATIONS

Underdeveloped countries are facing famine, malnutrition, poverty, disease, and economic paralysis. Cultural lags which restrict mobility and social cooperation further retard their economics. Their agriculture employs antiquated practices which keep crop yields low and which further impair the biological capital—soils, moisture supplies, fertility, etc. The combination of population crowding in areas low in agricultural output and drought force rural landholders, nomads, and livestock raisers to overcrowd land until water fertility and topsoils are exhausted. In the sub-Sahara, for example, overgrazing robbed vast areas of protective vegetation; this in turn reduces the amount of moisture that plants put back into the atmosphere. The land dries out more quickly, and when it does rain once again, the tightly packed sands and clays force the moisture to run rapidly off into the nearest stream bed or lake. The cycle repeats itself until the once-vegetated region eventually becomes a new desert. The vast sub-Saharan regions of Africa are becoming extensions of the Great Sahara Desert, which is moving south at a rate estimated to be 30 miles annually. This illustrates that poverty and environmental backlashes can become part of the calamity cycle that strikes underdeveloped countries much too often.

In the 1974 congressional sessions, the Department of Operations Subcommittee of the House Committee on Agriculture conducted hearings on world food shortages. Of those demographic and agricultural experts who testified at the hearings, Dr. Lester Brown, of the Overseas Development Council, described the basic causes of mass starvation in the world's underdeveloped lands:

> In the early 1970s the soaring demand for food, spurred by both continuing population growth and rising affluence, has begun to outrun the productive capacity of the world's farmers and fishermen. The result has been declining food reserves, skyrocketing food prices, and intense competition among countries for available food supplies. Fundamental changes in the nature of the world food problem have left governments, institutions and individuals everywhere unprepared and vulnerable.
>
> Finally, the ecological undermining of major food-producing systems also is beginning to have an adverse effect on the prospects of increasing world food production.
>
> The tragedy unfolding in the African countries south of the Sahara Desert is an example of another type of ecological overstress that is diminishing the earth's food-producing capacity, although the problem exists elsewhere as well. Over the past 35 years, human and livestock populations along the sub-Saharan fringe have increased rapidly, nearly doubling in some areas. As these populations have multiplied, they have put more pressure on the ecosystem than it could withstand. The result has been overgrazing and deforestation, encouraging the southward advancement of the Sahara Desert at rates up to 30 miles per year along the desert's 3,500-mile southern fringe, stretching from Senegal to northern Ethiopa. As the desert expands southward, human and livestock populations retreat before it. The result is ever greater pressure on the fringe area, which in turn contributes to further denudation and deforestation, setting in process a self-reinforcing cycle.[1]

A similar pattern of ecological ruin followed on the heels of overgrazing, deforestations, and cultivation in the Middle East, along much of the Mediterranean Sea coast, and in northern Africa (Carthage of Egypt) during the ancient dynasties of Babylonia, Persian-Medes, Greece, and Rome. While the patterns of environmental destruction can be traced far back historically, the lessons (or backlashes) learned by each generation seem brutally contemporary, especially when major climate changes switch off moisture supplies.

THE INDUSTRIALIZED NATIONS

The industrialized nations face scarcity and environmental problems as well. We employ natural resources in combination with large stocks of economic capital to stimulate growth and development. While we may understand how shortages—even famines—plague underdeveloped nations, we find it difficult to comprehend why raw material short falls sometimes cripple the economies of the wealthy nations. With the industrialized nations, the problems of resource shortages are very different from the impoverished countries. They are problems of growth and adaptation to finite environmental limits. Barkley and Seckler discuss this feature of growth and environmental adjustment:

> The spectacular growth of technology over the past few decades has created a state of mind basically counter both to the laws of physics and the life sciences and to the principles of economics. It is expressed in the idea that growth is free, that somehow goods are created from nothing and, after having yielded their benefits, vanish into nothingness once more. Modern growthmanship is a utopian fallacy resting on the premise of "something for nothing." The argument here has been that, on the contrary, for every benefit there is a cost; that in any growth process the value of additional benefits declines as the costs of obtaining them rise; that eventually a point is reached where the additional costs equal the additional benefits. That point is the place to stop. Perhaps modern industrial society has reached the state where the direct benefits of economic growth are being overwhelmed by the indirect costs of environmental degradation. That is the economic lesson.[2]

The United States is but one of the industrialized nations of the world that is experiencing a variety of raw material short falls. Our demand for raw materials makes us the largest world customer for energy, metals, and rare earths. While we make up only 6 percent of the earth's population, we consume 32 percent of the total world energy output. This energy is doing work that is equivalent to each American having 80 servants working for him 24 hours every day. The average U.S. citizen uses seven times as much energy as the average Japanese, four times as much as the average German, and three times as much as the average Englishman. The average American will use as much energy in the next seven days as the average citizen of the world will use in the next year. If projected demand estimates should come true, we will be using five times as much energy in 25 years as we consume today. We are not only straining the economic foundations of the world's trading system, but the fuel mix that we depend on is 95 percent fossil fuel; we require 18,000,000 barrels of crude oil daily. While we are 85 percent self-sufficient in petroleum reserves, the 6,000,000 barrels imported daily costs the United States an estimated $22.3 billion. The industrialized nations require energy amounts that are expected to deplete world supplies in less than 60 years. In the process of consuming fuels, we waste between 30 and 40 percent; the internal combustion engine alone wastes 80 percent of the energy it burns. The appetite and waste factors create the conditions for both inflation (crude oil price increases) and pollution (wastes released into the air, water, and land). A low-price energy alternative to fossil fuels is not within sight in this decade. Indeed, alternatives to petroleum are dependent on considerably higher levels of inflation just to make shale oil, tar sands oil, fusion, solar, wind, hydrogen, coal gasification, and geothermal power economically feasible on a large-scale production bases.

Other minerals are feeling the stresses of exponential demand rates from industrial nations of the world. The United States, according to Nicholas Wade (writing in the January 1974 issue of *Science* Magazine), is more autonomous in nonfuel minerals than any other country except the Soviet Union. But we began in the 1920s to be a net importer. For 20 nonfuel minerals, including such key metals as chromium, aluminum, nickel, and zinc, the United States already derives more than half of its supply from abroad. The Department of Interior estimates that nonfuel minerals that cost the United States $6 billion dollars in 1971 will increase to $20 billion by 1985 and $52 billion by the turn of the century. An increasing gap between rich and poor countries of the world and the growth in both affluence and population cannot help but intensify the competition between industrial nations for a finite quantity of natural resources. Our consumption of 27 percent of the earth's raw materials adds inflationary pressures to nonfuel minerals.

The American life style will continue to change in the near future as the nation pays the deferred social costs of past consumption and inequities in distribution and begins to calculate the costs of depletion, replacement of nonrenewable resources, and environmental restoration and protection. The National Academy of Sciences recommends that technology should be adapted to depend on widespread and abundant basic commodities such as iron, aluminum, magnesium, and the silicates. Failure to do so could result in economic colonialism, international friction, steadily deteriorating balance of trade, and the tarnished global image of the nation. Table 5-1 shows the dependency of the United States on foreign imports. Conserving demand, recycling discarded items, cutting down on wastes during production, and shifting from scarce minerals to more abundant items would reduce our vulnerability to mineral embargo tactics by other nations.

STOCKS AND FLOWS

In some primitive societies, stocks of stored-up goods are practically nonexistent. These tribal groups move where food is abundant, often following ancient game migration routes in harmony with the season. If one area contains little food, the tribes move to another location—sometimes as far as several hundred miles away. The nomadic societies are characterized by their constant movement, living off the

TABLE 5-1
PERCENTAGE OF U.S. MINERAL REQUIREMENTS IMPORTED DURING 1972.

Mineral	Percentage Imported	Major Foreign Sources
Platinum group metals	100%	U.K., U.S.S.R., South Africa, Canada, Japan, Norway
Mica (sheet)	100	India, Brazil, Malagasy
Chromium	100	U.S.S.R., South Africa, Turkey
Strontium	100	Mexico, Spain
Cobalt	98	Zaire, Belgium, Luxembourg, Finland Canada, Norway
Tantalum	97	Nigeria, Canada, Zaire
Aluminum (ores and metals)	96	Jamaica, Surinam, Canada, Australia
Manganese	95	Brazil, Gabon, South Africa, Zaire
Fluorine	87	Mexico, Spain, Italy, South Africa
Titanium (rutile)	86	Australia
Asbestos	85	Canada, South Africa
Tin	77	Malaysia, Thailand, Bolivia
Bismuth	75	Mexico, Japan, Peru, U.K., Korea
Nickel	74	Canada, Norway
Columbium	67	Brazil, Nigeria, Malagasy, Thailand
Antimony	65	South Africa, Mexico, U.K., Bolivia
Gold	61	Canada, Switzerland, U.S.S.R.
Potassium	60	Canada
Mercury	58	Canada, Mexico
Zinc	52	Canada, Mexico, Peru
Silver	44	Canada, Peru, Mexico, Honduras, Australia
Barium	43	Peru, Ireland, Mexico, Greece
Gypsum	39	Canada, Mexico, Jamaica
Selenium	37	Canada, Japan, Mexico, U.K.
Tellurium	36	Peru, Canada
Vanadium	32	South Africa, Chile, U.S.S.R.
Petroleum (includes liquid natural gas)	29	Central and South America, Canada, Middle East
Iron	28	Canada, Venezuela, Japan, Common Market (EEC)
Lead	26	Canada, Australia, Peru, Mexico
Cadmium	25	Mexico, Australia, Belgium, Luxembourg, Canada, Peru
Copper	18	Canada, Peru, Chile
Titanium (ilmenite)	18	Canada, Australia
Rare earths	14	Australia, Malaysia, India
Pumice	12	Greece, Italy
Salt	7	Canada, Mexico, Bahamas
Cement	5	Canada, Bahamas, Norway
Magnesium (nonmetallic)	8	Greece, Ireland
Natural gas	9	Canada
Rhenium	4	West Germany, France
Stone	2	Canada, Mexico, Italy, Portugal

Source: Mining and Minerals Policy 1973, a report by the Secretary of the Interior to the Congress.

land, and domesticated animal products (curd, cheese, meat). The cycle of weather patterns determines where grass and water can be found to sustain the herds of camels, goats, sheep, burros, reindeer (in northern arctic regions), and horses. Under these conditions, the human race is required to live in accordance with natural cycles, rhythms, and changes. The primitive society lacks capital goods (except for simple stone or metal tools, bowls, pots, dishes). Mobility in accordance with survival requirements often keep wilderness and nomadic societies from establishing permanent settlements.

FIGURE 5-1 Seasonal Migration of Rocky Mountain Indians and Big Game Herds

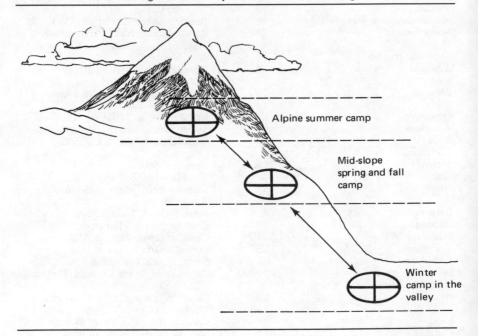

Alpine summer camp

Mid-slope spring and fall camp

Winter camp in the valley

In America, the early frontier period contained such diverse life-style characteristics as wilderness migrations among Indians, trappers, hunters, adventurers, prospectors, and miners; frontier settlements existed as self-sufficient homesteads living from the land (crops, domesticated livestock, wild game, and food). Here, each frontier family was expected to meet its own requirements by planting and harvesting grains, fruits, vegetables, and fibers, and by providing adequate shelter against the elements. The frontier settlement differed from nomadic wilderness life style in respect to the custom of storing away home-prepared foods for the long, barren days of winter. Small surpluses of food, tobacco, fur, and labor were exchanged for a small list of staple items required around the house and farm. Although these homesteaders worked diligently at maintaining self-sufficient stocks of foods for winter months, misfortune was not a stranger; the tradition of sharing goods with unfortunate neighbors during the frontier era remains to this day in many rural communities.

Frontier existence was characterized by irregular flows of goods along slow and often undependable natural avenues such as rivers, clearings, passes, and ancient migration routes of primitive Indian tribes and large grazing herds of buffalo, deer, elk, moose, etc. Unless frontier families were willing to work for self-sufficiency by storing-up their own stocks of goods, survival was at most doubtful. From Figure 5-1, one may detect the seasonal nature of migrations among Indian tribes in the West. Since high-altitude mountain peaks experience arctic-type winters, growing seasons are very short. The valley floors, however, have much milder winters and living conditions are less harsh than in higher mountain meadows, forests, streams, and cold lakes where wild game and wild fowl flourish on the rich, fertile, mineralized soils. Interim time in the swing seasons of spring and fall was spent on the mid-slopes. Storing large quantities of food or forming food stocks are not typical characteristics of these mountain-valley Indian cultures. Hand-to-mouth practices kept these societies in constant touch with nature's inventory, which sustained them on a day-to-day basis. From Figure 5-2, one may note certain

FIGURE 5-2   Self-Sufficiency, Land-Oriented Organic Homestead

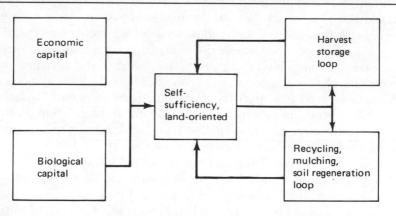

Characteristics: low capital use; production for consumption, no or small surplus for cash and barter; biological capital improved by soil nutrient; organic farming practices; little or no pollution; conservation oriented.

characteristic features of self-sufficient homesteads. These may be discussed in the context of frontier life or in the context of a current lifestyle trend toward organic farming which incorporates the frontier concept of self-sufficiency.

Produce grown on the farm unit provides the family with all its basic needs; food is grown, harvested, processed, and stored away in fruit cellars and utility cabinets. Surplus is sold or traded for staples. Under the present organic farming concept, the farm is both a way of life and the means to stock up on homegrown, handmade items required to subsist. This life-style choice is characterized by harmonious living with nature; land is revitalized and nutured by the practice of returning organic matter to the soil, plowing under green manure (legume crops), and mulching (providing protective covering over cultivated garden rows with straw, leaves, sawdust, spoiled hay, etc.). Nearly everything on both the frontier and the organic farms of today is reused or recycled, with almost no pollution leaving the farming unit. Small capital requirements provide low-budget agricultural operations. Hand labor and intensive growing of vegetables, fowl, pigs, cattle, and fruit grace the tables of many self-sufficient homesteads. The reliance on frontier skills and living in harmony with natural rhythms seem to re-establish self-esteem in a manner which many in the urban life-style are emulating.[3] While the urbanite enjoys many conveniences that technology provides, the self-sufficient homesteader trades convenience for naturally grown produce which is carefully stored away for later use. The urbanite is more vulnerable to interruptions and strong inflationary pressures on essential items such as food, which he tends to purchase frequently; the inventory of urbanites depends on distributors, who in turn must be regularly replenished from dependable industrial sources. Disruptions anywhere along the line interrupt the flow and may cause considerable inconvenience to consumers.

While primitive societies exist today in isolated regions of the world, they are becoming increasingly rare. By contrast, industrialized nations are accumulating huge stockpiles of capital goods. This allows contemporary mankind to depart from ancient living patterns. Capital goods provide the means by which society can move large quantities of raw materials to where people shop, live, work, and play. By specializing labor skills, capital goods become more productive; by combining the productivity increases by both labor and capital, we can build up large inventories of required items such as food, fuels, fibers, and finished goods. In this way we can adjust both supply and demand cycles.

Technological products which lengthen storage time of perishable products can offer us some protection in the event of supply disruptions or poor harvests. The presence of reserves stored in warehouses, factories, silos, and other locations helps to stabilize prices and economic planning. Surpluses can be absorbed gradually and can provide industry with a measure of economic stability; ideally, shortages can be managed from reserves which can sustain essential social functions even through a short-term crisis.

As an industrialized nation enters a phase that indicates that shortages are likely, stockpiling processes are set in motion. Larger inventories are built up at all levels, including the consumer's level. If sufficient time is allowed to lapse, stockpiling causes little disruption in the economy, but if an essential good, such as petroleum, experiences a sudden supply curtailment, the resulting hoarding and panic buying can be disruptive to all. Jobs, essential infrastructure maintenance functions, including military effectiveness, were involved during the Arab oil embargo during 1973–1974. Pressures to obtain new supply sources and to speed up the flow of raw materials accompany short falls; crisis-oriented acts often interface with environmental standards and safeguards. This, in turn, leads to new arguments to open up national parks, national monuments, and sensitive ecological areas to commercial exploitation.

From Figure 5-3, three demand and supply models may be noted. In part A, demand and supply are in equilibrium and stocks and flows are adjusted to provide necessary matching, sorting, and, quantity and quality dimensions. In this condition, there is little incentive to build up excessive inventories since speculative profits from hoarding are remote, as the price remains stabilized. In part B, market demand doubles, which forces distributors, producers, processors, and raw material developers to ·expand stocks and accelerate flows through the system. Strains on storage capacities, production capacities, distribution capacities, and raw material sources lag behind market demand; inflation, spot shortages, and work stoppages blot an otherwise vigorous growth phase. In part C, consumer demand declines rapidly. The supply system curtails production levels. Inventory stocks are gradually sold-off and reach record low levels. The entire system suffers from excessive industrial capacity.

This tendency for irregular supplies to encourage speculative hoarding and panic buying practices may be noted in Table 5-2, which reflects the influences of the Arab oil embargo on black market prices of selected petroleum derivatives. In the case of industrial firms with near-exhausted inventories, the costs of halting production while normal channels caught up with back orders would far out-weigh increased (and even black market prices) of one or half a dozen required raw materials. Once the scarcity syndrome produces speculative profits from hoarding, the conventional supply channels find it extremely difficult to catch up with demand at either the industrial or consumer end of the market. The value of dollars relative to holding goods, commodities, and stocks of raw materials drives up the inflationary spiral even higher.

During the selective price control phases of the Nixon Administration, an estimated 40 percent of industrial buyers were approached by black market sources; most black market prices were two to three times government-allowed prices. In the plastics industry nearly 3 percent of all

FIGURE 5-3 Exponential Expansion Cycle

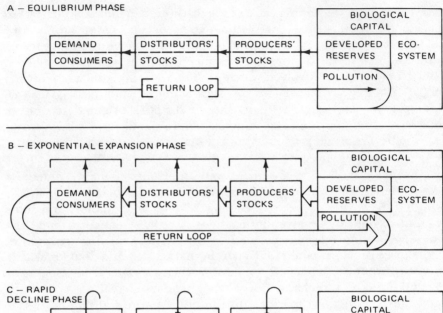

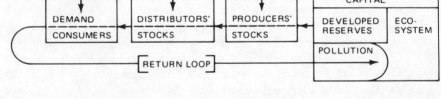

tonnage moved through black market channels.[4]

Later, as demand falls, a recession forces plants to close and drives up unemployment. Producers adjust to lower inventory levels; this may lead to excess capacity in the entire system. After supply-demand-economics problems are resolved, the model may move once again into slow growth equilibrium.

The important feature of a stock and flow illustration with component demand, distribution, production, and natural resource items is the necessary balance that an economic system must attain with the biological system. In the case of renewable natural resources (food, fibers, and timber), harvest yields require consideration of both demand levels and self-sustaining capabilities of the forest, fishing waters, and fields. Harvesting for demand may create the conditions for cannabalizing an entire forest or a wildlife specie (extinction), or exhausting soil nutrients through short-term destructive farming practices. If managed properly, forests can produce sustaining yields indefinitely; the oceans can sustain great schools of fish and other seafoods if they are not overfished, depleted, or destroyed by pollutants from other economic activities. But the wealth of natural stocks and their resultant abilities to produce high levels of harvestable items are not indestructable.

TABLE 5-2
BLACK MARKET PRICES, ARAB EMBARGO, 1973–1974

Item	Regular Market	Black Market
Polyvinyl chloride	$ .14/lb	76¢/lb
#2 oil	.26/gal	58¢/gal
#6 oil	13.00/bbl	$ 18.00/bbl
Benzene	.30/gal	$ 2.00/gal
Propane	90/gal	90¢/gal
Antifreeze	1.80/gal	$ 1.80/gal
Casing	565.00/ton	$565.00/ton
Steel pipe	5.75/ft	$ 5.75/ft

Item	Quoted Price	Old Black Market	New Black Market
Hot rolled steel bar	$10.50	$16.00	$20.00/cwt.
Hot rolled steel sheet	10.00	14.00	$17.50/cwt.
Steel reinforcement bars	9.50	14.50	$22.00/cwt.
H S plate	16.00	18.00	$22.00/cwt.
Zinc anode	27.00	80.00	$74.00/cwt.
Styrene	.17	.60	$ 1.00/lb.

Source: Ted Schafers, "No 'Recession' on Supply Front," *St. Louis Globe Democrat* (March 4, 1974) p. 16B.

CONCENTRATION OF POWER

Continuing concentration of economic power in the hands of giant international corporations has become both a social and an economic problem. Conglomerate firms (consisting of several subsidiary corporations or corporate divisions) have molded organizational systems which now control most major industries in the business system. Verticle integration is particularly important as a means for controlling resource flow. (This type of growth allows firms to control their business systems from raw material exploration-discovery-development stages to processing, production, distribution, and postsales servicing.) The practice of acquiring raw material reserves assures vertically integrated firms of supply sources.

As the economy has moved to the trillion dollar GNP plateau, raw materials have become increasingly important to these corporate giants.

For example, the petroleum companies are really energy firms with huge investments in the coal industry; research and development projects in solar, nuclear, wind, and geothermal energy sources are conducted by these firms. Petrochemicals, plastics, natural gas, and related product categories fall under the interests of energy firms. The largest energy giants also control a large part of the international oil trade.

The presence of concentrated power in the hands of a few corporations in key industries tends to distort the democratic process, tie up large reserves of raw materials and natural resources under single ownership, and regulate demand and supply factors to produce desired profit levels. Environmentalists are quick to recognize the influence of large firms in lobbying concessions from Congress with respect to public lands which hold promising economic deposits of minerals.

OVERCONSUMPTION AS A WAY OF LIFE

The wealthy nations of the world combine the factors of production with natural resources to expand economic activity. Capital, technology, specialized labor, raw materials function in economic balance to produce vast amounts of goods and services; raw materials flow into producing nations from worldwide networks of distribution systems controlled by multinational corporations. Material acquisition in the production sense and material acquisition in the consumer consumption sense have stimulated economic growth objectives that encourage wasteful management of raw materials and natural resources. The flow of raw materials from virgin sources (from mines, forests, and wells) is encouraged by low prices, tax incentives, transportation rate breaks; and processing advantages (ores, petroleum, fibers, grains) can be processed in large quantities with efficient standardized processes.

In the United States, consumption is encouraged for both economic and cultural reasons. Consumption enhances employment and, in turn, allows for the efficient use of large production facilities. In some respects, both consumption and production are subsidized. Waste, use-and-discard, emphasis on virgin raw materials, pollution, and abuse of the environment are linked to economic expansion and wealth.

The cumulative abuses to the environment and to the nation's finite stockpiles of raw materials are responsible in part for inflation and renewed concerns for mankind's survival on this planet. The efficient use and careful management of our natural resources have traditionally lacked economic and cultural incentives; but as resource accessibility becomes more limited in world markets as a result of economic and political motives, the incentive to reduce wastes and inefficiencies will rise sharply.

TECHNOLOGICAL AND FASHION OBSOLESCENCE

The fashion cycle, innovations, fads, and growth incentives account for many product changes. New products are more profitable than older products, which tend to lose innovative and fashion appeal. New technologies create opportunities for manufacturers to change products and to expand into other lines of business. These factors operate more smoothly in stimulating economic expansion when consumers are affluent (seeking to satisfy physiological, sociological, and psychological needs and requirements). The innovative and fashionable item lends support to the consumer's own identity with his life-style patterns. Hence, satisfaction itself may become closely identified with innovation.

Technology can be innovative; it is also an expression that appeals to consumer tastes. In this respect manufacturers link technological improvements with fashion trends. New products are both innovative and fashionable. New styles, accessories, and features are incorporated in products to accent contemporary tastes. Increased product size, greater horsepower, more accessories, and increased fuel requirements are often promoted as representing actual product improvements.

Psychological obsolescence is linked to innovative and fashion cycles; as such, products become old or obsolete in many instances well before functional fatigue. Old products are traded in, discarded, or junked, and become additional items in solid waste heaps. Our emphasis on new products adds exciting dimensions to the marketplace, but has also encouraged waste, pollution, and depletion.

When new technological advances are incorporated in products simply to conform to model changes, consumer safety and product performance may suffer. The culmination of science and technology in commercial innovations seems to have advanced faster than performance and safety standards. In this respect the wide range of toxic substances that consumers (and nonconsumers) come in contact with on a daily basis pose health hazards that may not surface for several years. Food additives, pesticides, herbicides, and numerous industrial solvents find their ways into the environment well after initial use.

CONCLUSIONS

Underdeveloped nations are caught in a vicious cycle or circle of poverty. As rangelands, ore fields, and food-producing areas become subject to increasing pressures, the environmental backlash actually reduces supply capacity. Stripping rangelands of vegetation accelerates moisture depletion and soil losses. Food production drops further as the remaining grasses are consumed by starving herds. Other items, such as minerals, can be depleted by domestic and foreign users; this often means the end of economic activity in those regions having an economy based around a single mine. Inflation and population pressures further impair the economic and environmental resources. Since underdeveloped nations trade raw materials for finished goods and currency, higher costs for energy and vital industrial goods can all but halt economic growth.

Industrialized nations are having their problems as well. Rapid increases in world demand for finite metals, energy (fossil fuels), fibers, and other materials have dramatically inflated prices. Rapid inflation is a threat to industrial nations; it robs them of their economic vitality and monetary stability. In order to control inflation and maintain environmental safeguards, conservation strategies are required. The elimination of wastes and long-term resource planning are key features of conservation strategies.

Case 9
The Case of the Living Organisms Outstripping the Carrying Capacity of Their Environment

On February 4, 1974, Russell E. Train, Administrator of the Environmental Protection Agency, testified before the Senate Subcommittee on the Environment. He was invited to develop his thesis on the interrelationships of energy and environmental problems.

"The energy crisis, particularly in the longer term aspects, is actually an environmental problem of a most fundamental kind," testified Train. He maintained that the real cause of our energy problem is wasteful growth in demand and that our energy needs and environmental concerns are not in conflict, they are both real and must be solved together, the solutions go hand in hand.

According to Mr. Train, our energy problem springs from patterns of consumption, rates of growth and demands created from the fundamental imbalance of our environment, and our available resources. In many ways this is the most basic of environmental problems as a whole, ". . . the case of the living organisms outstripping the carrying capacity of their habitat."

Environmental concerns matter in the short-term, immediate energy picture. All forms of energy production that are presently available to any substantial degree involve environmental costs of various kinds, such as degradation of landscapes, public health in cities, and stresses in the biocommunities of our oceans. He stressed the fact that these concerns and problems are real.

However, Mr. Train took care to point out that lack of energy production due to the delay in the Alaska pipeline, the switch from coal to gas

Conservation Reports, Report No. 4 (February 15, 1975), pp. 49–50.

power generation in industries, and the shortages of refining capacity was not the fault of environmental endeavors. The delay of the Alaska pipeline, he claimed, was a result of a realistic appraisal by the Department of the Interior many months before NEPA had been enacted. Had they gone ahead with the 1969 plans, very serious problems of an environmental nature and in the " . . . basic integrity of the pipeline itself" would have developed. The switch from coal to gas power generation was primarily for economic benefits rather than environmental concerns. And the lack of refinery capacity was a result of economic opportunities in foreign investment and the poor planning of industry and the government in underestimating the increases in energy demand—not a result of environmental blockage.

Substantial energy costs in environmental programs such as auto emissions, lead regulations, stationary controls, effluent guidelines in the water field, and municipal treatment were not overlooked. The administrator of EPA estimated that by 1980, when these environmental measures might be fully effective, their net energy cost would be under 2 percent of the total energy bill. However, he projected that the energy saved in such environmental programs as recycling, smaller automobiles, and auto fuel economy measures would outweigh the cost.

The main factor in correcting the energy shortage and environmental problems is a decrease in demand, emphasized Train. No matter what energy alternatives may be considered—increases in oil production, other continental production, shale production, geothermal power or nuclear power development, there will still be a substantial gap between available supply and projected demand.

In order to reduce the rate of growth in the consumption of energy, Russell Train proposed a national strategy for a more "energy efficient society." The main focus would be (1) increase mass transit, (2) increase recycling, and (3) develop a strong land-use policy. All of these factors would greatly reduce the demand of energy consumption. Mass transit would be the greatest potential for energy savings due to the reduction of individual fuel consumption. Recycling would reduce energy waste.

"The better the land-use planning and the more efficient land-use regulations, the more efficient will be the consumption of energy," Mr. Train stated. He estimated that the average suburbanite uses approximately 50 percent more energy than the city dweller. A sound land-use policy could reduce the present growth of energy consumption from 5 percent to less than 3 percent.

Mr. Train viewed the fuel shortage as a " . . . warning to both our own society in the United States and to the world to put our houses in order and bring ourselves in better balance with the environment" in order that we may curtail the various resource and food shortages accompanying the energy crisis.

"We should act as a nation united," Train said, "to declare war on waste, and that theme brings together the energy and environmental concerns."

According to Mr. Train, the energy problem results from the wasteful uses of energy. The environmental problem, especially pollution, results from the wasteful uses of our natural resources. "A more energy efficient society will be a cleaner, healthier, less polluting, and environmentally far more acceptable society. The problems of environment and energy are closely related, and in many cases are the same problem, simply the different sides of the coin. The solution to both must go together."

Case 10
BLM Rides to Improve the Range

Approximately one-fifth of the total land area in the United States is federally owned, with 62 percent of it under jurisdiction of the Bureau of Land Management, or about 470 million acres. A recent in-house study on the effects of livestock grazing on wildlife, watershed, recreation, and other resource values on a few areas in Nevada, conducted by the BLM, presents a dismal picture. The facts in the report, not surprising to experienced observers of western rangeland conditions, clearly shows much amiss out there in the wide open spaces. Too many hungry critters, domestic livestock, free-roaming feral, or wild horses and burros, deer, antelope, and other wildlife, and man—the intruder in many ways, coupled with a lack of long-range management, show abuse and deterioration of an environment naturally harsh and unforgiving.

This report, which caused a stir in some quarters, may be the reason why BLM Director Curt Berklund announced he is "ordering immediate actions to intensify management" of grazing lands.

In initiating the six-point conservation-enhancement program, Berklund ordered (1) increased supervision of range use to control livestock trespass and assure compliance with grazing programs; (2) readjustment of grazing privileges to balance use and forage production; (3) apportionment of "realistic" forage use for wildlife and wild horses and burros; (4) adjustment and enforcement of seasonal livestock grazing to protect vegetation; (5) classification of ranges for use by types of domestic livestock; and (6) BLM employees to fully consider environmental impacts of competing land uses.

Conservationists are applauding the BLM Director for his refreshing candor in airing the unflattering report which is critical of range conditions, detailing destruction of trout streams and other losses of wildlife habitat, and for his prompt efforts to resolve the resource management problems described in it.

Literally tons of range condition studies, reports, recommendations, and public announcements have been made by the BLM, special study commissions of the Congress, by private organizations, foundations, and by individuals, as well as educational institutions. This flood of material has been accelerating since the passage of the Taylor Grazing Act in 1935, which established the Bureau of Land Management. In addition, at the 1974 Western Governors Conference, BLM focused its attention on the public land situation and the program resources needed to reverse deteriorating range trends. At that time, it was conceded that rehabilitation was essential. In spite of all the talk and written reports, though, any range resource college student can readily ascertain that few of the good management intentions ever result in improvement on the range.

The simple reason for the continuing failure is that the Bureau of Land Management lacks the basic organic act which would give congressional authority for the BLM to become a management agency rather than maintaining a custodial function. Livestock domination of decisions at the district grazing level, coupled with insufficient budgets, lack of personnel, and little continuity from one federal administration to the next has kept BLM in the orphan child category.

With the energy and protein shortages prevalent, increased demands upon all public domain lands are going to find them in short supply. Not only does the Nevada BLM study show deterioration of rangelands but other careful ecologists are now presenting unmistakable evidence that management of publicly owned wildlands in many areas leaves much to be desired.

Richard J. Vogl, a professor of biology, California State University, Los Angeles, writing in *Western Wildlands,* says, "A recent trend in resource management has been the modeling of approaches after those found in agriculture and business. The facts that most resources cannot be successfully viewed as business ventures and that modern agricultural 'improvements' upon nature have their shortcomings, limitations, and ecological complications (to the point where continued modern operations are questionable) have done little to discourage this trend. Foresters are now talking about a 'third forest' and are treating forests more like agricultural lands; some range managers are promoting overgrazing and the eliminating of native grasslands in the name of conservation; mineral resources are becoming part of big business to be exploited or liquidated solely according to market trends; recreation managers are beginning to operate national forests and parks like drive-in movies or sport shows; wildlife managers are operating wildlife refuges as farmland cafeterias and shooting clubs; and sport fisheries are being managed more and more on a put-

and-take basis, while commercial fisheries managers are doing little more than monitoring the sickening races among counties and companies to see who will bring the final catch of a given species."

The Nevada evaluation report was prepared by a team of BLM resource managers with expertise in range, watersheds, wildlife, and recreation. It identifies 11 principal problems arising from present grazing administration practices: (1) livestock grazing systems in allotment management plans have not adequately considered other multiple uses (wildlife, recreation, etc.) in the planning stages; (2) land-use planning should be completed on critical areas as soon as possible so that action plans can be implemented on the ground; (3) significant increases in livestock grazing use have been authorized that cannot be supported by documented studies showing existing forage resources; (4) forage was allotted for livestock use without due consideration for wildlife, wild horses, and wild burro needs; (5) there was excessive livestock grazing in some areas; (6) reservation of grazing privileges in excess of any reasonable forage production potentials was carried on the books for future livestock use; (7) the Bureau's intensive livestock grazing management program (Allotment Management Plans) is not being effectively implemented. This has resulted in adverse impacts on the range resource; (8) range improvement projects, such as seedings and other vegetative conversions, have not been followed by proper grazing management techniques; (9) the increasing density of pinon-juniper stands has caused a loss of understory forage for all grazing animals including wildlife; (10) protection and enhancement of historical and archeological values have been diminished for the benefit of the range program; (11) BLM district offices have inadequate staffs to correct deficiencies in the grazing program. It is not unusual for a single employee to be responsible for the administration of multiple-use programs on a million acres or more of public land.

Berklund said the Department of the Interior will present a comprehensive report on the Bureau's range management program and on range conditions to the Senate Interior Appropriations Subcommittee early next year. This report will reflect the existing situation and define what needs to be done on public domain lands.

"Unfortunately," Berklund noted, "the attention given to the management of the western public domain lands, in terms of money and manpower needed to reverse . . . declining trends, has taken a back seat to every other national priority. Now, hopefully, with the increased impact of increased competition for public land uses and implementation of the National Environmental Policy Act, we will get the resources needed to provide adequate management and rehabilitation for public rangelands."

The Bureau of Land Management has on its staff, in the field and in Washington, D.C., an excellent cadre of highly qualified individuals. The failure of working with nature to improve wildlands cannot be laid only at their door. An indifferent general public is the real culprit. Citizen conservation organizations show signs of increasing efforts to change things around, but the success of any such program requires much more display of interest and action from the general public than has yet been evidenced.

TOPIC QUESTIONS

1. How are underdeveloped nations susceptible to environmental ruin and famine?
2. Is overpopulation by underdeveloped nations a greater threat to the world's finite resources than the material acquisitive industrialized nations? Discuss.
3. How can the United States, in order to fill domestic requirements, be both a major producer of metals and a major importer of metals?
4. Can a nation's distribution system soften the shocks of sudden shortages in strategic raw materials?
5 How does the consumer accelerate short-fall problems?
6. What accounts for black market operations during a short-fall situation (such as the Arab embargo)?
7. How can large companies control raw material acquisition and distribution in the United States.
8. How does the raw material acquisition process affect biological capital?

Case 9

9. How could a national strategy for a more efficient society improve our raw materials position in the world market?
10. How does land use affect resource use and environmental balances?
11. If economic incentives were responsible for the shift from coal to gas for power generation, how could the federal government encourage a return to coal?

Case 10

12. What should be the priorities in managing federally owned lands?
13. What raw materials are extracted from public lands?
14. Do finished goods that wind up in the hands of consumers find a use on public land? If so, what products can you cite as having important uses on large land tracts?
15. Why is the attitude of the public important in managing public lands?

RECOMMENDED READINGS

Louis W. Stern and John R. Grabbner, Jr., eds., *Competition in the Marketplace* (Glenview, Ill.: Scott, Foresman and Company, 1970).

Ronald R. Gist, ed., *Marketing and Society* (Hinsdale, Ill.: Dryden Press, 1974).

Betsy D. Gelb and Ben M. Enis, *Marketing Is Everybody's Business* (Pacific Palisades, Calif.: Goodyear, 1974).

Gene Logsdon, *Homesteading: How to Find Independence on the Land* (Emmaus, Pa.: Rodale Press, Book Division, 1973).

FOOTNOTES

1. Dr. Lester Brown, Overseas Development Council, described the roots of the world food shortage before the House Committee on Agriculture hearings, as reported in *Conservation Report* 28, 93rd Congress, 2nd Session (August 9, 1974), pp. 383–384.
2. From *Economic Growth and Environmental Decay* by Paul W. Barkley and David W. Seckler, pp. 46–47, © 1972 by Harcourt Brace Jonanovich, Inc., and reprinted with their permission.
3. For those readers interested in learning more about alternative life styles, see Helen and Scott Nearing, *Living the Good Life* (New York: Schocken Books Inc., 1970) and Samuel Ogden, *This Country Life* (Emmaus, Pa.: Rodale Press, Book Division, 1973). A third choice is recommended for persons who wish to recapture frontier skills: Eliot Wigginton, ed., *The Foxfire Book I and II* (New York: Doubleday and Company, Inc., 1972).
4. From Ted Schafers, "No 'Recession' on Supply Front," *St. Louis Globe Democrat* (March 4, 1974), p. 16B.

PART THREE
THE
SOLUTION

CHAPTER SIX

THE CONSERVATION ETHIC

AND THE

MARKETING CONCEPT

MARKETING MYOPIA: A DEFINITION

Contemporary society is pushing against natural limits with unparalleled speed. As the earth becomes more toxic and as basic raw materials become more scarce, planning time likewise shortens, forcing us to find solutions to more complex problems in shorter time spans. While utopians and proponents of unlimited economic growth and development may look to science and technology to fill environmental and economic voids, difficulties seem to be accumulating faster than solutions. Society is accruing deferred human costs (biological and economic) which rank right alongside other national problems.

Ironically, new health worries about respiratory illnesses and cancers, which are being linked more closely to toxic substances, lagged behind rapid expansion phases of such industries as tobacco, chemicals, petroleum, automobile, metal processing, and nuclear fission. The tremendous spin-off of vast product lines associated with these industries introduced pollutants with more toxic properties; these substances have the capacity to combine and form new chemical compositions in the air, water, and soil.

The complexities of integrating social, environmental, and marketing information into working models are indeed challenging. Figure 6-1 illustrates the macro information-communication flow relationships. Biological capital and life style choices are integral parts of the total information system.

FIGURE 6-1

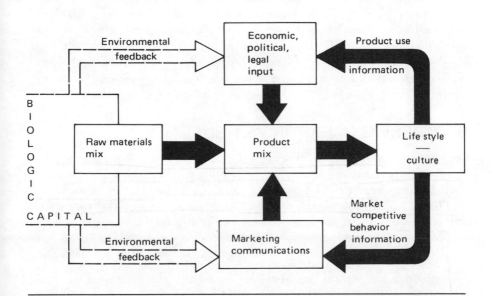

In the economy, economic cycles, changing consumer tastes, life-style alterations, wars, and fashion transitions are responsible for major shifts in growth patterns. As a result, some industries adapt to change and continue to survive and expand, while others pass into oblivion. Many industries that suffer greatly when trends shift fall victim to their own myopia. Defining industries, products, markets, and legal, political, and social boundaries too narrowly further undermines adjustment of change. Levitt presents four conditions leading to self-deception:

1. The belief that growth is assured by an expanding and more affluent population;
2. The belief that there is no competitive substitute for the industry's major product;
3. Too much faith in mass production and in the advantages of rapidly declining unit costs as output rises;
4. Preoccupation with a product that lends itself to carefully controlled scientific experimentation, improvement, and manufacturing cost reduction.[1]

Firms that enjoy strongly entrenched positions in well-established industries can deceive themselves into thinking that technical, specialized, and narrow solutions can be applied to abstract social influences. The result often leads to ineffective responses and even damaging public relations; social responses to myopic industrial practices is often manifested in such dimensions as antitrust indictments; legislation unfavorable to the industry; consumer boycotts of products; labor unrest; adversities in financial markets; relaxed tariffs for foreign competitors; unfavorable publicity; and criminal prosecution of executives involved in price fixing, collusion, bid rigging, and illegal political campaign contributions. Societal influences are being transferred more rapidly into legislation, administrative positions (especially by governmental agencies), congressional concerns, and organizational responses (by voter, environmental, consumer, racial, ethnic, and cultural blocs).

BROADENING MARKETING'S ROLE

Fortunately, marketing is viewing contemporary social problems with increasing concern. Marketing is being defined in broader terms, encompassing a developing field defined as social marketing. External variables and limits to behavior are considered in relation to economic incentives and cost limits. Lazer discusses social marketing in these terms:

> Social marketing suggests that marketing decisions cannot be justified on economic costs and profits alone. It indicates that some products and services should be marketed where there is little or no economic profit. It holds that marketing has dimensions that extend beyond the profit motive. It maintains that management know-how must be applied to the solution of society problems. It is in marketing's best enlightened self-interest to do so, for the alternative consequences of society's negative reaction, government regulations, administrative rulings, and an expanded posture are not desirable alternatives.[2]

Social marketing or social aspects of marketing seeks to examine broad social issues in context with causes and ideals. Since environmental issues represent a categorical array of interrelated causes, a composite of ideals, a portfolio of diverse remedial plans, and a powerful influence on market freedoms, ecology has become a much discussed social aspect in marketing literature. Environmental debates that evolve from societal interfaces with business and economic processes will continue to sharpen in intensity as natural backlashes (economic and biological) continue to accumulate around us. America is approaching an age that holds unparalleled dangers to its survival as a sovereign people. The options open to a contemporary society seem to preclude the existence of a readily available solution. For this reason we cannot afford to be myopic in our conceptual understanding of external relationships. The eventual solution to the complex ecological-social-economic problems confronting us will most probably stem from several approaches. The important point to consider is the time variable. If crises culminate too quickly for science or technology to contribute its share of solutions, if social disruptions preclude effective leadership at all levels of government, and if ecological impairment passes a point of no return, then the world is heading for a collapse condition.

In terms of the time factor, conservation is widely discussed as one means for bringing social behavior and market demand into balance with resource short falls, inflation-recession pressures, and natural resource policies. While conservation is not the complete answer to all environmental problems, it does provide alternative approaches that can be enacted and can be put into general use in both short-run and long-run dimensions. These approaches require adjustments in demands and efficiency improvements in the state of the arts.

THE CONSERVATION ETHIC DEFINED

Conservation is generally thought of as a means of allocating scarce goods and as a conceptual guide for managing economic and natural resources. Throughout history, mankind has been faced with shortages and famines. When confronted with sudden and catastrophic scarcities, entire cities, regions, and nations have been forced to conserve, ration, and allocate available supplies of food, water, military weapons, shelter, and clothing. Under this survival challenge, mandatory conservation generally exists and the free rider is all but eliminated. Even hoarding is viewed under these conditions as being a serious crime. In this instance, the resource problem becomes so critical that serious disruptions in social and economic processes occur. Trading centers, transportation routes, mercantile patterns, and social order have been known to fall victim to the great famines and panics of history.

Conservation under crisis conditions is at best a short-term survival or expediency matter. In World War II the United States emphasized war goods production, and consumer goods become scarce; rationing programs determined the manner in which many categories of consumer products could be distributed. New automobiles and many large appliances were very scarce, because civilian production virtually ceased. Tires, gasoline, meat, butter, and many other products required rationing coupons. Black market merchandise could be purchased, but at considerably higher prices.

Conservation is a conceptualized view of managing natural resources against a broad scenario of ecological, social, and economic considerations and is considerably more than a short-term, crisis-oriented field. Often conservationists view developing problems over time spans much longer than the 5-, 10-, or 15-year planning cycles of industry; therefore, valuable lead time can be provided a nation to avoid a catastrophy or a disruptive crisis.

The conservation views that follow typify energy, resource, and ecological positions.

Something for Our Critics to Ponder[3]

Advocates of conservation are often vigorously criticized, especially in highly industrialized societies, for holding so steadfastly to viewpoints which seem to be contrary to the trend of social or economic needs.

We have been called obstructionists, and worse, for urging caution in approval for such projects as the trans-Alaskan oil pipeline, or the proliferation of nuclear-fired power plants, off-shore oil wells, strip mines, larger airports, colonization schemes in tropical rain forests, super highways, dams, and scores of other projects which result in environmental degradation.

In the words of some highly placed officials, we do little good and enormous harm once our interests go beyond such relatively "harmless" activities as holding scientific meetings, writing textbooks, bird watching, and making lists of endangered species. Presumably, wider concerns should be none of our affair, but left entirely to the good judgment of politicians, businessmen, and those governmental agencies which are the official guardians of the public's interest in resource use.

Conservationists also are criticized for views which seem simple-minded to people who have never known anything under their feet but hard surfaces. To hear these critics, it would seem the real world is paved or walled, trees confined to tubs or planting margins, animals to feedlots or zoos, and wild nature to worthless and unknown or, at best backward, places. To suggest that there are paramount values in wilderness, for instance, in the views of many seemingly intelligent people would be a priori evidence of a feeble mind.

Indeed, throughout a large part of the world the dominant drives are destruction of wilderness and consumption of basic resources at ever increasing rates, in the process of which economic growth and relative prosperity—and even something called "the good life"—have resulted for part, but far from all, of the world's people.

Some conservation advocates have challenged the economic theories of increasing use and continuing growth as invalid for the long term. For decades they have warned of coming troubles, urging moderation in the consumption of nonrenewable resources—including land—and care in the harvest of such renewable resources as fisheries and forests.

In general, these warnings have had few receptive listeners and many critics.

Where rational use of resources—in the full realization that these resources are limited in supply—has been conservation's rallying cry, many of our critics have advocated precisely the opposite action.

Where conservation has demonstrated the ecological truth that diversity results in strength, many critics have advocated systems of monocultures, in human activity as well as in agriculture. Even in the field of ideas, diversity has been shunned and contrary opinion persecuted.

Where conservation has urged that development programs, fully conceded to be necessary in many cases, take ecological considerations into account in the planning stage, the critics usually have ignored this advice, in spite of ample evidence that to do so imperils the success of the program concerned. Ironically, when a program goes sour, ecologists usually are the first experts called in to find a remedy.

Where conservation has urged societies to keep open options for future resource use and not to foreclose choices for coming generations, our critics have advocated policies that will preclude such choices.

Where conservationists have proved the destructive effects of chemical pollution, critics seem quite willing to accept this destruction as the price—but only part of the price, it must be reminded—of so-called economic growth and expansion of markets, or simply of business as usual.

A few decision-makers have listened to these warnings, but in general they have paid little attention. Far too many people have held to the belief that technology and science would miraculously produce substitutes in good time. This has yet to be convincingly demonstrated.

And now the world has come face to face with the bitter reality of an energy crisis. This is a reality with sufficient impact to convince even the most skeptical that there are limits to growth.

One would hope the lessons of this crisis would be taken to heart by those who make the decisions that shape our world. These are the lessons of nature and they extend to the societies of men and the system they create with the same force as they work in the natural world.

Ecologists know that when a group of living things becomes too successful—in terms of numbers, at least—it tends to destroy itself by the sheer weight of its mass and inability to satisfy its needs for food and habitat. Has mankind become too successful?

Ecologists know that there is strength in diversity. Have our enormously complicated economic systems become too rigidly dependent on a few raw materials? Have we put too many of our eggs in one basket? Do we rely too heavily on too little? Are we attempting to lift ourselves by our own bootstraps?

Sadly, the answer appears to be "yes" to all these questions.

For at least 20 years conservationists have warned of serious trouble ahead in the matter of energy use and production. These warnings have been borne out, and the future appears dim indeed for a large part of the industrialized world.

Conservationists must reiterate that there are no easy answers, no panaceas, no magic replacements for exhausted resources that can issue from factories or laboratories.

Hope for the future does not lie in the panic reaction of further environmental destruction and minor modification to the policy of "business as usual," which appears to be one immediate response to the crisis.

Genuine hope lies only in the imperative and urgent necessity that men and nations honestly begin to practice conservation in all its creative aspects. Realigned priorities, a genuine end to waste, significant retrenchment in levels of consumption, recycling, environmental restoration and repair, and careful planning in all we do must now be the goal in societies where men have long forgotten the feel of the earth under their feet. Ultimately mankind must find the way to live in dynamic balance with the only source of his own strength, which is the natural world.

As they always have, conservation's critics will no doubt call these actions simple-minded and too radical for the "practical" needs of today. No conservationist would suggest they will be easy to accomplish, especially where so much major effort has been spent in the opposite directions. Nevertheless, these are ideas whose time is long past due.

Can the world afford further delay? Perhaps. But only at the risk of enormously greater disruption and difficulty when the start is finally made, as inevitably it must.

Fundamental Changes Needed for Energy Conservation Success[4]

If we are going to make a real impact to achieve energy conservation, certain fundamental changes must be made throughout our social and economic structure. Lip service and token gestures will not suffice. Patterns of industrial development and personal consumption have dynamics of their own. They move forward on their established courses with momentum and with force. Many existing market forces encourage waste. To change these patterns—to truly hold back the flood—a public decision must be made and nailed down in firm legal terms.

My own judgment is that there is much that we can do and should do to ensure energy conservation—much that we can do without disrupting standards of living or imposing real hardship. For example, unless the auto makers give a full and firm assurance that they will meet the president's request to improve fuel economy, we should adopt a flat regulatory requirement that all cars produced after 1978 achieve at least a minimum standard for fuel economy, and this bottom floor requirement should be coupled with a further incentive in shift toward smaller cars in the form of a surtax on all cars weighing more than 3,000 lb escalated upward to as high as $1,000 tax on the big cars over 5,500 lb.

We also should continue to consider the need for additional gasoline taxes or some form of rationing to cut down on excessive automobile use. We should abolish the Highway Trust Fund, so that federal money for highway construction would go through normal appropriations scrutiny. We should increase governmental support for public transportation. And we should establish measures along the patterns of the air pollution transportation control plans to reduce individual automotive use in metropolitan areas where public transportation can be provided.

None of these proposals would be popular. But such a package of governmental action would reflect a judgment by society that a real change should be made. Short of commitments of this depth, success will not occur.

I do not mean to zero in only on the automobile. A great many similar changes should be made to deal with energy extravagance in other forms. But the automobile sits in the center of the stage in this drama of energy conservation. It is a big part of the problem in and of itself. And it is a symbol for all the rest. If we are unwilling to face up to the problem of the automobile and do something about it, we might as well forget about the goal of energy conservation. We are kidding ourselves if we think the job can be done without attacking the problem at its core.

The underlying issue posed by the energy crisis is whether a fundamentally new approach must be taken to cope successfully with this national problem. In the past we have always met problems of shortages by reaching out for more production. We have never really tried to scale down the demand.

Our whole American history has been a march against the frontier. We have set out to subdue the wilderness, to control our natural surroundings, and to exploit our natural resources. Progress and prosperity have been our slogans. GNP has been our yardstick of success. Constant increase of production has been the engine that has kept the whole show moving down the road. It has been the answer to every problem.

The basic division on this problem today is between those who see the future as an extension of the past and those who see the future as fundamentally different from the past. Many disturbing signposts indicate that we cannot keep going on our present course. We are pushing past the limits of our finite resource base. Problems are jumping up at us faster than we can solve them, but we are keeping our foot pressed down on the throttle. We have breezed past the environmental crisis, and we are racing through the energy crisis. Our lights flicker. Our air smells foul. Our streets are choked with traffic. Our land is jammed with buildings. No matter. Full speed ahead.

A day will come when we shall rue our recklessness. A day will come when we shall look back in wonder that we didn't use more care. We are whizzing past so many opportunities to make small adjustments that would give us more time to find long-term solutions. In our heady self-assurance we cannot be troubled with such restraints. We may be heading for national disaster, but that isn't in our minds right now. In the meantime, we are doing just fine. Speeding past the danger signs, the American Joy Ride runs on.

A Comment on Natural Resources[5]

Our national park system is incomplete. Several new parks (Big Thicket, Prairie, Sawtooth) and significant additions to existing parks (Grand Canyon, Redwoods, Everglades) are needed. National park management is unduly influenced by concessionaires. We are fighting for new parks and additions; we are pushing for park management practices that will preserve this heritage.

Our national forests are being mined—and not just for minerals. Present forest practices mine the trees, too. Timber must be treated as a renewable resource and not just extracted. We believe in true sustained yield forestry. We believe in true multiple use.

Recreation vehicles are tearing up our deserts, grasslands, and forests. The Bureau of Land Management and the Forest Service are unable to prevent this destruction because they have lacked both money and direction. We are trying to educate people to provide the public support necessary to control the ORV's.

The development of a rational energy policy can wait no longer. The walls are falling down, but it's not too late to rebuild on a solid policy foundation. We must conserve energy, while supporting research and development to increase the supply. Present nuclear energy technology is clearly not adequate and is filled with danger. Clean fossil fuel resources are diminishing rapidly, yet we possess vast coal reserves. Technology is needed to extract coal in a less destructive manner than by strip mining; then the coal must be cleaned. Again, research and development are necessary.

Are Conservationists Obstructionists?

Conservationists depict the natural world in the context of values that often conflict with narrow, specialized, and short-term economic, political, and profit standards used by industry, government, and technological optimists. Since the United States has enjoyed a long era in which basic energy and other raw material resources were cheap, expansion and economic development have traditionally reached out into the surrounding environment to acquire more raw materials. Suburbs moved out from central metropolitan centers because urban renewal is more expensive than using out-lying farmlands. Municipal dumps made use of open space in adjacent areas. Likewise, roads, shopping centers, and industrial parks have employed open spaces beyond urban centers to expand.

The treasure chest holding our reserves of natural resources has, by design, been restricted. Muncipal parks provide open space even within the most densely populated city centers; national parks provide scenic beauty, wilderness regions, watersheds, and deposits of raw materials. The national park system represents a resource that cannot be evaluated strictly in terms of an economic yardstick. The system represents a heritage open for all to use with activities that are compatible with environmental requirements of park management. As minerals, timber, and open space grow more scarce, increasing pressures to open up parks to mining, timbering, and commercial operations evolve from specialized economic sectors within society. When commerical interests collide with the preservation philosophy of national parks, conservationists lead the fight to eliminate such projects.

Not all natural resources should be open to commercial exploitation; national parks represent a unique national resource which meets collective social needs. Wilderness areas are unique and offer society a collective good that requires protective measures to safeguard its features. Other open space, green belts, and farm regions are less fragile; but disruptive and wasteful uses of open space by special interests which lead to pollution and conflicting land-use developments are opposed by conservationists.

Science and technology can play positive roles in our society in reducing blatant wastes through greater efficiencies, especially in energy use. Expansionary needs for natural resources and raw materials require long-term growth guides with environmental safeguards rather than immediate profit maximization goals.

THE MARKETING CONCEPT DEFINED

Marketing's expanding role in societal aspects is reflected in the growing list of areas that are becoming increasingly important to business. Lavidge suggests that marketing may serve society in the following categories of societal concerns:

1. Consumerism.
2. The struggle of the poor for subsistence.
3. The marketing of social and cultural services.
4. The day-to-day functioning of the economy.
5. The use and pollution of society's resources.[6]

During the 1960s, when raw materials were both plentiful and inexpensive, productivity increases and economic expansion promised to lift the impoverished out of ghettos and sharecroppers' squalor. The economy produced product lines that offered both excitement and economy. Market segmentation offered consumers increasing choices of brands and variations in models. Good times tended to conceal developing social and economic stresses, which had evolved into national problems by the 1970s.

The environment became not only a national problem, but a marketing concern as well. Pollution and resource use are linked to our production and consumption patterns. The nation's infrastructure (health and maintenance systems) is overloaded with social, economic, and environmental demands. Rising local taxes and mounting service costs are straining the financial integrity of many municipal and state service programs. Pollution levels have exceeded the effectiveness of our cleansing systems, and part of the problem can be traced to the products that industry designs and consumers use and discard.

New technology and new product additives are making the environment more potentially hazardous. The house is fast becoming a legitimate drug and chemical supply unit which inventories lethal products that can kill or seriously injure people who carelessly use them. The utility cabinet and kitchen storage shelves represent hazardous areas around the home for infants and small children. Industrial product users are required to take greater precautions in handling chemical solvents, acids, and radioactive materials.

Industrial effluents leak into the surrounding air, soil, and streams; these toxic substances combine with consumer effluents from automobiles, homes, and recreational sites to further tax natural and municipal treatment facilities in treating liquid and solid wastes in water resources. Other pollutants such as litter increase collection costs and rob scenic areas of their beauty.

Marketing becomes even more involved with environmental issues as raw material shortages force key industries to change traditional distribution practices. Strong inflationary pressures are forcing more families to spend higher percentages of income on such basics as food and clothing. The advent of "stagflation" (inflation and recession) combines high prices with high unemployment. In many respects the raw material short falls of 1973–1975 have opened a new era in resource utilization and attitudes. The societal problems of poverty, pollution, inflation, and consumer dissatisfaction are interrelated rather than existing as separate social issues.

In this age of enlightened social awareness, marketing should avoid myopic tunnel vision. Social issues should be incorporated into the corporate decision making processes. Unfortunately, many companies view marketing in rather narrow terms. Kotler and Levy comment on this problem in the following discussion:

> Modern marketing has two different meanings in the minds of people who use the term. One meaning of marketing conjures up the terms selling, influencing, persuading. Marketing is seen as a huge and increasingly dangerous technology, making it possible to sell

persons on buying things, propositions, and causes they either do not want or which are bad for them. This was the indictment in Vance Packard's *Hidden Persuaders* and numerous other social criticisms, with the net effect that a large number of persons think of marketing as immoral or entirely self-seeking in its fundamental premises. They can be counted on to resist the idea of organizational marketing as so much "Madison Avenue."

The other meaning of marketing unfortunately is weaker in the public mind; it is the concept of sensitively serving and satisfying human needs. This was the great contribution of the marketing concept that was promulgated in the 1950s, and that concept now counts many business firms as its practitioners.[7]

The second view of marketing is potentially useful in the integrative processes that focus on exploring long-range solutions to national, industrial, and human needs. In this context sales goals and corporate profits are viewed in relation to actions that contribute to resolving human problems; or, if not, which actions by industry need modification so that dangerous trends leading to serious environmental and human confrontations can be curtailed while acceptable options can be found. The avoidance of collective bads in private-goods marketing can further the advance of market freedoms and individual choice. This is the real task of social marketing.

A TRANSVECTIONAL VIEW OF MARKETING

The societal emphasis offsets the manipulative and transactionally oriented image of marketing. The broad conceptual view of marketing is not something new in the literature. A. W. Shaw, a pioneer in marketing thought, described marketing as "matter in motion." The movement of material through distribution channels in synchronous harmony with services, promotional concepts, and functions symbolizes Shaw's approach to the study of marketing. Indeed, the profession developed in the early years around the analysis of commodities, functions, and industrial distribution techniques. The cycle of harvest, shipment, storage, classification, processing, distribution, sale, and consumption tends to position the product in the context of material flow.

Wroe Alderson continued the flow idea, developing a concept known as transvections, which is defined as follows:

> A transvection is the unit of action for the system by which a single end-product such as a pair of shoes is placed in the hands of the consumer after moving through all the intermediate sorts and transformations from the original raw materials in the state of nature. The choice of a word which would sound something like the word "transaction" was deliberate since the two ideas were obviously closely related.

A transvection is in a sense the outcome of a series of transactions, but a transvection is obviously more than this. The transactions as such are limited only to the successive negotiations of exchange agreements. A transvection includes the complete sequence of exchanges, but it also includes the various transformations which take place along the way. The pair of shoes in the hands of the consumer is obviously a very different thing from the raw materials in the state of nature. The student of transvections is interested in every step along the way by which this flow through the marketing system was accomplished.[8]

Marketing has tended to dwell on the consumer product phase in the transvectional sequence. Finished goods represent an economic investment for firms, consumers, institutions, and government units; finished goods are at the top of the ladder in the chain of events that transform raw materials into finished goods. Products sold in marketplaces carry raw material, energy, labor, social, and environmental costs. Unfortunately, products often bear prices below their full costs (which include depletion, pollution, and environmental clean-up costs) when purchased by consumers. Until recently, consumer involvement with products ended with their disposal. Today, postconsumption dispensation of solid wastes is a growing national headache.

The Product of Marketing

The product of marketing is more comprehensive than packages, promotions, or physical or psychological dimensions. Indeed, products are designed to satisfy human needs, to meet life-style requirements, and to resolve living, working, and recreational problems. But in the process of placing ever widening arrays of items in the hands of consumers who seem to share more individualized and diverse attitudes, increasing difficulties arise in our social structure that limit and prohibit consumer usage of products. Although consumers are encouraged to develop individual tastes for consumption decisions, they are more aware than ever of growing scarcities in open space, scenic beauty, clean air, water, and living "elbow room." While decisions to purchase products are often left to the individual's own discretion, his use of those goods may be rigidly restricted; highly toxic chemicals, drugs, automobiles, snowmobiles, mobile home, firearms, aircraft are but a few such products. Our world tends to shrink as technology spins off products that penetrate protective spatial cushions between countries, regions, states, localities, neighbors, and individuals within the same house. Pollution of all kinds—noise, air, water, and soil—link people who involuntarily share collective bads; for example, aboard a passenger aircraft nonsmokers chose to segregate themselves to avoid a pollutant—smoke. Those persons with acute lung congestion or with respiratory illnesses must avoid air pollution of all kinds, including cigarette smoke.

Natural areas in many parts of the nation's public domain are becoming off limits to over-the-road vehicles (ORV's) because of ecological damage that careless drivers impart. Snowmobiles have broken the traditional quiet of the north country, creating problems in protecting wildlife and in protecting against crime in unguarded cabins, resorts, farms, and businesses located in remote areas. Real estate developers are restricted by zoning and environmental regulations from constructing incompatible developments in many areas. (Unfortunately, zoning ordinances are often manipulated to allow for "exceptions." While flexibility allows cities to adjust to dynamic conditions, some exceptions are ploys motivated by leverage of the purse.) Collectively, living and consumption patterns share available natural resources; this, in turn, spawns confrontations between those holding differing views, attitudes, philosophies, and temperaments about the role of such products in the environment.

Consumer Convenience

The transformations and transactions that constitute the transvectional flow of natural resources to consumer markets are influenced by convenience dimensions of the product. Convenience is achieved through market mix, promotion, and systems designs that facilitate the ease and use of products by consumers. The trend toward convenience is accompanied by additional processing, individualized packages, product-brand proliferation, multiple outlets, new innovations, and technology. Duplication, litter, disposal complications, energy wastes, higher unit prices, and environmental pollution are often linked to convenience dimensions in products. The "use it once and throw it away" attitude is blamed for rising demands for the nation's timber, minerals, fibers, and water resources. Convenience for the consumer often means that additional functions must be assumed by firms higher up in the distribution system; other infrastructure burdens on society and on the environment increase the cost of convenience.

As material shortages and inflation further limit economic expansion (in the growth phase of the business cycle), marketing mix trade-offs from convenience to utility, function, conservation, and pollution control may alter the essential character of many products.

SOCIOECOLOGICAL PRODUCT

Products undergo physical changes while moving from natural states, to raw material components, to finished goods, to consumption, to postconsumption disposal, to recycling, and to eventual return to nature. Transformations within the flow cycle from nature to consumer and back to nature suggest that interdependent, sequential relationships exist throughout the system. Economic resources, societal goods and bads, and physical and psychological dimensions become interdependently linked to product flow.

While products are generally considered to be private goods, their intended and unintended uses in society have collective consequences. In this context, Cracco and Rostenne suggest that the Alderson's transvection evolves into an "ecological transvection" which encompasses a broad range of facilitating or multidimensional aspects; the socioecological product of marketing is described as follows:

> If, for example, we look at the system of which the car is a part—rubber plantations, oil fields, refineries, manufacturers, new cars, roads, service stations, pollution, noise, mobility, junk—it is clear that no part exists separately from the others. They must be considered as one entity, a total product which encompasses all the elements of the system from nature back to nature and which also takes into account the effects upon the entire social structure. The overriding components of this system are the time, physical, psychic, and social dimensions of the socioecological product.[9]

Industrial facilitating links are supportive to distribution and consumption; this interdependency, in turn, influences how resources are extracted from their natural states and the form that products eventually take in satisfying human needs. Since marketing traditionally focuses on product use by consumers, the wider societal-environmental impact of transvectional transformations is often overlooked. Negative attributes are often associated with product flow in both the direct and residual dimensions. Hence, decisions involving price, package, promotion, market, and suggested uses of products have positive-negative factors relative to direct users; the positive and negative product features leave an imprint on others as well. Pollution, resource depletion, destruction of ecologically unique area, losses of privacy, injury, and even death spill over market boundaries, thus affecting the lives of nonusers.

PROLIFERATION

As a matter of routine business, marketing influences product development; selection of brand names, trademarks, determination of market targets, pricing, packaging features, material selections, channel decisions, and purchasing arrangements are representative decision areas that mold product characteristics. The choices that firms make in formulating product characteristics tend to be limited to rather narrow market and profit determinants. Products are designed to satisfy consumer wants and to resolve consumer problems; but consumers are increasingly segmented into specialized market niches (or micromarkets). An emphasis on micromarkets has the advantage of customizing product characteristics to customer needs; but the inherent disadvantage of myopic vision (relative to broad market trends) can be dangerous to the product's competitive environment. New technologies, shifts in social priorities, international trade imbalances, shortages, and special interest legislation can make products obsolete almost overnight.

Along with rising product and market specializations, our market economy is becoming increasingly dependent on facilitating, interrelated, and complementary business units. Enterprise differentiation determines or assigns organizational roles and resource allocations within our economic structure. Research and development, mineral leases, functional specialization, manufacturing efficiency, and capital-raising capabilities provide unique areas of expertise that, in turn, contribute to the effectiveness of the entire system. An interwoven market structure has contributed immeasurably to the nation's economic growth; however, this specialized role assignment function has a major flaw: sudden shocks, changes, disruptions, and crises which alter industrial alignments and markets represent serious adaptive threats to the survival of many firms. Alderson comments on this adaptive role in the following:

> In general, firms do not respond to opportunity unless they possess some significant part of the required resource pattern. They have the production facilities they need, they have experience with the appropriate trade channels, or their product research and development department has special skills in the proposed field. There are rare exceptions in which a firm is prepared to enter almost any field but on the ground that the truly basic pattern of resources for them is capital and management ability. Experience in trying to rehabilitate ailing companies might well lead to a rule of thumb as to whether they should be revived or liquidated. For illustration, if a firm already possessed 50 percent or more of the assets it would need to fulfill a new assignment, there would be a good chance for it to obtain the other assets required. If it did not stack up so well against any new assignment considered, it might be wiser to liquidate.[10]

Major conglomerate corporations, operating holding companies, multinational firms, and basic industries play central parts in both role assignments for other business units and allocation of raw materials that flow into the nation's economic system. Concentration of mineral reserves, capital reserves, management skill, technological specializations, research and development talent, organizational systems, and market dominance allow giant corporations a certain degree of flexibility in planning for change. Their ability to shift directions within a reasonably short time frame is directly linked to both the capital and managerial resources that large firms possess.

Smaller firms lack this advantage in adapting to change. Large firms can leverage production, and financial and market resources to reach growth objectives that may be measured in percentage of market control, total assets, numbers of subsidiaries, sales, profits, and control over competitive and supply dimensions; planning time often extends into decades for major capital expenditure projects.

Market opportunity for smaller firms can often be directed to limited consumer markets that large corporations may not have detected or may consider unattractive. In industrial markets, smaller firms perform many subcontracting supply tasks and complementary functions in assigned channel roles.

The combination of capital, management, and control over vast reserves of natural resources (economic deposits) gives large corporations adjustment advantages over smaller business units. When market demand expands and raw material supplies are abundant and inexpensive, most complementary and facilitating roles assigned to smaller firms are both profitable and conducive to growth. During periods when industrial materials and consumer products become scarce, however, smaller firms (independents in the case of petroleum distributors) face sudden interruptions in operations. Large firms can virtually choose under which circumstances and according to which profit goals scarce inventories can be distributed to industrial and consumer markets.

Social priorities on growth have encouraged large corporate enterprises, extravagant use of virgin resources, and loss of market competition in basic industries. Depletion and other tax incentives favor verticle integration to natural resource supplies. Large firms enjoy the capital needed to acquire and exploit large holdings in known ore fields. This has tended to increase the flow of raw materials through the production and distribution system. Product decisions that encourage larger, more expensive units are related to both financial incentives to deplete natural resources and to the economic rewards of near-full utilization of manufacturing and distribution capital units.

The traditional patterns of waste are bringing instability to both the economic system and the nation's monetary standing in the international community. During the past two years alone, the economy has suffered shortages in such product areas as food, chemicals, textiles, natural gas, paper, metals, plastics, cotton, wool, wood, ceramics, leather, cement, rubber, lard, blue jeans, diapers, wire, twine, toilets, cardboard, belts, stationary, furniture, burial caskets, automobile parts, structural steel, musical instruments, starch, chlorine, soda ash, phenol, newsprint, hides, insulating materials, ethyl alcohol, tallow, fuel oil, diesel fuel, fertilizers, to name a few.

Stresses caused by shortages are being reflected in the business system, with smaller firms facing the greatest challenge to survival. Larger firms, on the other hand, experienced disruptions, but their profits (derived in part from speculative profits on inventory stocks) have soared well beyond traditional industry boundaries. Consumers, too, found even routine living patterns disrupted; inflation and job losses are threatening to reverse gains in living standards.

In this period of transition, proliferation of opportunity may quickly shift to market needs emphasizing product savings in costs, operation, and servicing. Societal aspects would become essential factors in formulating marketing mix dimensions. Adaptation to changes in traditional distribution practices may well alter complementary and facilitating role assignments. Major revisions in antitrust and legislative policies, and new social values may in turn modify the power base of major corporations over markets and sources of raw materials.

INFLUENCES OF THE CONSERVATION ETHIC ON THE MARKETING MIX

The conservation ethic can be readily applied to the distribution system to stretch out raw materials, improve technological efficiency, and preserve the environment. Market strategy that employs the conservation concept can influence the product mix in several respects. These include the following:

1. Lengthening product life by emphasizing function, efficiency, simplicity. Less stress on mere style change for energy-using products.
2. Emphasizing lighter models of automobiles, appliances, power equipment, which use less fuel to operate.
3. Employing new technology to provide *real* improvements to products in terms of performance, safety, durability, dependability, and efficiency.
4. Thorough, new-product market testing, including an impact analysis on the social services, technology, resources, and consumer uses.
5. Encouraging consumers to carefully match the quantity of purchase with their needs and requirements.
6. Promoting conservation in the use of products requiring energy.
7. Redesigning the product line to eliminate wasteful and unnecessary product duplication.
8. Promoting packaging decisions that more easily incorporate materials recycled or returned, and establishing the return channel by which consumers, businesses, and government services may collect and sell back the cans, bottles, and boxes to the originating industry for reuse.
9. Formulating communication strategies that fuse social issues, ideals, concepts, and stresses with corporate responsibility and consumer life-style requirements.

Promotion

The essential task of promotion is product demand stimulation. Advertising and sales programs incorporate marketing mix factors which encourage consumer response in the market. Advertising budgets are often tied in directly to sales volume, and salesmen are compensated in many firms by commissions and bonuses. Rising sales trigger dynamic growth processes in firms, leading to expansion in employment, factory capacity, office space, broadened distribution channels, and product offerings. Promotion characteristically does more than describe product features to customers. Abstract concepts are applied to the advertisement and sales presentations to relate psychological and sociological attributes to consumer use and enjoyment of the product. Employing symbols and images with life-style associations further links the product with consumers' living patterns. The encouragement of material acquisition, fashion conciousness, technological innovation, and individual choice in turn influenced frequency of purchase, product use (and discard), and life-style values.

The potential influence of ecological transvections or the socioecological product on promotion strategies is considerable. The rapidly changing economic situation is forcing the United States to institute sweeping reforms. These reforms, which include voluntary and mandatory conservation programs, are destined to alter business systems and consumer life-style concepts.

Broad social changes carry adjustment risks as well as create new market opportunities. Firms that adapt policies with the dynamic forces that move within our society can likewise adjust products, marketing strategies, and promotional emphasis toward the emerging market requirements. Conversely, those firms that refuse to adjust marketing plans with developing social trends may lose markets because of consumer attitudes, legal restrictions, or lack of raw materials. The impact of emerging social changes for advertisers is discussed in the following:

> The scope of this new Age of Alternatives boggles the mind. For advertisers, we must again stress our belief in the urgent need to "sell real, meaningful, and quality differences." Some critics of the "limits of growth" concept have pointed out that human beings can make value judgments that alter their behavior, thus rendering invalid the forecasts of doom. We are now into that process of altering behavior and priorities. We will have to do more about selective growth, not about accelerating disposables.[11]

For over 20 years, marketers have largely ignored the conservation ethic. Our entire distribution philosophy seemed to be based around waste, duplication, and oversubscription of raw materials incorporated in the vast array of products produced for the United States and for world markets. Social critics have pointed to this waste in a variety of ways. Obsolescence through calculated strategies designed to shorten product life prematurely increased replacement sales. Style, fad, fashion, and gadgetry are manipulated to produce obsolescence well before the product physically breaks down. Products are traded in, discarded, and junked at higher rates than would be the case if *function* were the primary feature of the product. This results in shorter product life and, in turn, requires more of the nation's resources.

We have encouraged the consumer to buy larger quantities of products than are required; we have encouraged the market to purchase the luxury or premium brands of products, which require more accessories, parts, fuel, etc.

Packages are becoming so varied and sophisticated that they have assumed as important a role in merchandising products as advertising. These packages require vast quantities of aluminum, steel, plastics, and paper. For the most part, these packages go far beyond the protective function for ingredients with the wrap. Discarded packages end up as trash, litter, and solid wastes.

Advertising Stragegy

Opportunities for economic growth present themselves in different guises from period to period. For the next decade or two we are likely to enter a fast-moving transitional era that offers business new challenges and new dangers. Advertising techniques and emphasis are likewise subject to dynamic social pressures. In order to avoid obsolescence by way of self-deception, firms need to broaden product and market perspectives to catch glimpses of new market opportunities emerging from social changes.

Advertising strategies may likewise reflect an expanding view of consumption, competition, credibility, social service, and product-use impact. Such strategy decisions may well be guided by (1) life-style diversities, (2) growing demand for services, (3) developing public markets for beneficial private goods, (4) expanding concepts of human needs and satisfaction. These subjects embrace ecology, social responsibility, market service requirements, and research and development emphasis.

During the next 20 years new industries are predicted to emerge from new service and public market requirements. The environment may well produce new service and public market requirements. The environment may well produce new socially directed programs that not only resolve ecological imbalances but also improve overall efficiency in both industrial and consumer sectors of the economy.

Innovative advertising directed toward expanding public market opportunities is expected to become more important. Corporate advertising that relates social responsibility to products, services, research, innovation, and managerial philosophies should facilitate marketing and advertising plans for products having public market potentials. Consumer education can provide useful product information directed as prolonging beneficiary attributes, while minimizing associative hazards or negative features (both in product content and use). Credibility will become an essential market factor, especially for those firms in key market areas that offer solutions to collective bads plaguing society. In this context, psychological advertising will not disappear, but rather be directed toward influencing ideals and concepts.

Point of Purchase

The point of purchase location represents the last stop in the distribution channel before products are sold to consumers. Retail shopping facilities have undergone extensive and sometimes elaborate change within the past 20 years. The corner store, the neighborhood shop, and the small-town shopping center have evolved into shopping centers and malls covering may acres of land. The point of purchase represents an essential part of the manufacturer's distribution system; it represents the focal point in the consumer-product transactional process.

Volume movement depends on ample inventory levels. Inventories, inventory replacement, and inventory mix strategies are the life blood of retail establishments. In periods when shortages suddenly erupt, transactional patterns are disrupted, leaving consumers and retailers frustrated and angry. Panic buying and hoarding further complicate retailers inventory management practices. Unethical price advances allow some retailers speculative profits on items in short supply. In some instances retailers are often asked to allocate goods in short-fall categories as a part of their business responsibility to the public.

Nonprice Competition

Quality, service, and brand reputation allow firms to de-emphasize price as being a competitive advantage. In fact, price cuts are often matched anyway, leaving competing firms with lower profit margins. Psychological advertising relating status, living patterns, peer groups, social affluence, esteem, and fashion consciousness represents synchronous competitive variables that constitute the nonprice competition model. In periods of rising income, abundant resources, and expanding market demand, profit objectives are refined from volume, share-of-the-market goals, and cost trends. Prices are selected in conjunction with product innovation appeal, identification with specific market targets, with psychological price niche options, and by competition.

Nonprice competition is extensively practiced by large firms which must balance large capital expenditures with market volume and profit expectations. One of the criticisms of nonprice competition is its slowness to pass on cost savings to consumers in the form of lower prices. Corporations often prefer to use profits derived from improving revenue-cost margins to develop new technologies or further improve internal operations. In periods of rapid inflation consumers become price sensitive, and even relatively inelastic products may reflect buyer unwillingness to purchase items they consider too high in price. Consumerism and buyer reluctance to purchase some artificially high products may soon force firms to become more competitive in price.

Brand Names

Brand names are essentially linked to market mix strategies. The brand name gives the manufacturer and the distributor the means of communicating with consumers and of establishing reputation, quality dimensions, and perceived value. Branded products were originally established as a way to improve product dependability and corporate reputation for fine craftsmanship. Performance, function, consumer use, and derived enjoyment are described in conjunction with brand products.

Marketers and consumers alike are not likely to lose brand conciousness; but in periods of shortages and high prices, consumers tend to shift brands in order to obtain the generic product. Product shortages have disrupted traditional brand choice patterns in such basic industries as gasoline, food, textiles, and chemical products.

Pricing Strategy

An affluent society is characterized by numerous product choices in the marketplace. Although the number of firms competing for consumer purchases is small in basic industries, technology, innovation, and psychological purchase appeals have stimulated multiple-product lines and numerous brand choices. In most instances traditional industry boundaries no longer exist; interrelated research and development expertise and market opportunities allow firms to diversify well beyond original product and industry limits.

Pricing strategies followed in such diversified corporations likewise follow pricing patterns quite different from classical economic models. Such variables as costs, volume goals, profits, market share objectives, competitive moves, market trends, and brand-oriented advertising represent trade-off dimensions to pricing decisions. Firms may elect to price products low to achieve market penetration and to build strong brand identification. Market penetration pricing discourages competition by keeping profit margins relatively low (in relation to capital investments needed for market entry). A second pricing strategy involves market skimming. This practice allows firms with high research and development costs to recover initial investments in new products quickly through high prices (wide profit margin per unit). New products tend to be purchased by innovative consumers who delight in setting fashion trends and living patterns. These consumers are often willing to pay higher introductory prices in order to obtain satisfactions from market innovation. Since affluence is characterized by rising income levels, market-skimming pricing strategies often result in large volume and large profits.

Shortages, allocation requirements, ecological aspects, and inflation are introducing new pricing problems for business. If raw material short-

FIGURE 6-2

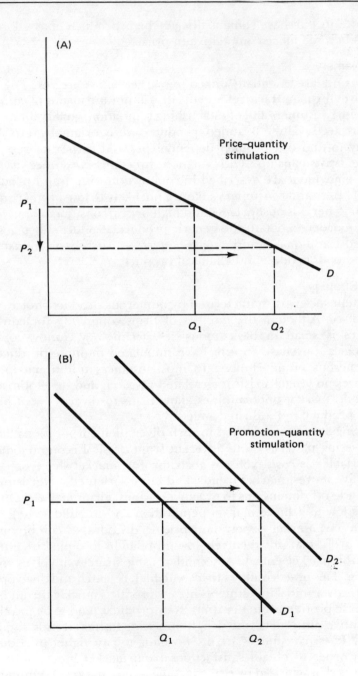

In part A, a cut in price from P^1 to P^2 stimulates an increase in demand from Q^1 to Q^2. Price is used to stimulate an increase in demand, whereas in part B, price P^1 remains the same, but promotion and advertising campaigns build the market to the point at which a new demand curve (D^2) is established.

falls etablish demand ceilings well below optimum production levels, firms may decide to protect profits by increasing prices. The market is vulnerable to pricing spirals during short-fall situations; consumers (especially industrial customers) are often willing to pay higher prices rather than do without. While higher prices may "ration" smaller quantities of scarce products over a short-fall crisis, societal problems enter into the picture. Allocating basic products (such as food and energy) by price hikes forces low-income consumers either to go without the needed product (and to resort to charity or crime) or to shift drastically their purchasing patterns to acquire needed items (to cut purchases for children's clothing, health care, school requirements). In addition, sudden price increases may dramatically distort profit margins. Swollen profit margins enjoyed by firms during periods marked by economic crisis and consumer sacrifices lowers public confidence in business motives.

SOCIOECOLOGICAL INFLUENCES ON THE MARKETING CONCEPT

Marketing's impact on society is stretching well beyond the traditional boundaries that divide market segments, industries, distribution channels, and product classifications. Marketing puts into motion economic stimuli that influence both culture and ecological relationships. Often, the effects of marketing action on society are felt or shared far outside of ordinary firm-customer transactions. With accelerating scientific innovations on product development and with continuing specialization of interlocking business systems, marketing executives are experiencing growing social restraints on the one hand and narrowing organizational constraints that limit product mix choices on the other. The impersonalized conglomerate structure limits both marketing's influences on product planning and consumer responses to product-use situations. In many companies the marketing concept has proven to be a valuable product growth guide. Unfortunately, it has been overly committed to leveraging financial goals (rather than satisfying customer needs in the broader sense).

The distribution function is more than transactional in nature. The transvectional impact permeates through both the economic and social dimensions of the marketing effort. The ability of marketing to satisfy social and human requirements and to perform its designated tasks efficiently will be greatly hampered by system-wide corporate bureaucracy and narrow, short-term profit goals. The marketing concept has exhibited an amazing degree of adaptability since its general usage began in the 1950s; invariably, the organizational emphasis placed on consumer satisfaction determines (in part) its breadth and its contemporary value.

Since the advent of raw material shortages (in such categories as petroleum, scarce metals, sporadic food crop failures, etc.) and tightening pollution control standards, the role of business in our democracy is under serious pressures to respond quickly to social problems. To meet this complex challenge, organizations need to consider the broad impacts that business systems impart to economic, social, and environmental factors.

Firms need to adjust organizational emphasis. Resource allocations are no longer strictly a matter between producers and consumers. The transvectional view suggests that resources and their relative efficient deployment take on socioecological significance in both the product-planning and product-use stages. In the 1950s and 1960s, when resources were relatively abundant, product decisions favored quality, top-of-the-line, expensive units. As our national budget for resource use becomes more limited, products will reflect more modest size and weight, and improved energy-use efficiencies.

The marketing concept is really an extension of organizational influences on economic and social behavior. Firms that conduct social audits, improve organizational responses to economic and social problems, and improve communications are in an excellent position to broaden the marketing concept and make it an effective part of new growth emphasis. In the final analysis, the most crucial marketing task for the future may well be directed toward revitalizing the image of the corporation and assisting in giving it a public responsibility "brand." This task cannot be achieved with mere "lip service"; the growing undercurrents of social anxieties will not be relieved unless demonstrated results can be achieved from business firms.

CONCLUSIONS

Marketing enjoyed abundant raw materials, rising consumer affluence, favorable monetary policies for growth, and supportive political programs during the 1950s and 1960s. The marketing concept was first viewed in a narrow transactional sense; profit maximization became the primary motivational force behind technical product decisions. Utopian influences, rising consumer purchasing power, increased leisure time, and mobility supported product decisions that led to larger units which used more natural resources and became more inefficient.

During the 1970s, the nation's raw material budget tightened, the environment became an explosive issue, and international trade became linked to national economic survival. Highly educated consumerism groups, environmentalists, government officials, and professional groups have become increasingly critical of business methods that continue to contribute to social problems. Even while many firms lack the resources to correct many product-spawned problems contributing to collective bads, the social mood is nonetheless requiring some kind of behavior modification—even on the part of small businesses.

The age of social awareness has passed into an age of social action. Marketing is broadening its emphasis to include human satisfaction, improved marketing communication, and responsive product changes. The roles of science and technology may rapidly shift toward product innovations that resolve rather than contribute to social problems. The effectiveness of the marketing profession's response to the new challenges of the 1970s is directly linked to organizational emphasis. Corporate-wide planning and control programs will need to incorporate financial requirements with resolving human needs.

The influence of the conservation ethic promises to eliminate substantial resource wastes now produced in the economic system. Conservation practices, whether voluntary or part of a mandatory rationing system, can give science extra time to resolve energy and raw material shortages in conjunction with environmental requirements. Consumers may soon be confronted with difficult choices involving life-style trade-offs that affect their everyday existence. Marketing is not wedded to any one kind of life-style concept; rather, the taste counselor role of marketing executives requires careful analysis of human needs evolving around contemporary distribution, economic, cultural, environmental, and behavorial problems.

Case 11
Escaped Parakeets: A New Threat to Crops

Our affluent society is constantly searching for ways to find companionship and unique ways to differentiate one individual or group from another. Not many products sold to consumers can qualify on both these dimensions at the same time. Exotic pets are purchased by the millions to resolve both the need for companionship and for individual identity. More than 36,000 pet dealers in America distribute exotic or foreign species in our domestic markets. The aquarium trade alone has reached the $560 million level; more than 20 million citizens now own tanks.

Unfortunately, the trade in exotic pets has led to the introduction of disruptive fish, reptiles, animal, and bird species to our own native ecosystem. Disruptive exotics include the Oriental carp, walking catfish, giant toads, African snails, tigers, kinkejous, leopards, iguanas, boas, monkeys

"Escaped Parakeets," *Conservation News,* Vol. 39, No. 9 (May 1, 1974), pp. 11–12.

and chimpanzees, pythons, gorillas, parrots, kangaroos, and a wide variety of tropical fish. This list is by no means complete; one specie missing is the monk parakeet. This bird is a handsome, foot-long bird which has found great market appeal and acceptance in the United States.

This exotic bird, which graces many cages in our affluent homes, is a serious pest in Argentina, Bolivia, Brazil, Paraguay, and Uruguay. Ripe grain and fruit are its favorite foods; farmers have been using bounties, traps, poisons, and guns to control this multi-million dollar pest in Argentina since 1947. Even these measures to eradicate these fast-flying birds have failed, the result being that between 3 to 15 per cent of the food crops in Argentina are destroyed annually.

Although the United States now bans further importation of the monk parakeet, a number of the estimated 50,000 birds brought into our country since 1968 as pets have escaped or been freed by their owners. In one accident, 50 or more parakeets flew from a shattered crate at Kennedy International Airport and settled on Long Island. Although the parakeet normally lives in tropical or subtropical climates (they do not migrate) they have been know to live in chilly Andean foothills in South America. U.S. authorities believed that the Long Island colony of monk parakeets would not survive our New England winters. They have, and now flocks of the birds are being observed in Connecticut, Maryland, New Jersey, and New York. They have been sighted as well in Alabama, Arizona, Arkansas, Delaware, Florida, Illinois, Kentucky, Maine, Massachusetts, Michigan, Minnesota, Nebraska, New Hampshire, North Dakota, Ohio, Pennsylvania, Rhode Island, Tennessee, Texas, Vermont, and Wisconsin. The native-born monk parakeets have shown the surprisingly adaptable nature of their specie. The distinct threat of damage to U.S. grain and fruit crops now confronts our farmers. Like other exotics, such as the English sparrow and European starling, monk parakeets have few natural foes which can control or balance their numbers.

Ironically, the exotic pet starts his journey to satisfy a consumer market need, but turns out in the final analysis to be an ecological problem. Exotic species of fish are endangering the freshwater sports fishing industry in the state of Florida. The adaptable nature and absence of predators in these waters allow massive increases in the population of exotic fish. By their very nature, exotics are not a part of our ecosystem; disruptions to native wildlife can have a devastating effect on long-term balances which control the productivity of agriculture and recreation industries. The monk parakeet is a symbolic part of the exotic pet problem which is plaguing the United States today. The problem is further complicated by smuggling an exotic past custom officials. The accidental introduction of foreign diseases, insects, and animal pests concealed in large shipments of grain, fruit, vegetables, and timber (primarily) account for one additional avenue by which exotics enter our ecosystem.

Case 12
Powerline Pollution—A "Hot" Issue

Everyone agrees that electric transmission lines are appallingly ugly, but suggesting that they are health hazards and sources of environmental pollution is surprising to most people. But the extremely high-voltage lines which are currently being constructed in many places around the country are causing side effects which are degrading the quality of life and may be endangering the health of the people living nearby.

Transmission technology has now reached the point where lines carrying 765,000 volts are operating in a number of states, and lines designed to carry up to 2,000,000 volts are being perfected for the near future. These very high voltages are carried on bare, unshielded conductors that pass in many places just 40 or 50 feet above roads and farms. In the vicinity of these lines there is a very intense electric field which causes small but continuous currents to run in everything near the line—the ground, the plants, the farmer on his tractor. There is a surprisingly large voltage difference between one point in space and another, say a yard away. The difference between these two points may be as high as 50,000 volts under a 765,000 volt line. This electric field can be made visible in a rather dramatic way by carrying an ordinary fluorescent bulb in your hand as you walk in the vicinity of the line. The bulb lights up without benefit of batteries, cords, or metalic connections to ground.

Most people who see this experiment immediately ask what effect currents and fields of this strength have on people and other living things. Considering the importance of this question, one might assume that it had been quite thoroughly investigated by the power companies before building such lines; but a search of the scientific literature reveals the fact that this subject has not been adequately studied. The few research projects that have been done show that there may be profound effects caused by these fields.

About 8 or 10 years ago, when American utilities were starting to use extra-high-voltage transmission, two tests were conducted by the companies. In one experiment they exposed 22 mice to strong electric fields for a portion of each day over a 10-month period. The results showed a statistically significant reduction in the size of the male progeny of the exposed mice. The other study involved 10 linemen who did repair work on 345,000-volt lines. The company watched these men for 9 years, doing

Louise B. Young, "Power Line Pollution—A Hot Issue," *Conservation News*, Vol. 39, No. 20 (October 15, 1974), pp. 2–5.

seven complete medical examinations on them. At the end of that time, three of the 10 men had significantly reduced sperm count. However, since sperm count had been quite variable throughout the various medical examinations, the report stated that it would be hazardous to draw any conclusion on the significance of these facts from such a small sample. Studies of this type, of course, should examine a much larger number of people over a longer period of time.

A much more thorough examination of this problem, however, has been conducted in Russia. In 1962, after the first Russian 500,000-volt lines had been operating for several months, men working at the substations began to complain of headaches and a general feeling of malaise. They associated these symptoms with exposure to the electric fields. The Russians made a long-term study of 250 men working at extra-high-voltage substations. These results were compared with medical examinations of men working at lower-voltage substations. The studies concluded that long-time exposure to intense electric fields without protective measures resulted in "shattering the dynamic state of the central nervous system, heart, and blood-vessel system, and in changing blood structure. Young men complained of reduced sexual potency." As a result of these tests, the Russians have set up safety standards for maximum exposure to strong electric fields. The fields which they begin to consider dangerous are approximately those that will light up a fluorescent bulb in your hand. A farmer on a tractor under a 765,000 volt line is exposed to fields so strong that the Russians would not allow it for even one minute. In this country, we believe that we have more respect for human rights and human life than the Soviets have, yet we have not made as much effort as they have to protect people from this type of damage.

Recent laboratory studies in the United States have also turned up positive evidence of biological effects from similar electromagnetic fields—effects ranging from chromosome damage to high blood pressure and alterations in levels of blood protein, fats, and cholesterol. Neurological tissue appears to be particularly sensitive, confirming the fear that long-term exposure may damage the nervous system, as well as cause changes in cellular chemistry and the genetic structure in human beings. Some of these experiments were conducted in connection with Project Sanguine (the enormous low-frequency antenna which the Navy would like to build in order to communicate with its submarines around the world). Some have been independent university research projects.

The other principal pollution hazard from high-tension lines results from the fact that they generate ozone and other highly reactive chemicals. These electrochemical reactions are caused by the corona discharge that occurs continuously along the conductors. Walking under these lines, even in good weather, you can hear a crackling, sizzling sound which is the audible manifestation of this electric discharge. In fog, rain, or snow, the corona increases by as much as a hundred-fold. This discharge causes the air to break down as an insulator and the space around it becomes a veritable seething cauldron of electrical and chemical activity. There are many processes involved, and some of the chemicals formed are considered to be particularly damaging to living things. Ozone, one of the principal products, is the most common "photochemical oxidant" present in polluted air. Research into this phenomenon has shown that chronic exposure to concentrations of ozone over 0.05 parts per million causes lung tissue damage, increased incidence of sterility, and defective offspring in laboratory animals. It affects the growth and yield of many plants.

Regular monitoring stations for ozone levels in the atmosphere have only been operating in a few locations during the last two or three decades, and it has only been in the last year or so that monitoring has been conducted in many cities and rural locations throughout the country. But several surprising and interesting results have already emerged from this monitoring. Concentrations in rural areas are found to be regularly higher than they are in the cities. And levels in both city and country throughout many states exceed the National Air Quality standards for photochemical oxidants on a very large number of days. Furthermore, over the past few decades the average levels have been increasing throughout the industrialized parts of the world. No one really understands the reasons for the high levels that are being recorded. The chemistry is complex and a large number of factors are probably involved, but power lines and other high-voltage equipment are certainly among the contributing factors. Transmission lines do generate ozone; even the power companies admit that. They argue that the amounts are very small, but the studies that they rely on in making this statement are neither definitive nor conclusive. The field measurements, for example, were made under lines that were not energized to the full-rated voltage. The amount of corona discharge is very sensitive to changes in voltage as well as to certain weather conditions such as rain or snow. A much more careful and impartial evaluation of the problem is needed. In view of the fact that ozone concentrations already exceed danger levels, we should know exactly how much these lines contribute to the concentrations before any more of them are installed.

Plans reported by the Federal Power Commission call for more than 10,000 miles of lines rated 765,000 volts or higher by the year 1990. A $5 million research and development program is currently in progress, perfecting lines that will carry 1,000,000 or even up to 2,000,000 volts, yet there is no federal or state agency that is taking responsibility for assessing the safety of these installations. In the absence of regulatory protection, much more public awareness and public pressure is needed to insist that the impact of these big lines be thoroughly evaluated before this construction plan is carried any further. Once the enormous financial investment has been made, we will be irrevocably committed to this technology.

TOPIC QUESTIONS

1. What are the two diverse views of marketing?
2. Is the conservation ethic incompatible with the marketing concept?
3. Has the ecological question become an important marketing issue?
4. What is the socioecological product of marketing?
5. Does Alderson's transvection concept view resource acquisition as a requisite part of the finished product?
6. Can consumer abuse of products lead to collective "bads" in our society?
7. How is the environmental debate affecting marketing mix decisions?
8. Is nonprice competition an appropriate marketing strategy in our contemporary environment?

Case 11

9. Are exotic pets an environmental problem or a social problem? Discuss.
10. How does marketing stimulate consumer demand for exotic pets?
11. What often happens when exotic species are introduced into the United States?
12. What is the role of the pet dealer in controlling exotic pet trade in the United States?

Case 12

13. How is power line pollution related to the broader problem of air pollution?
14. What biological hazards exist near the extra-high-voltage transmission lines?
15. What arguments could you give for curtailing a utility company's advertising (designed to increase the demand for electricity)?
15. What other social and environmental problems exist in relation to electrical utilities and the public?

RECOMMENDED READINGS

Louis E. Boone and David L. Kurtz, *Contemporary Marketing* (Hinsdale, Ill.: Dryden Press, 1974).

Eugene J. Kelley and William Lazer, eds., *Social Marketing* (Homewood, Ill.: Richard D. Irwin, 1973).

Eugene M. Johnson, Ray S. House, and Carl D. McDaniel, Jr., eds., *Readings in Contemporary Marketing* (Hinsdale, Ill.: Dryden Press, 1974).

Raymond A. Bauer and Dan H. Fenn, Jr., *The Corporate Social Audit* (New York: Russell Sage Foundation, 1972).

FOOTNOTES

1. Theodore Levitt, "Marketing Myopia," *Harvard Business Review*, Vol. 38, No. 4, (July–August 1960), pp. 45–56.
2. William Lazer, "Dimensions of Social Marketing," *Social Marketing*, William Lazer and Eugene J. Kelly, eds. (Homewood, Ill.: Richard D. Irwin, Inc., 1973), p. 48.
3. Robert I. Standish, "Something For Our Critics to Ponder," *Conservations News*, Volume 39, No. 11, (June 1, 1974), pp. 8-10.
4. John Quarles, "Fundamental Changes Needed for Energy Conservation Success," *Advertising Age*, (November 11, 1974), p. 16. Reprinted by special permission.
5. Sanford Tepfer, "Why You Should Join the Sierra Club?" *Sierra Club Bulletin*, January 1974), p. 39. Reprinted by special permission
6. Robert J. Lavidge, "The Growing Responsibilities of Marketing," *Journal of Marketing*, Volume 34 (January 1970), pp. 25–28. Reprinted from the *Journal of Marketing* published by the American Marketing Association.
7. Philip Kotler and Sidney J. Levy, "Broadening the Concept of Marketing," *Journal of Marketing*, Volume 33 (January 1969), pp. 10–15. Reprinted from the *Journal of Marketing* published by the American Marketing Association.
8. Wroe Alderson, *Dynamic Marketing Behavior*, (Homewood, Ill.: Richard D. Irwin, Inc., 1965, pp. 86–87.
9. Etienne Cracco and Jacques Rostenne, "The Socio-Ecological Product," *MSU Business Topics*, (Summer 1971), pp. 27–34. Reprinted by permission of the publisher, Division of Research, Graduate School of Business Administration, Michigan State University.
10. Wroe Alderson, *op. cit.*, p. 201.
11. Editorial Viewpoint, *Advertising Age*, (December 3, 1973), p. 12.

CHAPTER SEVEN

THE

REVERSE CHANNEL

STRATEGY

DEFINING THE STRATEGY

If some distant civilization should someday explore our landscape for raw material, it might well discover (presumably among ruins) deposits of minerals very near the surface; these large buried mounds of metal bits and pieces (as well as numerous other materials) would not constitute some new natural resource find; instead, these would be the remnants of land fills that twentieth-century man popularized.

While science fiction writers might speculate on the dimensions of some future civilization, the prospect that raw material scarcities and wastes will alter our concepts about dumping is fast becoming an economic reality. Nor is the economic factor alone the basic issue in controlling resource wastes in our disposal system. The question of how the nation's burgeoning solid wastes are managed ranks in importance along with land use planning, strip mining regulation, and energy research and development as among the top environmental issues. The 4.5 billion tons of solid wastes involve such key problem areas as (1) protection of public health and the environment; (2) recovery of energy and valuable materials; (3) conservation of natural resources; and (4) disposal of urban wastes. In 1974 alone, Congress worked on over 25 different solid waste management bills. The most comprehensive legislation would greatly extend the federal role to include (1) redefinition of federal procurement policies, freight rates, and taxation to encourage recycling of recovered materials; (2) regulation of waste generation and its disposal; (3) development of standards for manufacturing and distributing products; and (4) mandatory state and regional planning.

The successful management of solid wastes, effective resource recovery, and a beneficent materials policy requires a public, industry, and government commitment to (1) return organic wastes (from animals, crops, food processing, sewage sludge) to the soil; (2) return metals, glass, and natural fibers to their producing industries for recycling; (3) reclaim nonmetallic substances (glass, fly ash, mine tailings, ceramics) for new uses, such as construction materials; (4) convert fibers, textiles, and synthetics (plastics, tires, textiles) into new by-products; and (5) recover energy from mixed combustible wastes. The principal salvage operations may be noted in Figure 7-1.

FIGURE 7-1 Principal Salvage Operations

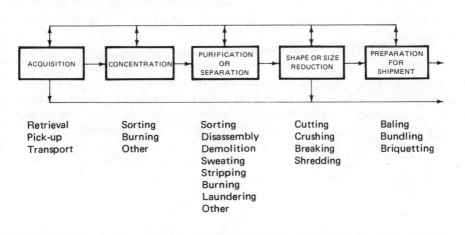

Source: Arsen Dornay and William E. Franklin, *Salvage Markets for Materials in Solid Wastes* (Washington, D.C.: U.S. Government Printing Office, U.S. Environmental Protection Agency, 1972), p. 30-1.

Solid waste management requires a socioecological approach to distribution planning. One of the deficiencies of present product planning policies is the dominating emphasis on promotional appeal, which often leads manufacturers to overpackage, use assorted product package materials (making recycling more difficult), and select product components that are difficult to treat, sort, or move through the reverse channel. Manufacturers have helped to instill in the minds of consumers a preference for products made of primary materials (in comparison with reused or secondary fabric, fibers, and related materials).

While waste disposal and recovery issues have not affected market mix planning and decision making for most firms, the prospect that sweeping legislation will soon revolutionize secondary material handling and influence even day-to-day business practices is very real indeed.[1] The public will have an increasing responsibility to follow reverse channel guides, laws, and programs that are postconsumption in nature. Too, reverse channel systems will not be composed of completely separate channel members. Rather, dual roles for some channel members will be performed, while in other instances, new specialized channel members will perform return or recovery tasks exclusively (such as industrial collection centers). This realignment of channel tasks will require important margin adjustments as well.

OLD BUSINESS—NEW ROLE

Historically, resource recovery was mainly limited to gleaners, pickers, scrap dealers, and merchants who sold scrap metals to those engaged in smithing, armaments, jewelry, and similar businesses. Even the ancients emphasized primary sources of raw materials.

Cities grew along trade routes that brought economic goods aboard ships, camels, horses, and other conveyances. Civilizations developed rapidly in those regions that not only remained in close contact with traders but also contained fertile lands for fiber and food production. The ancients also worked deep shaft mines and moved many other kinds of materials from concentrated natural deposits to population centers. For the most part, resource recovery was not emphasized.

The industrial revolution brought scrap and recovery into a slightly more important economic position. At times when iron production lagged behind industrial demand, the scrap business flourished; but this boom period was soon followed by severe price declines.

The problems of price fluctuations, low capital business units, low social standing, unfavorable tax and transportation rates, and unsystematic methods have characterized the recovery business until the most recent times. Only in today's scenario are recovery businesses taking on the form of larger and more efficient commercial units. Science, technology, and more equity financing are slowly becoming prominent in the recovery industry. This new emphasis is only in the infancy stage. Much more needs to be done to encourage more rapid growth. An old business is, indeed, on the verge of performing a new role for the economy and for society. The basic structure of the salvage industry may be seen in Figure 7-2.

FIGURE 7-2 Structure of the Salvage Industry and Flow of Commodities

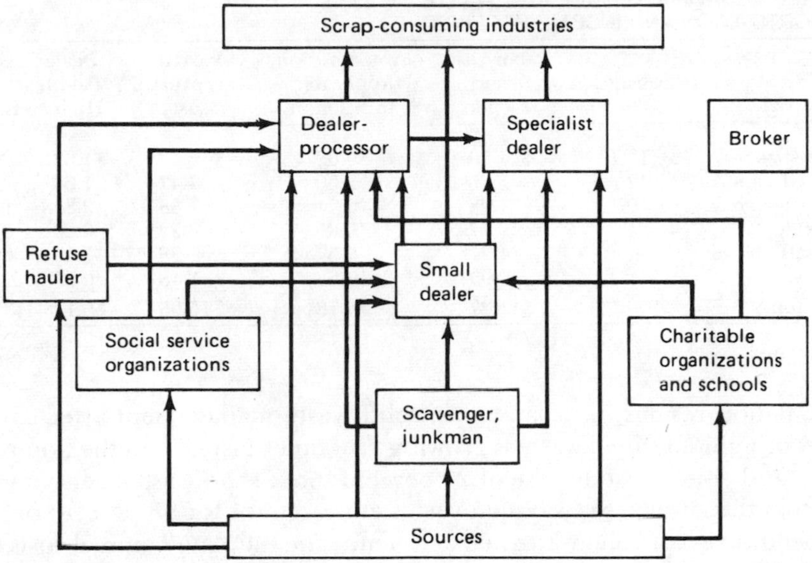

Source: Darnay and Franklin, *op. cit.*, p. 19-1.

THE CONTEMPORARY SCENE

Rising waste piles, the climbing costs of land, and the unsafe disposal of hazardous materials are important reasons for finding alternatives for taking care of the nation's solid wastes. The energy crisis sparked special interests in resource recovery and energy recovery. Organic wastes have a fuel potential which, if burned under controlled conditions, would equal about 1.5 percent of the nation's annual requirements, or more than half of the oil imported from the Middle East in 1972. The Solid Waste Management Task Force of the National League of Cities estimates that millions, if not billions, of dollars worth of metals are thrown away annually. The economic losses of dumping recoverable materials are not the only costs that the nation bears. The principal solid waste catagories for the U.S. and municipalities may be noted in Tables 7-1 and 7-2.

The Plight of the Cities

Urban waste constitutes less than 10 percent of the total waste generated annually in the United States. The other 90 percent comes from agriculture and mining. Since population and distribution systems are concentrated in urban areas, the solid waste handling problem of cities has both economic and health aspects. Since roughly 74 percent of the nation's

TABLE 7-1
ESTIMATED SORTING COSTS OF A COMPOSITE TON OF SALVAGE
TAKEN FROM MIXED MUNICIPAL WASTE, INCLUDING PLANT
AMORTIZATION AND INCOME RECEIVED

Material	Salvage (%/ton)	Labor cost to sort fraction	Amortization applicable to fraction	Partial recovery cost	Dealer price paid/fraction High	Low
Newspaper	13%	$ 1.50	$0.62	$ 2.12	$1.82	$0.52
Mixed paper	42	5.46	2.00	7.47	1.68	—
Corrugated	19	1.98	0.91	2.88	2.85	1.90
Textiles	1	0.17	0.05	0.22	0.60	0.10
Metals	14	1.21	0.67	1.88	1.40	0.70
Glass	11	0.95	0.53	1.48	0.77	0.55
Per ton	100%	$11.27	$4.78	$16.05	$9.12	$3.77

Source: Darnay and Franklin, *op. cit., p. 30-5.*

population resides in urban areas, solid waste management affects the lives of millions. Solid waste is growing five times faster than the population, and cities must dispose of 20 percent more solid wastes per person than in the rural areas. Local governments account for 98 percent of all expenditures for solid waste management. The estimated annual costs to these local government bodies amount to about $6 billion. In the nation's 48 largest cities, nearly 50 percent of their environmental budgets goes to solid waste management. It is no surprise, then, that in a survey of over 1,000 municipal officials (1974), the majority ranked solid waste management their most pressing problem.[2]

Land values continue to soar in price in urban areas; communities are becoming increasingly sensitive to the presence of dumps and landfills. As a result, over half of the U.S. cities are expected to run out of landfill sites within less than 5 years. More rigid environmental regulations (particularly concerning open burning) further limit disposal options.

The costs of solid waste control go even farther. Capital investments in solid waste recovery technologies have, historically, been discouraged by the inexpensive landfill operation. There was little incentive for cities to make large (and often risky) investments in recovery facilities. But with the skyrocketing costs of collection and of acquiring new land for disposal sites, resource and energy recovery systems are becoming more attractive. While landfills yield no recoverable scrap (and thus no income), resource recovery operations pay for at least part of disposal costs. While they are seldom self-paying, their costs are becoming competitive.

According to the EPA, more than 30 communities have expressed interest in establishing systems that burn wastes to generate heat for steam and electricity production. Connecticut is implementing a statewide solid waste management plan that coordinates waste collection and disposal throughout the state. Energy recovery centers at key locations are expected to provide the state with a new source of power.

For many smaller communities, resource recovery and energy recovery continue to be an impossible dream. Large expenditures for expensive facilities that process waste materials are simply beyond the means of many local governments. The scale of operations and the market conditions represent economic factors that smaller communities find difficult to manage. Like any other raw material flow problem, production capacities must be harmonized with supply. If solid wastes are too limited in quantity, production processes that recover energy must likewise halt; if recoverable energy is intended for rise in power utility furnaces, enough combustable material must be available on a round-the-clock basis to efficiently function. By the same token, large-scale recovery processes that salvage metals, for example, must have a reliable market with steady prices. Large fluctuations in prices, or a boom-and-bust situation makes recovery risky.

Health Hazards

Waste materials collected into large dumps represent an ecological imbalance which carries biological hazards to surrounding populations. The natural environment is constantly changing. Rain, wind, sunlight, soil conditions, vegetation, microbes, wildlife—all influence ecological balances or, in some cases, imbalances. Trash provides food and shelter for disease-carrying rodents and their ubiquitous parasites, fleas, flies, and lice. Microbes multiply rapidly and make unsanitary areas subject to outbreaks of diseases from bacteria and virus infections. Concentrated piles of minerals, acids, solvents, and other contaminants follow the scientific law of dispersion—leaching into surrounding areas; these substances, in turn, pollute soils, lakes, rivers, and streams. In the case of open burning, the air becomes polluted with ash, sulfur, and many other particulates. The EPA reports that of approximately 16,000 authorized land disposal sites and of another estimated 160,000 unauthorized dumping grounds, nearly half were polluting water resources. Nearly three-fourths of these dumps were polluting the air.[3]

When rain water filters through garbage and trash heaps, the leachate (or drainage) is often more contaminated than raw sewage. Even groundwater or underground water supplies can be polluted from open dumps. Even the "sanitary" land fills, which control daily burying of trash in layers separated by soil and clay, often cause serious leachate problems. This is especially true where landfill sites are poorly suited for containing trash materials. But such restrictions further limit potential landfill sites, thus driving up further the costs of finding additional locations. All too often the decision on landfill locations is made politically rather than in context with scientific reasons. "Who wants to live next to a garbage pit?" is not an easy question to answer politically.

TABLE 7-2
COMPOSITION OF MUNICIPAL WASTES

Composition — Percent by weight

Origin and references	Date	Food wastes/garbage	Yard/garden wastes	Paper wastes	Plastics	Rubber and leather
New York City[a]	1939	17.0	3.2	21.9		
Chandler, Ariz.[a]	1953	21.8	1.3	42.7	0.4	1.0
Chicago, Ill.[a]	1957	3.2	19.7	53.3		
	1957	2.3	3.7	59.3		
	1958	1.5	–	63.7		
	1958	0.8	34.4	54.7		
Oceanside, N.Y.[b]	1966	9.6	33.3	32.8	2.4	
	1966	10.2	19.0	39.8	3.4	
Cincinnati, Ohio[d]	1966	28.0	6.4	42.0	1.6	
Wayne, N.J.[c]	1966	22.5	–	53.7	2.4	
Passaic, N.J.[c]	1966	21.4	–	44.4	2.3	
Clifton, N.J.[c]	1966	26.8	–	46.8	2.3	
Patterson, N.J.[c]	1966	20.2	–	39.8	3.0	
Quad-City, N.J.[c]	1966	21.0	–	46.0	2.0	
Oceanside, N.Y.[b]	1967	16.7	0.3	53.3	3.5	
Flint, Mich.[d]	1967	29.1	26.7	13.0	1.9	
Johnson City, Tenn.[d]	1967	21.1	0.9	59.8	0.9	0.6
Russell H. Susag[e]	1967	25.7	4.1	41.2	0.7	
San Diego, Calif.[d]	1967	0.8	21.1	46.1	0.3	4.7
Flint, Mich.[d]	1967	24.0	–	57.0	1.0	
Berkeley, Calif.[f]	1967	25.1		44.6	1.9	0.3
Raleigh, N.C.[h]	1967	31.8	8.4	38.9		
Santa Clara County, Calif.[i]	1967	2.1	34.5	36.2	1.5	1.1
	1967	45.9		28.6	0.4	
Flint, Mich.[d]	1968	36.0	0.3	21.1	2.6	
Weber County, Utah[d]	1968	8.5	4.2	61.8	2.5	
Johnson City, Tenn.[d]	1968	34.6	2.3	34.9	3.4	2.4
New Orleans, La.[g]	1968	18.9	9.2	39.4	1.5	
Alexandria, Va.[d]	1968	7.5	9.5	55.3	3.1	
Atlanta, Ga.[d]	1968	12.3	1.6	58.6	3.0	
	1968	17.5	2.8	53.2	2.6	
New Orleans, La.[d]	1969	11.0	9.8	44.9	3.5	
John Bell[j]	1959-62	12.0	12.0	42.0	0.7	0.9

a American Public Works Association. Municipal refuse disposal. 2d ed. Chicago, Public Administration Service, 1966. p. 47, 48, 52.

b Kalser, E. R. Composition and combustion of refuse. In Proceedings; MECAR Symposium; Incineration of Solid Wastes, New York, Mar. 21, 1967. Metropolitan Engineers Council on Air Resources, 1967. p. 1–9.

c Quad-city solid wastes projects; an interim report, June 1, 1966 to May 31, 1967. Cincinnati, U.S. Department of Health, Education, and Welfare, 1968, p. 181.

d Bureau of Solid Waste Management. Unpublished data.

e Susag, R. H. Developing classifications for refuse. Solid Wastes Management/Refuse Removal Journal, 11(3); 20, 37, Mar. 1968.

f Golueke, C. G., and P. H. McGauhey. Comprehensive studies of solid wastes management; first annual

Textiles	Glass/ceramics	Metals	Wood	Ashes, brick, rock, dirt and miscellaneous	Type of waste and comments
	5.5	6.8	2.6	43.0	Municipal — year's average based on monthly sample
1.9	7.5	9.8	2.5	11.3	Residential only
	5.9	9.3		8.6	Municipal — April
	6.5	5.2		23.0	Municipal — November
	5.8	8.1		20.9	Municipal — April
	3.5	6.2		0.4	Municipal — June
3.0	9.7	8.0	1.2		Municipal — June
3.3	9.5	8.2	6.6		Municipal — June
1.4	7.5	8.7	2.7		Residential — October
1.7	5.4	7.0	1.7	6.2	Municipal
7.8	5.2	8.7	3.6	8.6	Municipal
2.2	3.7	7.0	3.2		Municipal
5.1	10.0	12.9	3.4	7.0	Municipal
4.0	7.0	8.0	3.0	8.0	Municipal — regional composite
2.2	11.9	10.6	1.5		Municipal — February
0.3	12.7	14.5	1.0		Residential — June
1.3	7.0	7.5	0.3	0.6	Residential and commercial — October
	12.8	2.7	12.8		One week's accumulation of a family of six — June
3.5	8.3	7.7	7.5		Residential and commercial
1.0	6.0	6.0	2.0	3.0	Commercial — estimate
1.1	11.3	8.7		7.1	Residential and commercial
	11.9	9.2			Domestic refuse
1.3	10.9	7.4		0.5	Residential
3.6	5.8		4.2	11.5	Supermarket wastes
0.8	23.2	14.5	0.8	0.7	Residential — January
2.0	4.6	8.4	2.2	5.9	Residential and commercial — April
2.0	9.0	10.4	0.8	0.2	Municipal — July
2.6	16.2	12.2			Municipal
3.7	7.5	8.2	1.7	3.4	Residential and commercial — May
1.8	10.3	8.6	0.4	3.4	Municipal — December
2.0	6.5	8.8	3.2	3.4	Municipal — December
3.2	9.5	8.1	3.1	6.9	Municipal — February
0.6	6.0	8.0	2.4	15.4	Composite based on several city surveys

reports. Berkeley, Sanitary Engineering Research Laboratory, School of Public Health, University of California, 1967. p. 34.
g City of New Orleans. Unpublished data, May 13, 1968.
h Department of Public Works, City of Raleigh. Evaluating alternatives in refuse disposal; progress report, Jan. 1, 1967-Dec. 31, 1968. Unpublished data.
i Systems analysis for solid waste disposal by incineration. Prepared by FMC Machinery/Systems Group, Engineering Systems Division, FMC Corporation, for the City of San Jose and the County of Santa Clara, Nov. 1, 1968. p. 167
j Bell, J. M. Characteristics of municipal refuse. Presented at National Conference on Solid Waste Research, University of Chicago Center for Continuing Education, Chicago, Dec. 2-4, 1963. American Public Works Association, Special Report No. 29. p. 37.

As scientific advances produce new substances (used in industrial and consumer markets) new health hazards have become evident. The disposal of wastes inherently "hazardous" (toxic, chemical, biological, radioactive, flammable, and explosive) is a growing health worry for the nation. Current management practices in hazardous material disposition are largely deficient.[4] Uncontrolled discharges of such wastes are encouraged by inadequate legislation, economic expediencies, and high costs of expensive technical equipment needed to process toxic materials.

One of the principal difficulties in hazardous material legislation and control programs is defining what constitutes nonhazardous wastes. What might have been classified nonhazardous earlier might well become hazardous shortly after scientific inquiries discover some new danger. This is the case with such substances once considered "safe"—DDT, vinyl chloride, and freon. In a sense, the practice of dumping carries a delayed health hazard. Discarded materials, industrial effluents, municipal leachate, raw sewage pollutants, and feed lot drainage filter into the air, water, land, and underground streams. These toxic substances in turn find their way into our food, water, and oxygen supplies; such agents interfere with biological functions and, in the case of certain toxic minerals and chemical compounds, are stored in human tissues. The toxic build-up process may not produce symptoms of serious diseases for 10 or more years. Lung diseases, heart and circulatory ailments, nerve disorders, and liver cancer are environmentally related illnesses in instances where the human body absorbs such substances as asbestos, vinyl chloride, mercury, lead, many hydrocarbon pesticides, radium, and biological agents.

Source Reduction Versus Resource Recovery

The issues associated with waste management are complex and affect our society in many ways. The material acquisition philosophy, convenience living emphasis (use it once and throw it away), multiple packaging, and built-in obsolescence contribute to the growing trash problem.[5] Additional wastes come from industrial sources such as farming, mining, production, and transportation. For example, during the past 15 years, the nation has witnessed a major shift in manufacuturing and consumer preference toward disposable, convenience packaging. Between 1959 and 1972 the per capita consumption of beer and soft drinks in the United States increased 33 percent, but the total number of containers jumped 221 percent (from 15.4 billion to 55.7 billion). By 1980, the total number is expected to soar to 80 billion containers. Beverage containers are the fastest growing portion of all municipal wastes, accounting for more than 8 percent. Containers account for 20 percent of the total number of litter items. In terms of raw materials, an average worth of $300 of aluminum, $30 worth of steel, and $20 worth of glass can be found in a ton of municipal wastes. The beverage container illustration provides a timely example of one problem in controlling wastes, that is, handling increasing volumes of trash.

Source reduction represents one method for controlling waste levels; if manufacturers and consumers cooperated in holding down the volume of wastes, municipal collection, disposition, and recycling processes could be more efficiently controlled. Returnable bottles are filled an average of 15 times before final disposition. Not only does the returnable require 50 to 85 percent less energy than a one-way container, but in the state of Oregon, container litter fell 70 percent after the flip-top can was banned.

Proper waste control systems must be developed from two essential directions—source reduction, and resource recovery and reuse. The problem touches all aspects of our society; the solutions will require increased use of new technologies, systems management, expanded markets for secondary materials, and sound environmental planning. According to the EPA:

> There is a generation of hard work ahead. Each of us must make his own contribution. But the task will seem less arduous if we focus on those opportunities for betterment which present themselves from day to day. The combined efforts of individuals, industries and governments at all levels—though they may seem small when viewed in isolation—can make an enormous collective impact. A national commitment, involving each American, will not only lift the veil of pollution from our skies and cleanse our turbid waters, it could help propel this nation toward a new era of social amenity for transcending the proud achievements of the past.
>
> If we act wisely and with speed, we can extract long-range social dividends from our resources as well as short-term private conveniences. We can elevate the quality of life as well as expand the quantity of goods.[6]

THE POTENTIAL: HOW LARGE?

The economic impact of the reverse channel on resource management (recovery, reuse, and recycling) will remain of minor importance as long as consumers, industries, and municipalities continue to emphasize the dead-end approach. The entire waste handling system at all levels must be directed toward recovering, reusing, and recycling materials that play an economic role in the distribution system. Source reduction, heat (or energy conversion), and practices that convert organic wastes into soil conditioners and fertilizers have socioecological importance and economic value, and that reduces environmental abuses as well.

The dead-end approach to waste disposal techniques simply accelerates depletion rates in the case of nonrenewable stocks of minerals, metals, rare earths; the one-way channel likewise accelerates the depletion of renewable resources which are being harvested at rates that exceed natural replenishing cycles. Within the 1980s the dead-end channel will become uneconomical and will, in itself, represent an important growth barrier principally because vital raw materials will be scarce and expensive. The Department of the Interior has indicated that metals will be critically short by the 1980s unless conservation measures are introduced soon. The one-way channel is, unfortunately, very much in business today. Many municipalities have no recovery programs, nor can such local governments afford the direct investment costs involved with establishing such programs. Recycling programs are often beyond the financial means of individual businesses, but industrial wastes represent the greatest environmental threat to natural resources. Consumers often find that in their communities no means exist to return packages, bottles, cans, paper, and other materials to a collection center. If the nation is to convert a one-way channel into a return channel, consumer cooperation and support is absolutely essential.[7]

Recovery processes may be classified into the following general categories:

1. *Energy recovery processes:* Processes that recover the energy content of mixed municipal wastes in the form of steam, electricity, or fuel.
2. *Materials recovery processes:* Processes that separate and recover the basic materials from mixed muncipal wastes, such as paper, metals and glass.
3. *Pyrolysis processes:* Processes that thermally decompose the mixed muncipal waste in controlled amounts of oxygen and produce such products as oil, gas, tar, acetone, and char.
4. *Compost processes:* Processes that produce a humus material from the organic portion of the mixed waste.
5. *Chemical conversion processes:* Processes that chemically convert the waste into protein and other organic products.[8]

NATIONAL POLICY CONSIDERATIONS FOR RECYCLING[9]

In general, the nation should employ a systems approach to recycling policy in which all pertinent aspects of recycling are given a fair hearing. Recycling should not be viewed solely as a materials conservation activity or only as a solution to solid waste management problems, but should be viewed broadly under the subject of resource conservation, with "resource" understood to include both tangible and intangible values.

Today roughly 25 percent of paper, metals, glass, textiles, and rubber are recycled through the market (Table 7-3), or approximately 48 million tons of materials that need not be handled as solid waste. If other materials are also included, such as plastics, wood, ashes, stone, brick, and

TABLE 7-3
DOMESTIC PROMPT AND OBSOLETE SCRAP CONSUMPTION IN SELECTED
COMMODITIES, 1967, 1968, OR 1969, IN 1,000 TONS AND PERCENT*

Material	Year	Total material consumption 1,000 tons	Prompt and obsolete scrap consumption for recycling–1,000 tons	Recycling as percent of consumption
Paper and board	1967	53,110	10,124	19.0
Ferrous metals	1967	105,900	33,100	31.2
Nonferrous metals	1967	9,775	3,006	30.8
Glass	1967	12,820	600	4.2
Textiles	1968	5,672	246	4.3
Rubber	1969	3,943	1,032	26.2
Total		191,220	48,108	25.2%

*From Midwest Research Institute; excludes exports of scrap materials; but in some instances includes imports of scrap for domestic consumption; excludes scrap materials reused (such as textile wastes for wiping rags); nonferrous metals include only aluminum, copper, zinc, and lead; rubber recycling includes tires retreaded for resale as tires.

Source: Environmental Protection Agency

the like, the recycled proportion is much lower, of course, but no reliable estimates of the quantities of these latter materials involved are available.

Why can't we recycle a larger proportion of our wastes and thus unburden our waste management systems? The reason is that demand for scrap materials is limited. These commodities compete with primary natural resources, whose use and processing have become rationalized and institutionalized in large part because in earlier decades wastes were not available in sufficient quantities to satisfy demand for materials while virgin materials were abundantly available. Scrap recovery techniques — in the broad sense of acquisition, upgrading, processing, and distribution — have not changed significantly in the 20th century. In the meantime, the mining or harvesting, purification, upgrading, and processing of primary materials have made dramatic technological and economic strides forward.

Today scrap use is frequently uneconomical because the productivity of labor associated with acquisition and processing of primary materials is greater than labor productivity in scrap acquisition and processing. For instance, a steel producer finds it cheaper (1) to mine, beneficiate, and ship ore; (2) to mine and transport fluxing materials; (3) to produce coke from coal (which was also mined and moved); (4) to produce pig iron from these materials; and (5) to produce steel from pig iron (sometimes using oxygen extracted in air liquefaction plants) than to acquire, remelt, and reformulate steel scrap.

In addition to greater labor productivity consequent upon use of advanced materials processing technology, processors of primary materials also enjoy depletion allowances when extracting these materials.

Where primary processors do not meet air, water, and solid waste standards in manufacturing (or where these standards are leniently set) the processors do not pay the full environmental costs created by pollution and waste generation associated with their virgin materials uses. Many raw materials, also, come principally from foreign sources (like bauxite), and their use contributes to a foreign trade imbalance.

By contrast, secondary materials are not generally credited with conserving natural resources, receive few credits for contributing favorably to our foreign trade balance, receive little credit for removing materials from the waste stream, and receive no credit for providing materials whose processing usually pollutes the environment less than the comparable processing of virgin materials.

When all the costs of primary materials use—including those usually disregarded—and all the benefits of secondary materials are considered, secondary materials would probably turn out to be less uneconomical than they appear to be from an examination of the status quo. Little information is available to establish whether or not this judgment is accurate and, if it is, how it can reorder our economic accounting structures to bring about greater use of secondary materials. Public policy can be directed toward gaining a more comprehensive knowledge of total costs, both tangible and intangible, of various materials processing systems.

Why Policy Considerations?

Legislation to increase the quantities of waste materials recycled appears justified if the total socioeconomic costs of using virgin raw materials are higher than costs of the alternative use of secondary materials. Given our traditional economic accounting methods, manufacturers experience only a portion of the real or total costs of their materials; some part of total costs occurs externally to industry and externally to the seller-buyer relationship wherein the market value of materials is determined. Any costs that are not incurred directly in a formal financial accounting sense go unrecognized in the commercial system. In this sense, the cost of environmental pollution may be passed along to the population in dirty water, dirty air, and polluted land if the dollar cost of physical control of effluents is not borne by the polluting industry. Thus the market mechanism is not a sufficient guarantee that those materials will be used that have the lowest total cost. It is in these instances that governmental intervention is desirable, to make the best use of natural resources.

Resource Versus Materials Conservation

In line with this analysis, public policy aimed at increasing the proportion of secondary materials recycled must be considered within a broad context. The appropriate context is that of resource conservation, whereby resource is defined broadly to include all substances, energies, manpower, and conditions that we value.

Given a resource conservation context, some products are probably "cheaper" if made from virgin materials; others are cheaper if made from secondary materials. It would clearly be undesirable, for instance, to recycle an abundant material if in so doing two or three times more energy, water, and manpower are expended and if more pollution is generated than in obtaining the same material from natural deposits. Materials conservation is not necessarily identical with resource conservation.

The concept of resource conservation also permits taking into consideration certain intangible values that are not usually counted in normal cost estimates. For instance, maximum recycling may require an extremely high degree of governmental intervention in industrial decision making. While this may be desirable in order to conserve fossil fuels, scarce materials, and environmental purity, the nation's commitment to a free-enterprise economic system may be viewed as a value or resource too great to be sacrificed.

Cost Allocation Issues

Public policy to increase recycling, framed within the context of resource conservation, will necessarily be based on the assumption or on the finding that on a national basis, if not on an industry basis, recycling is less costly than use of virgin materials.

Pollution control legislation requiring manufacturers to clean their effluents, changes in import/export regulations, and a host of other legislative changes (whose objective is something other than recycling of wastes) may gradually result in a reallocation of costs. Changes in economic factors such as price increases for fuels, primary raw materials, or transportation brought about by scarcity, technological changes, or increased labor costs may result in a shift in values favoring secondary materials.

In order to bring about the recycling of secondary materials, cost allocation must necessarily work out so that the internal as well as the external costs of materials use will be internalized by industry. This means that manufacturers (and in turn final consumers) must pay, directly or indirectly, costs created by their materials use that arise from environmental quality preservation, material and energy conservation, defense posture, social welfare, or other considerations.

Such cost criteria are already recognized by manufacturers; one example is the minimum wage. Legislation requiring recognition of external costs not now borne by industry would thus be the extension of precedents already established. From industry's viewpoint, of course, any such legislation would represent a further constriction of the magic circle within whose boundaries freedom of economic choice is still possible.

Always assuming that total cost of virgin materials use is greater than secondary materials use, legislation will necessarily have the effect of restricting virgin materials use by rendering its use actually more expensive than use of waste commodities. This can be accomplished, in practice, (1) by making the acquisition, processing, and distribution of virgin-based products more expensive in some way while maintaining the costs of secondary raw materials unchanged, or (2) by putting on the market secondary materials technically equivalent to virgin materials at a cost sufficiently low so that manufacturers can avoid waste use only at their economic peril.

Raising primary material prices vis-a-vis secondary material prices can be achieved directly in the form of tax on any material obtained from natural resources, or indirectly by forcing the manufacturers to spend more in the form of pollution control expenditures, transportation charges, environmental maintenance (mine-site landscaping, for example), higher energy cost, longer depreciation schedules, lower depletion allowances, etc.

However achieved, higher primary materials costs would also require some control over secondary materials costs as well. Otherwise, secondary materials prices might simply rise in proportion to virgin materials prices as a result of increased demand and might stabilize at a new and higher level without net changes in the actual consumption ratio of secondary to virgin materials. The net effect would then be higher prices for the consumer. This requirement implies at least some additional direct or indirect governmental control over the secondary materials industry—at least during the period of transition between the current situation and a period in which waste materials are used in a significantly higher proportion.

The other major approach—that of creating a supply of technically acceptable secondary materials at irresistibly low prices relative to virgin materials—can be achieved by fostering the development and use of technology to acquire and process such materials and by achieving an economic relationship on the price of such materials so that they are cheaper than equivalent virgin materials. The amount of subsidy that may legitimately be made available for this purpose should be no more than the difference between the market cost of virgin materials and their real or total cost including external cost.

The Need for Demand Creation

Demand for waste commodities is limited; the low demand is not caused by a lack of supply but by other factors. This is not generally understood. Rather, researchers frequently encountered the opinion, in the course of the Darnay and Franklin study, that ". . . if only waste commodities were made available, they would be consumed." This opinion is quite natural.

The supply of waste commodities is not the critical aspect of secondary materials use. Instead, the critical parameter is the demand for waste commodities relative to virgin resources. Unless secondary materials are viewed more favorably as a raw materials supply by industry and unless the relative value relations are changed to help bring this about, then the demand for waste materials will either remain stationary in relation to total consumption (at best) or it will decline.

In such a situation, programs to remove saleable materials from municipal wastes may actually succeed, but they will do so by taking existing markets from the secondary materials industry. This is illustrated by the following hypothetical situations. The situations assume conditions of steady need or demand for 100 units of a given product.

Situation one (Figure 7-3) represents a hypothetical condition today in which total need or demand for a product is 100 units. After the 100 units are discarded, the manufacturing sector recovers 10 units for recycling while 90 units are added to the municipal disposal inventory. Manufacturing withdraws 90 units from the virgin material inventory for manufacture and distribution to customers of 100 new units for use and discard; the cycle repeats.

FIGURE 7-3   Situation One: Constant Demand 100 Units; Recycle 10 Units.

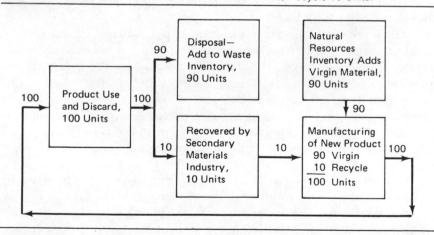

Source: Darnay and Franklin, *op. cit.*, p. 95-1.

In situation two (Figure 7-4), the municipal waste sector invests sufficient capital in technology to recover 5 units from its 90 units of waste stream in order to effect resource recovery and to reduce solid waste disposal quantities. Since demand for recycled units remains at a grand total of 10 units, the traditional secondary materials handling system loses

FIGURE 7-4 Situation Three: Constant Demand 100 Units; Recycle 20 Units

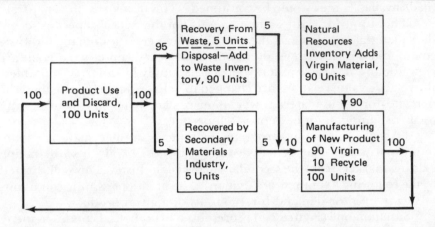

Source: Darnay and Franklin, *op. cit.*, p. 95-3.

markets for 5 units that can no longer be sold to industry. Thus, the 5 units no longer economically recoverable by industry are instead diverted into the waste stream. The waste system then must really process a total of 95 units (instead of 90), 90 of which it disposes just as before, and 5 of which it recovers, which it sells to industry. The net result is that the waste system must handle 5 more units of waste and must still dispose of the same quantity as before. The secondary materials industry loses its ability to collect and process 5 units.

The point of situation two is that the expenditure of capital and the development of waste processing technology do not necessarily lead to greater recovery of secondary materials and may lead to greater quantities handled by the waste system while the supply of recovered secondary materials remains unchanged in the whole system. Simply making a supply of material available does not assure its consumption. Demand for this material must increase in concert with or in advance of the actual recovery or else the system does not change the total waste disposal quantities.

In situation three (Figure 7-5) demand for recycled units is increased to 20 units while total product demand remains at 100 units. A new situation now arises. In this case, the manufacturing sector has a demand for 20 recycled units. The effects are as profound as in situation two. Assume that the traditional secondary materials industry sector can recover economically an additional 5 units, bringing its recovery to 15 units. The waste system's load is then reduced to 85 units collected instead of 90 units. In addition, assume that the waste system invests capital in technology to recover 5 units so that it then disposes of 80 units and can sell 5 units to industry. If the system is to stay in balance, the primary supply sector of

FIGURE 7-5   Situation Three: Constant Demand 100 Units; Recycle 20 Units

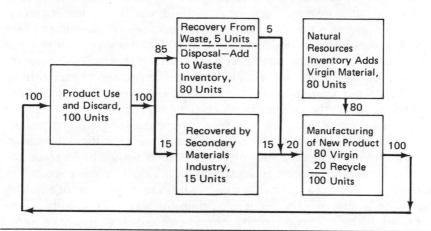

Source: Darnay and Franklin, *op. cit.*, p. 95–3.

manufacturing gives up 10 units and now supplies 80 units, compared with 90 previously.

Obviously, in situation three, the burden on solid waste systems is reduced substantially, and both the solid waste and the traditional secondary materials sectors recover more materials. The primary materials producers are penalized because they must give up 10 units of output but the system still supplies the 100 units of demand. The recovered materials consumed for a complete cycle reduce the waste disposal inventory by 10 units over the original condition, while 10 virgin material units need not be taken from the virgin material inventory. Both disposal capacity and virgin resources are conserved by increasing the number of recycled units.

At present, it seems that far too few people recognize the importance of the demand parameter and far too many place blind faith in technology and capital to increase the supplies of secondary materials not needed or demanded by the materials processing sectors under current economic relationships and industry structures. Recognition of demand as an unforgiving system element in the whole recycling question is simply not present to the degree necessary in the current rush to recycle resources. What looms, then, is a potential imbalance of supply and a shift or dislocation of supply of secondary materials from traditional systems to waste management systems and an even greater burden on solid waste management systems as a whole. Simplistic assumptions about demand taking care of itself or being easy to change are not realistic. This supply push approach is analogous to pushing on a string when, in fact, it appears that demand pull would more effectively bring about the desired increase of secondary materials consumption.

To bring about a desirable change (situation three) requires that virgin material use be displaced. In a situation of increasing consumption, this means that waste recycling must grow faster than virgin materials use. Today the reverse is the case. Since the proportions of waste to primary materials are ultimately determined by the relative cost of each as set in the market, creation of demand necessarily dictates that the cost structure of virgin and secondary materials be changed in relation to each other.

The role of waste processing technology in meeting increased demand depends on the manner in which demand is increased. If primary resources are made more costly or scarce, by whatever means, manufacturers will seek secondary raw materials and will develop the needed technology for processing and upgrading such wastes to increase the secondary materials supply. If demand is increased by making secondary materials available at a cost below that of virgin materials and of a quality equivalent to that of virgin materials, then the waste commodity sellers and possibly the solid waste management establishment will have to develop and use the processing technology for materials upgrading. In any case, waste processing technology is a vitally important part of increased recycling.

The key point about waste processing technology deployment is that its use will not in and of itself bring about an increase in demand but must be accompanied by actions that will bring about a change in the relative consumption ratios of primary and secondary materials—in favor of waste commodities.

Intermaterials Competition

Legislation to bring about recycling in one material category must take into account the relative competitive position of that material with respect to other materials. Perhaps the single most important trend in materials used today is the penetration of synthetic materials based on hydrocarbons into markets dominated by traditional substances—cotton, wool, paper, wood, glass, steel. Unilateral legislation aimed at paper alone, for instance, may well simply intensify the competition between paper and plastics, making the latter materials, which are not now recycled in any significant quantity, more competitive in paper markets.

Obsolescence

One way to reduce solid waste generation is to use materials for longer periods of time. If a refrigerator is used for 15 years instead of 10, its continued use represents reduction of waste at the source, a form of recycling—without any materials collection, scrap processing, materials reprocessing, fabrication, or redistribution having taken place. Efforts to increase the life-in-use of products would thus result in resource recovery. The classic example of long-lived and short-lived products in an identical application is the use of returnable and nonreturnable containers in soft drink and beer packaging. New design criteria for products (such as modular components) that make repair rather than replacement more attractive would have the same effects.

Energy Recovery

Combustible materials need not be recovered as materials; their resource value may be extracted in the form of heat energy. This is a particularly appropriate way to use materials whose recycling in more conventional ways is impractical, such as plastics, wood, and paper products contaminated by laminants, coatings, and adhesives. In this type of recovery, combustible materials would displace fuels—coal, gas, and oil. Because energy demand is large and growing and because low-sulfur fuels are in short supply, the impact of energy recovery from waste would have little effect on traditional energy industry alignments; the alternative of recycling such materials as materials would have a far greater impact on present industry structures.

Secondary Recycling

Materials produced by one industry need not necessarily re-enter the same industry. Waste rubber and waste glass could be used in road construction, for instance, displacing asphalt and concrete. Organics such as rubber can be converted to crude oil by pyrolysis and could displace well oil. Organics can be composted and used to displace a portion of soil conditioners used. The key is that a product is created from waste that competes with or displaces another product used in other applications. To bring about secondary recycling of materials will be equally as difficult as effecting their primary recycling, but such programs are nevertheless a distinct legislative option.

Recycling in Key Industries

Paper. Paper is the largest component of municipal waste collected (40 to 50 percent by weight). Fairly large quantities of paper are recycled. In 1969, 53 million tons of fibrous materials were consumed in paper making; of this, 10.1 million tons, or 19 percent, was waste paper. But paper's recycling rate has been declining steadily since 1945. Generation of paper waste is growing more rapidly than waste paper consumption. Mills using virgin pulp have been built in preference to those consuming waste paper to tap abundant sources of low cost primary raw materials—trees.

The demand for products made of pulp fiber has increased about three times as rapidly as the demand for products made of secondary fiber in the past 15 years. Virgin fibers are also used to upgrade the appearance of products that traditionally have been made exclusively of waste.

Higher recycling rates in paper are limited by economics (wood pulp is inexpensive in relation to waste paper), logistics (manufacturing plants are far from cities, in which waste paper occurs), and the fundamental pulp wood materials orientation of the paper industry and its customers.

Ferrous Metals. Approximately 7 percent of collected municipal waste is ferrous metal. The iron and steel industries use large quantities of scrap metal in their operations—33 million tons of purchased scrap supplied 31 percent of the industry's total metallics demand of nearly 106 million tons in 1967. In addition to this demand, 7.6 million tons of scrap were exported.

Of the 33 million tons of domestic scrap demand, obsolete scrap, such as automobile hulks and other discarded iron and steel objects and structures, accounted for 21.4 million tons, equivalent to 20 percent of total domestic metallics demand. The remainder was supplied by fabrication wastes.

In addition to some 33 million tons of scrap acquired by the industry from external sources, the industry also used 52 million tons of internally generated scrap in 1967, called home scrap. Over the past decade, home scrap use has increased at the expense of obsolete scrap.

Ferrous metals occurring in municipal waste consist largely of tin-coated steel cans. These materials are not suitable for recycling in steel furnaces because the tin cannot be removed from the cans and contaminates the furnace products. Small quantities of obsolete steel cans are consumed in copper mining operations in the refining of low-grade copper. The demand for cans in this application is not sufficiently large to consume more than a small fraction of available cans.

Total demand for iron and steel scrap by industry here and abroad falls short of the tonnage actually available. In 1967, between 52 and 68 million tons of obsolete scrap were available by our estimate. Total domestic and export demand for obsolete scrap was 29 million tons. Closing the gap between available scrap supply and demand requires lower rates of iron ore consumption. At this time, ore-based operations are more economical than scrap-based operations for most of the industry. Collection of scrap occurring in dispersed locations and removal of impurities (such as tin) are more costly than mining and processing ores.

Nonferrous Metals. The major nonferrous metals—aluminum, copper, zinc, and lead—constitute less than 1 percent of collected municipal waste. All of these materials are valuable as scrap and are recycled within economic limits. In 1967, nearly 9.8 million tons of these materials were consumed; 30.8 percent of this consumption, 3 million tons, was provided by recycled materials.

Aluminum is the only nonferrous metal encountered in municipal waste in significant quantities. Approximately 680,000 tons of aluminum cans, food trays, and packaging foils were part of such waste in 1968. As a consequence of various legislative pressures on the packaging industry, three aluminum companies have entered the field of aluminum packaging reclamation by starting can reclamation centers. These programs depend on delivery of the cans by the public to a central collection point, where they are processed for shipment to a smelter. Success of the programs turns on these points: (1) collection must be by the public; (2) sufficiently high quantities must be brought in to operate the collection centers economically; (3) the aluminum is valuable, worth about $200 per ton, thus permitting processing. The Reynolds Metals company has the oldest successful program in operation. A "successful" program is unlikely to recover more than 10 to 15 percent of available aluminum packaging in an area.

Glass. Glass, largely discarded containers, makes up about 6 percent of collected municipal waste. All segments of the glass industry use waste glass known as cullet. But most of the cullet is derived from internal plant operations. Very little comes from outside sources. Cullet is an accepted component in glass making provided that it is clean, free of contaminants, and color sorted. Glass containers constitute by far the largest share of total glass production tonnage (about 70 percent) and represent about 90 percent of the glass found in municipal waste.

In 1967, 12.8 million tons of glass were consumed. Of this total, 600,000 tons were purchased cullet from external sources, equivalent to 4.2 percent of consumption. The use of purchased cullet has declined because predictable supplies at prices competitive with basic raw materials (sand, limestone, and soda ash) have all but disappeared. The few surviving cullet dealers face rising costs and dwindling supplies.

It is not economically or technically feasible to recover glass from mixed wastes at present. However, technology for separation is being tested. The glass industry could absorb large quantities of cullet if the various technical and economic problems of cullet supply could be overcome, and indeed glass collection centers have been organized recently at glass container plants around the country under the leadership of the Glass Container Manufacturers Institute to induce the return of waste glass by consumers. Incentives for increased glass cullet use by industry are not present; virgin raw materials are inexpensive and abundant.

Textiles. The occurrence of textiles in waste is relatively low—about 0.6 percent of collected municipal wastes. Textile wastes are not normally returned to the industries that produce them with the exception of a small amount of wool that is rewoven. The chief uses of textile wastes are in paper and board products; furniture stuffings, fillings, and backings; export for resale; production of wiping cloths; and resale in secondhand stores. In 1968, nearly 5.7 million tons of textiles were consumed and

246,000 tons of textiles were recycled, a recycling rate of 4.3 percent of consumption.

Rubber.   Rubber is around 1 percent by weight of collected municipal wastes. Tires are the principal source of waste rubber. About 1 million tons of rubber were recovered in 1969, 26.2 percent of a total consumption of 3.9 million tons. Retreading is the principal form of rubber recycling (75 percent); rubber reclaiming accounts for a substantial share (24 percent); tire splitters—who cut tires into various products like gaskets—take less than 1 percent of the recovered tonnage.

There are definite technical limitations to recycled rubber, since it cannot be successfully mixed with virgin rubber in large percentages nor can it be substituted for virgin rubber. Retread tires are losing markets to new tires, and this decline is expected to continue; rubber reclaiming is also in decline.

Since rubber recycling is experiencing decline as markets dwindle, the rubber content of solid waste can be expected to rise. Use of waste rubber to produce new materials (for example, oils) or energy appears to offer the best hope for recovery of this waste category.

Plastics.   Plastics are increasing rapidly in waste because these materials are growing in a number of consumer product markets. Obsolete plastics are not recycled. The immense number of different formulations of plastics and the near impossibility of sorting these materials after discard prevents their reuse. A small market exists for fabrication wastes. These are purchased by waste plastics processors who regrind, color blend, and remelt plastics for low-grade applications. The demand for secondary plastics made from fabrication wastes falls short of the total supply of such wastes, and many fabricators haul their wastes to dumps and landfills.

CONCLUSIONS

Our economic system has encouraged the one-way or dead-end disposal philosophy. Organic materials, synthetics, metals, industrial chemicals and solvents, biological agents, and radioactive wastes travel the dead enroute. These substances end up in landfills, rivers, lakes, underground water reserves, and oceans. Dangerous substances such as atomic wastes are simply stored either in specially constructed facilities or in deep wells inside of impervious rock formations. But, atomic radiation, like so many highly toxic materials, manages to leak out into the environment, posing health dangers for mankind. Metals and chemicals from pesticides, herbicides, and industrial processes are increasing the chances of severe illnesses and a wide variety of diseases as drinking water, food, air, and soil absorb higher levels of pollutants.

Behavior modification proponents suggest than the human race can avoid an environmental collapse; altering or changing customs, viewpoints, habits, and values can contribute to a cleaner environment and an economic system that maintains growth potential. Rapid resource exploitation and the practice of dumping drain the earth of its finite riches and pollute the ecosystem with toxic wastes. In many respects, the issues swirling around resource recovery are associated with the willingness of society to modify its behavior. Resource recovery stimulates the return of finite resources back into the economic system. The development of a reverse channel that can transform, sort, and facilitate the movement of secondary products to industrial users has lagged behind other innovative distribution changes; but the time is apparently right for the reverse channel to become that much needed link that can close the circle in the distribution system. The socioecological aspects of the reverse channel are most important to the conservation of the nation's raw material reserves and for the nation's environmental health.

Case 13
A Dead Sea in New York Bight

Just off the coasts of New York and New Jersey lies a 20-square-mile "dead sea." This spreading, oily black body of sludge kills virtually all sea life in its path. The sludge is organic and inorganic solid waste—the residue from sewage-treatment plants in an area where 13 million people live. These toxic substances (in high concentrations) are dumped by barges in the ocean first 10 miles from shore. This oceanic dumping area has overwhelmed the ecosystem; these pollutants (some 500 million cubic yards are dumped annually—enough to cover Central Park with a four-foot layer of sludge) can not be dissipated or absorbed by the ocean's maintenance system. As a result, concentrations of pollutants increase, spreading out into larger pockets. Marine scientist Dr. William H. Harris suggests that the sludge poses a threat to New York and New Jersey beaches.

The case of New York Bight is part of a growing worldwide practice of using oceans as dumping grounds for toxic substances. According to the Council on Environmental Quality, some 10 million tons of industrial wastes and sewage sludge were disposed of at sea in 1968 from our nation alone. By 1973, that figure had grown to 12 million tons.

In recognition of this problem, the government passed the Marine Protection, Research, and Sanctuaries Act in 1972. Its primary intent is to prevent or strictly limit ocean-dumping of harmful materials and to prevent

Conservation News, Vol. 39, No. 6 (March 15, 1974), pp. 8–10.

unreasonable degradation of the marine environment. To that end the Act places a strict ban on the ocean-dumping of "high-level radioactive wastes" as well as "chemical and biological warfare agents." Other wastes (with the exception of dredged materials, which fall within the purview of the Army Corps of Engineers) may be dumped only in accordance with permits issued by the Environmental Protection Agency (EPA). These permits are issued following an assessment of dumping need, effects on marine ecosystems, resource values, the availability of alternative methods, and locations of waste disposal or recycling installations.

Ocean-dumping regulations and criteria, which were not finalized by EPA until October 15, 1973, set up a system of permits to control the dumping of four categories of wastes. At the extremely toxic level we find high-level radioactive substances and chemical and biological warfare agents (CBW). At the other extreme we find a category of wastes so innocuous that they may be dumped freely in most locations; these include rubble, construction debris, rocks, and boulders. In between these two extreme ranges are two other groups of toxic materials. The first category includes compounds of mercury, cadmium, and DDT, which may be ocean-dumped only as "trace contaminants." The second group are designated as "materials requiring special care" and includes arsenic and lead compounds. These substances may be dumped in levels determined by the amount of dilution occurring at the disposal site and on the basis of laboratory tests of biological toxicity.

Other provisions in the Act cover "general," "emergency," and "research" permits. Permits are valid for up to three years and renewals are relatively easy to obtain. But the program has not gone smoothly. Ocean dumping has run head-on into a knowledge vacuum. After more than 20 years of virtually unrestricted dumping, the oceans have almost overnight come under a regime of virtually total regulation—at least in theory. Although the oceans have been the subject of numerous scientific studies, not enough data exists, even today. These tremendous bodies of water are more difficult to research than air or inland waterways. For the most part scientists are at the stage where many complex questions are being raised concerning the future of oceans. For example, scientists have no reliable yardstick capable of evaluating ecological disruptions which emit from continuous ocean dumpings. It is not surprising, therefore, that ocean-dumping permits are being issued in a variegated manner.

Years of neglect have brought about the present widespread pollution of the seas; the seemingly infinite ocean has turned out to be vulnerable after all. The future promises much more marine pollution under the pressure of our constantly expanding populations and even faster-growing industries. Moreover, because the regulation of ocean dumping lags behind efforts to control pollution in other media, the by-products of effluent and emission treatment procedures all too often become candidates for ocean disposal. This vicious cycle will continue and worsen until adequate and economically feasible technologies are devised to recover and reuse much of the material now discarded as waste. Industrial refining and chemical processes are evolving new generations of highly toxic agents used in commercial and consumer markets. These new substances are too dangerous to dispose of in traditional dumping sites on land and in freshwater locations. Since it is more economical to ocean dump these agents, our great marine resources are bearing the burden of mass disposal requirements, especially along the East Coast. The New York Bight is but one example of pollution which threatens the ecosystem of the sea.

Case 14
The Case of McDowell County, West Virginia

The many environmental, economic, and social problems associated with the coal mining industry are generally well known. The need for a national severance tax on coal is well illustrated by the case history of McDowell County, in southern West Virginia, which has produced more coal than any other county in the United States. In describing that case history, the Sport Fishing Institute wishes to emphasize that it is not our purpose to deride McDowell County or its friendly, energetic, and resourceful people. The County has a variety of fine institutions, a colorful history, and a potentially bright future. It does, however, have great environmental problems which are symptomatic of the entire Appalachian coal fields.

In 1858, when McDowell County was organized out of 538 square miles of beautiful and inaccessible hill country of the state of Virginia, by fewer than 300 residents, it was almost entirely in public ownership. Virtually the entire county was covered with a virgin stand of hardwood timber. Even at that early date, the settlers were aware of the abundance of coal in the county; however, they made little use of it.

In 1863, McDowell County became part of the new state of West Virginia. However, few changes took place in the life style of the people until the arrival of the Norfolk and Western Railroad in 1888. The "boom and bust" story of the McDowell County economy in the 85 ensuing years is a prime example of what can happen when an apathetic public tolerates governmental failure to protect the public interest in dealings with an aggressive natural resource exploitative industry.

In the past 85 years, McDowell County has produced 1,320,533,000 tons of coal, worth an estimated $5 billion when mined. That staggering quantity would fill a string of coal-gondola rail cars reaching 10 times around the earth, equivalent to the distance from earth to the moon. With such fantastic wealth flowing almost endlessly from its underground coal

Conservation News, Vol. 38, No. 19 (October 1, 1973), pp. 8–13.

reservoir, one could easily imagine McDowell County as the 20th century "Garden of Eden," with all of the public facilities and opportunities that money could buy and an environment to match. Nothing could be further from the truth.

In 1971, public welfare costs in McDowell County were $3,747,104, computed at $73.90 per county resident—twice the statewide average. It is worthy of note that the total 1971 tax collections from all property classes in McDowell County amounted to $3,525,000. That amount is roughly $225,000 less than the cost of the county's welfare alone.

In 1970, the per capita income in McDowell County was $2,763. By comparison, the West Virginia statewide average is $3,034; the U.S. average is $3,933.

The average unemployment rate in McDowell County over the past 15 years was 14.6 percent. That rate far exceeds the corresponding averages for either West Virginia or the United States as a whole.

McDowell County contains five sizeable streams having an estimated surface water area of 554 acres, 57 percent of which is so grossly polluted that fish life cannot be sustained. The remaining water is affected to a lesser degree. Per capita hunting and fishing license sales in McDowell County are less than one-third the statewide average for West Virginia.

McDowell County's population declined from 71,359 to 50,666 (29 percent) between 1960 and 1970. This represents the sharpest decline of any of West Virginia's 55 counties. Unhappily, McDowell County lacks its full share of cultural opportunities, has no commercial airports, no public golf courses, and extremely poor roads.

Unfortunately, McDowell County has far more than its full share of streams poisoned by mine acid and black with coal washings. There are an abundance of huge, ugly slate dumps, many of which have been burning and sending off acid-forming sulfur fumes for years. Abandoned coal tipples, conveyor systems, and mine buildings are plentiful. Hillsides are permanently marked by countless strip mining scars and broken stands of timber smashed by small avalanches of rocks and boulders that now fill the valleys.

How, one might ask, is it possible for an area to produce such fabulous wealth and be left so devastated, destitute, and neglected in the process? It is simply because the coal industry has not been required to pay a share of the tax load sufficient to ameliorate the environmental consequences of its activities. Huge profits have been quickly channeled out of the county and out of the state by nonresident corporations which have not been required to accept their responsibility to the land and to those who occupy it now and who will occupy it in future generations. There is little possibility that McDowell County and the hundreds of other coal-mining counties of Appalachia can ever be restored to their pristine conditions. However, it is by no means impossible or too late to reverse past trends and to correct much of the damage that has been wrought.

In McDowell County, the 25 largest landowners (all of whom have direct coal interests) own 70 percent of the land. It is a fact that the West Virginia legislature has provided that land must be assessed at its true value. It is another fact that undeveloped coal lands are sold on the open market for very large sums. Regardless, the value of the known coal reserves in the ground is not considered in establishing property tax assessment levels. Much acreage in West Virginia is reportedly on the tax rolls at $1.00 or less per acre. As a consequence, the coal industry pays only minimum real estate and property taxes.

The coal industry does pay a state business and occupation tax, just as does every other business or industry. Ironically, however, the rate charged to the coal industry is less than for most other categories. One hundred and forty-five million tons of coal were extracted from West Virginia's deep mines in 1968. The value of that coal was $725 million, yet the industry paid only $11.6 million in direct taxes. It is interesting to note, by comparison, that West Virginia's taxes on liquor and cigarettes were roughly $13 million each in the same period.

McDowell County's estimated recoverable coal reserves are 1,898,232,000 tons, sufficient to last about 125 years at present rate of extraction. The estimated reserves for all of West Virginia are a staggering 58 billion tons. Coal has historically been in keen competition with oil; however, the growing national energy shortage virtually guarantees that demands for vast quantities of coal will continue for many years.

It is our opinion that a national coal severance tax should be imposed as quickly as possible. Such a tax appears to be the only practical source of funds to repair the environmental devastation resulting from the extraction of coal. A severance tax has been proposed in West Virginia on many occasions. Each time, however, the industry has defeated the move by protesting that such a tax would destroy the competitive position of coal. Each time, the specter has been raised of a rapid decline of the industry with mass unemployment. The facts do not support the industry's contention, as is amply demonstrated by the experience of the United Mine Workers.

In 1946, the United Mine Workers, after a long and bitter contract dispute with the coal industry, won coal production royalty payments of 5 cents per ton for the Union's Welfare and Retirement Fund. The industry fought the proposal with every weapon available to it. Only after the government had taken over the operation of the mines did the industry agree to the 5 cent royalty as a condition of their return. In reluctantly agreeing to the new terms, the industry forecast a dark future and gradual demise of the coal business.

In the first year (1964) the UMW Welfare and Retirement Fund earned $1,266,000 from McDowell County production alone. In 1947, when the contract royalty increased to 10 cents per ton, the UMW received

$2,522,000. The 1948 agreement specified 20 cents per ton, and the Fund earned over $5 million from McDowell County alone. The royalty payments were increased to 40 cents per ton in 1952; they remained at that figure until 1971, when they were increased to 60 cents. In May of 1974, the royalty will increase to 80 cents a ton, with the Welfare and Retirement Fund earning $12 million annually from the coal production in McDowell County, West Virginia, alone.

In the past 27 years, altogether, the United Mine Workers Welfare and Retirement Fund has earned about $165 million from McDowell County coal production. Imagine the extensive environmental improvements that could have been funded with such a comparable sum!

The U.S. Soil Conservation Service estimates that McDowell County has 10,000 acres of unreclaimed strip mines. Based upon a $3,000 per acre reclamation cost (as estimated in a 1973 CEQ/Senate Interior Committee report), those 10,000 acres could be reclaimed and reseeded for $30 million. There is no accurate count of the total number of abandoned and active underground mining operations in McDowell County but it most certainly numbers in the thousands. Every one of these mines has, at a very minimum, one slate dump to despoil the landscape. It is entirely feasible to remove these dumps or to level and cover them with topsoil. A spokesman for the U.S. Bureau of Mines has advised that many of these slate dumps contain up to 35 percent or more of usable coal. In many instances, that wasted coal may be economically feasible to recover.

A modest severance tax could long ago have eliminated those dumps—plus the abandoned rail and conveyor systems, unused coal tipples, and the countless other scars left by the industry. When all the reclamation work was completed, there would have been ample money left over to build public fishing lakes, golf courses, picnic areas, and the other public facilities which, we contend, a portion of the coal wealth should justifiably have provided.

The time for a national severance tax on coal is long overdue, but it is not too late. Theoretically, McDowell County could pass its own tax but, as a practical matter, this does not appear to be politically feasible. The same might be said for a state severance tax but, again, the strong local influence of the coal industry makes passage doubtful in the important coal-producing states.

A few states already have coal severance taxes but most are at ridiculously low rate levels. Furthermore, they occur in states having relatively little coal production. Ohio has a 4 cents per ton tax; in Arkansas the tax is 2 cents per ton; in Idaho it is 3 cents per ton. Tennessee charges 1.5 percent of gross income, up to a maximum of 10 cents per ton; New Mexico collects one-eighth of one percent of gross income; Utah collects 2 percent of gross income over $50,000 per year. Alabama receives 13.5 cents per ton; Montana receives an average of 27 cents per ton; Kentucky, one of the top producing states, made a major advance in 1972 by levying a severance tax of 30 cents per ton.

The major coal-producing states of West Virginia, Pennsylvania, Illinois, and Virginia, where the problems are the greatest, collect no severance taxes. The few existing state severance taxes need not complicate a national tax for it would be relatively simple to provide for appropriate deductions. In addition, a national tax would tend to discourage the coal industry from "shopping around" for states and localities with the lowest severance tax or with the least effective environmental safeguards.

The paradox of McDowell County's wealth-producing/poverty-stricken circumstances is almost incredible, yet it is very real and by no means unique in principle. No possible explanation can vindicate it, and the conscience of an aroused citizenry should demand that it be corrected.

A national severance tax—with the receipts specifically earmarked for environmental reclamation in coal-producing areas—is, in our judgment, the best available answer even though, naturally, the cost of coal would rise correspondingly. Our energy requirements are such that we doubtless must use the coal regardless of price. At the same time, our environmental requirements are such that we simply must rehabilitate ravaged lands. In the final analysis, the public will be paying the bill, as it always does, and they will judge whether the added cost will be worth it.

TOPIC QUESTIONS

1. Is resource recovery a channel of distribution problem or an environmental concern?
2. What distribution factors discourage resource recovery in municipal disposal systems?
3. Is product choice at the marketplace associated with the concept of waste reduction in the postconsumption phase?
4. Do primary commodity price fluctuations influence secondary material recycling?
5. Why are plastics especially difficult to recover and/or recycle?
6. Should firms be responsible for careless product use by consumers which leads to litter and waste disposal problems?
7. How should firms in the container beverage industry respond to legislative pressures to control nonreturnables?
8. What is intermaterials competition and how does it influence market demand for secondary materials in the reverse channel?

Case 13

9. Which groups are responsible for polluting New York Bight?
10. How is ocean pollution associated with waste management practices on the shore?

11. Why should ocean dumping be viewed as a pollution threat to our civilization?
12. What are the economic incentives which promote ocean dumping?

Case 14

13. In your opinion has McDowell County's natural wealth been well managed? Discuss your views.
14. What happened to the ecosystem in McDowell County?
15. Why does McDowell County have such impoverished citizens?
16. How could land surface recycling benefit a strip mine area? Who should pay for land reclamation?

RECOMMENDED READINGS

Arsen Darnay and William E. Franklin, *Salvage Markets for Materials in Solid Wastes* (Washington, D.C.: U.S. Environmental Protection Agency, 1972).

Midwest Research Institute, *Resource Recovery* (Washington, D.C.: Council on Environmental Quality, 1973).

Environmental Protection Agency, *Toward A New Environmental Ethic* (Washington, D.C.: U.S. Government Printing Office, 1971).

FOOTNOTES

1. Don R. Webb and John R. Darling, "The Post-Use Problem—A Response from Management," *Journal of Business Research* (Summer 1973), pp. 49–56. The increasing interest and growing pressures on behavior modification designed to encourage more effective disposal management are being felt by business. The authors suggest:

   One need only make a brief study of the increasing interest and initiative being taken by pressure groups on the environmental litter issue to conclude that the disposable packaging–litter issue is not a transitory thing. For example, more than 70 percent of the respondents in a study of the food service industry stated their beliefs that community and national social pressures will force better disposition of disposables. In addition, in a recent survey of its 287,000 members, the National Federation of Independent Business found 62 percent of the respondents were in favor of a federal ban on no-return soft drink and beer containers. The growing concern about the issue of solid waste disposal as a whole assures that, given present technology, this problem will continue to receive its share of attention by environmental critics.

2. Thomas L. Kimball, "Solid Waste Management," *Conservation Report* Situation Report No. 6, (July 26, 1974), pp. 1–7.
3. See the U.S. Environmental Protection Agency publication, *Mission 5000* (Washington, D.C.: U.S. Government Printing Office, 1972).
4. The Airlines Pilot Association has banned hazardous cargo aboard passenger airlines. The presence of industrial acids, solvents, biological agents, and radioactive materials posed increasing threats to passenger safety.

5. The Environmental Protection Agency's publication, *Toward A New Environmental Ethic* (Washington, D.C.: U.S. Government Printing Office, 1971) places a great deal of emphasis on changing consuming and disposal habits of society.

6. Ibid., p. 1.

7. See William H. Peters, "Who Cooperates in Voluntary Recycling Efforts," *Combined Proceedings* (American Marketing Association, 1973), p. 508.

8. Midwest Research Institute, *Resource Recovery* (Washington, D.C.: U.S. Government Printing Office, Council on Environmental Quality, 1973), p. 6.

9. National Policy Consideration for Recycling is adapted from Arsen Darnay and William E. Franklin, *Salvage Markets for Materials in Solid Wastes* (Washington, D.C.: U.S. Government Printing Office, U.S. Environmental Protection Agency, 1972).

CHAPTER EIGHT

ENVIRONMENTAL

LEGISLATION:

WHERE ARE WE HEADED?

DEFINING THE NEED

The pressures that stimulate new exploitations of natural wealth to simply satisfy exponential market demands are eventually self-destructive. If growth is not accompanied by sound pollution controls, compatible land-use planning, conservation practices, and long-term national policies to guide society, the processes of decay, and social disorientation become major problems. For example, the great urban centers of the nation sport lavish highway complexes, myriads of suburbs, shopping centers, factory districts (or industrial parks), and cultural activities. Municipal employees are specialized and professional. Many showcase exhibits dot the urban sprawl. In many respects these centers represent the last word in 20th century living. Unfortunately, urban centers are in deep trouble; crime, ghetto squalors, racial districts, fast rising municipal expenses, and disjointed land use patterns have created monumental social problems. Even the vast network of roads that embraces urban communities contributes to the decline of core or downtown regions. The presence of "country home" developments makes it possible for affluent persons to live well beyond urban districts.

A new migration back to rural areas is showing up in census reports; the large urban sprawl is in difficulty.[1] Municipal governments are being forced to cut back on vital education, health, safety, and sanitation services because of the heavy financial costs. Inflation has made it difficult for local governments to keep budgets trimmed; too, local tax rates (which represent one of the most rapidly rising living costs for citizens) have just about reached their ceilings in most areas.

It is becoming more evident that more growth will not cure the difficulties that urban communities are experiencing. In many respects, the problem can be traced to the loss of identity for both the community and the individual. Communities within communities, which in turn are engulfed by even greater suburban sprawls, represent ecological sterility which (to many persons) is both impersonal and hostile. The seeds of self-destruction are sown in the hodge-podge of modular developments which all too soon become obsolete and blighted. Reversing urban decay may well be one of the most challenging tasks undertaken by mankind.

The urban plight is a national problem. The culmination of population growth, exponential demands on land space, mushrooming, social services, ecological sterility, and pollution are problems that occur across wide belts of the United States. Resource decisions that we are making today can mean the difference between a socially viable and economically strong nation by the year 2000 or a nation experiencing environmental and economic collapse. Important policy decisions await us as we enter an era that offers little hope of reprieve if major mistakes are made.

THE ROLE OF SOCIOECOLOGICAL MARKETING

The socioecological product of marketing has important links with the major environmental issues. The marketing and physical distribution systems function within the socioeconomic framework affecting both resource allocation and resource utilization. Product mix decisions, the efficiency of transportation mode, inventory management, demand creation activities, and consumer post-use attitudes carry environmental impact price tags.

Marketing decision making involves a broad cross-section of society. In many respects, marketers serve as taste counselors and act as catalysts in creating time, place, and possession utilities. Society influences socioeconomic patterns; these, in turn, are evaluated by individual segments of our economic system. These decisions involve trade-offs at all levels in the industrial and consumer sectors. The basic problem in defining marketing's role in resolving distribution-related dilemmas is evaluating the often-obscured social responsibility factor. Firms find social trends difficult to evaluate in terms of major product changes. This is especially true in environmental matters.

Behavioral modifications are becoming increasingly necessary if society is to avoid a calamity. If distribution is to make effective modifications, major national policy guides will need to be established. This is especially important in the context of the federal and state governments. Such environmental policies will require the participation of the members of society, both in the formulation and implementation phases.

Environmental legislation currently reflects the difficult choices of options opened to our nation in establishing corrective policies on such major issues as energy, water quality, land use, reclamation, wilderness, and air quality. These policy issues may soon determine the basic character of our socioeconomic system and may ultimately affect the daily routine of most persons.

ENERGY POLICY ISSUES

The nation's dependency on inexpensive fossil fuels has delayed the formulation of a comprehensive energy policy. As early as 1952, the Paley Study Commission recommended an energy policy in its eight-volume report. Low prices for fossil fuels served to discourage energy exploration and development in the United States. The abundant world market supplies further dampened interest in domestic policies designed to more efficiently manage energy reserves. This abundance encouraged the wasteful practices which provided even more impetus to the exponential demands for petroleum products. It was not until the Arab oil embargo in September, 1973 that the illusion of abundance was shattered.

Project Independence

In January, 1974, the federal government embarked on Project Independence. In a detailed energy analysis, the 500 public and private professionals participating in the 15-volume study developed four major scenarios or options. These included the following: (1) a base case strategy that maps the consequences of continuing with existing policies; (2) an accelerated supply option that stresses concentrated resource development; (3) a conservation scenario that emphasizes elimination of wasteful consumption in the transportation, residential, and industrial sectors; and (4) an emergency preparedness strategy that derails stockpiling and standby emergency curtailment programs. Each strategy evaluates possible economic, environmental, and regional impacts assuming an import cost of either $7 or $11 per barrel of crude oil.[2]

For families caught in the Arab embargo short fall, the long lines and frequent fill ups at harried service stations seemed most unAmerican. The absence of an energy policy was largely ignored by the public until the harsh realities of international politics brought the oil issue home. In such an emergency situation as this, the primary emphasis is directed at cutting down demand. Unfortunately, without sound planning, the simple act of forcing back demand has a most serious affect on the economy. In a sense, this no-option enforced conservation of supplies is simply too disruptive. Since price rationing can be utilized to discourage consumption (even for inelastic goods such as gasoline), the steep price increases required to shut off excess demand can distort the nation's infrastructure and industrial processes. The sudden upsurge in oil prices in the autumn of 1973 led to unemployment and to dislocation of purchasing power (the less able bare the brunt of high price "allocation" rationing).

While Project Independence is viewed by some as a proper response to the energy crisis, environmentalists suggest that the plan relies far too heavily on developing energy supplies without corresponding improvements in efficiency in energy use, on conservation practices by industry and consumers, and on maintaining adequate ecological controls. The National Wildlife Federation suggests that major deficiencies in Project Independence can be found:[3]

1. *The environmental analysis is incomplete and far too general.* Individual supply areas lack specific data and estimates that would detail the intensity and chemical breakdown of each type of pollution. In many cases, major environmental concerns lose significance when placed side by side with those of minor importance, or else they are ignored entirely. For example, the problem of revegetation remains unmentioned in the oil shale discussion.

2. *Social and economic impacts are glossed over or are mentioned only superficially.* Although an entire chapter is devoted to this area, virtually no attention is given to food shortages, the impact of skyrocketing energy prices upon low-income areas, or disruptions in community life created by off-shore drilling and oil shale development. Alternative options (such as a fuel stamp program, a joint industry and citizen participation in community planning, or a negative income tax system) are needed to alleviate the expected adverse social impacts.

3. *Alternative energy sources such as solar, geothermal, tidal, and wind are downplayed.* These energy sources are relatively ubiquitous. Solar and wind represent energy source potentials that individuals could (with relatively low-level technology) use readily. These energy reserves do not readily appeal to corporate interests because they are not subject to patent or lease protection.

4. *Environmentally questionable, nonrenewable resources such as oil shale are given marked attention.* A 1,000-page task force report analyzes the future development of oil shale (as compared to a 135-page report on geothermal energy and a 550-page report on solar energy). Duke R. Ligon, the FEA Assistant Administrator for Energy Resource Development, recently emphasized to business leaders that the Ford Administration "does take seriously the need for oil shale development," while Secretary of the Interior Morton has emphasized the need for additional government subsidies and for expanding the prototype leasing program to ensure the development of oil shale. Thus the development of oil shale as an alterna-

tive energy resource is given priority despite the fact that it is a
resource which is (1) financially intensive (Atlantic Richfield recently had to suspend development on its 10-year oil shale plant
because of construction expense); (2) environmentally unsound
(after 10 years of experimentation revegetation is still unproven);
and (3) energy consumptive (it has yet to be determined whether
the amount of energy consumed for development will be worth the
net result).

5. *No consideration is given to the nation's energy industry market structure.*
   Neither the Federal Trade Commission nor the Justice Department
   were contacted to participate in studying monopolistic and anticompetitive practices within the oil industry. Despite the federal
   government's involvement in legal cases regarding anticompetitive
   action by the major oil companies in California, and the fact that the
   top five bidders in recent oil shale leases were representatives from
   those same companies, Secretary Morton recently insisted that "the
   oil industry is very competitive." A thorough examination of the oil
   industry's market structure is mandatory before firm energy
   policies are established.

6. *A financial analysis of the total Project Independence program is not
   included.* The report includes a budgetary review of federal energy
   research and development investments for fiscal years 1973, 1974,
   and 1975; all inclusive budgetary predictions analyzing the participation of both the public and private sectors through the year 2000,
   however, are excluded. The overall cost for Project Independence
   could run as high as $820 billion.

Thus it is clear that there are many reasons to be apprehensive about
the validity of Project Independence and its ultimate net worth. Nevertheless, one section, "Energy Conservation and Demand Management,"
which is clearly the most impressive section of the report, describes in
detail many of the conservation measures that can aid short-term efforts
to slow growth in energy consumption. Included are such options as a
gasoline tax, a 20-mile per gallon fuel consumption standard, residential
insulation requirements, and the recycling of solid wastes by industry.
According to the report, a substantial reduction in oil consumption could
reduce our national energy growth to 2.2 percent by 1985—a position
that was supported by the Secretary of the Interior as a viable alternative
to resolving the energy crisis.

Exploring the Options
The preliminary report of a group whose work has already had considerable effect on some energy legislation in Congress was released on March
31, 1974. The report, *Exploring Energy Choices,* is the first published review of the work being done by the Energy Policy Project, a Ford Foundation funded group headed by former presidential energy advisor S.
David Freeman. The EPP has been looking into the energy situation in the
United States for almost three years, and it was the group that contracted
with the National Academy of Sciences for the study on the reclamation

potential of western lands stripped for coal which has had such tremendous impact on both the Senate and House stripping regulation bills.

The preliminary report is a summary of much of the data uncovered
in the nearly 30 studies commissioned by the project.[4] Clearly, the part of
the report that will have the greatest impact on congressional energy
activities is that which lists three scenarios for future energy utilization in
the United States. One of the studies commissioned by the EPP is the
construction of a model to analyze the long-term implications of present
energy decisions. The EPP has been able to construct three "plausible but
different futures for the period through the year 2000." The study points
out that other scenarios might be plausible but that they are based on what
they believe to be defensible assumptions. The first scenario, which they
call "historical growth", assumes that energy use will continue in the
future at the same rate of growth as it has in the past. This scenario also
assumes that no policies will be imposed by government to change current
energy use habits but that a strong effort will be made to develop energy
supplies as rapidly as possible to match current and future demand. The
study concludes that even with domestic resources alone it is possible to
provide enough energy for unrestrained growth in this country through
the year 2000. It would require "very aggressive development of all our
possible resources—oil and gas on-shore and off-shore, coal, shale, nuclear power. If it proved feasible to increase oil imports on a large scale,
then the pressure on domestic resources would relax somewhat. Still, the
political, economic, and environmental problems of getting that much
energy out of the earth would be formidable." In this scenario, the energy
consumption in the year 2000 would be about 185 quadrillion BTU's as
compared with a current consumption of 75 quadrillion BTU's in 1973.

The second scenario outlined by the study is labeled "technical fix."
This scenario reflects "a determined, conscious national effort to reduce
demand for energy through the application of energy-saving technologies." While this scenario provides a similar level and mix of goods
and services to the historical growth scenario, the slower rate of energy
growth provides greater flexibility in terms of which resources will be
used to supply the needed energy. "Only one of the major domestic
sources of energy—Rocky Mountain coal or shale, or nuclear power, or oil
and gas—would have to be pushed hard to meet the energy growth rates
of this scenario," the study concludes. The technical fix scenario, however, "still provides a quality of life at home, travel convenience, and
economic growth that, to our minds at least, differs little from the historical growth scenario." The energy demand in the year 2000 under the
technical fix scenario is 118 quadrillion BTU's.

"Zero energy growth" is the third scenario. The study points out that
it represents "a real break with our customary way of doing things. Yet it
does not represent austerity. It would give everyone in the United States

more energy benefits in the year 2000 than he enjoys today, even enough
to allow the less privileged to catch up to the comforts of the American
way of life." The study emphasizes that the zero energy growth scenario
does not preclude economic growth. The hypothesis is that such a
scenario might come about if society became enough concerned about the
social and environmental costs of energy growth and if it appeared that
technology could not solve problems associated with energy growth. Such
a scenario might also reflect broader social concerns, ". . . like uneasiness
about the dehumanizing aspects of large, centralized institutions. Zero
energy growth would emphasize durability, not disposability of goods. It
would substitute for the idea that 'more is better,' the ethic that 'enough is
best.' " The energy demand under the zero energy growth scenario in the
year 2000 is estimated to be 100 quadrillion BTU's. According to the
study, ". . . all three scenarios share certain characteristics. They all assume household comforts and conveniences greater than today's; no one
must live in a lightless shack or a sweltering tenement because of energy
scarcity. Every American would have a warm home in winter, air conditioning in hot climates, a kitchen complete with appliances. He would still
drive a car and have a job although he might drive less or have a different
job depending on the scenario the nation follows."

The growth rates used in suggesting these scenarios were not arbi-
trarily chosen, the study points out. Instead, they represent the sum of the
growth which the research done by the EPP has shown to be likely in all
energy-using components of our society. Government data on population
forecasts were used, and forecasts for transportation needs and energy
requirements of home appliances and industry were developed by the
staff for the various scenarios.

The description of the various scenarios follows the discussion of
several other aspects of the energy situation. The first section outlines
current patterns of energy consumption broken down by residential
energy use, commercial energy use, transportation energy use, industrial
energy use, and electricity. This section also looks at the status of energy
supplies. Specifically considered are oil, natural gas, coal, and nuclear
power. An outline of the reasons for the current energy problem facing
the United States is given. Another section of the study looks at various
objectives of a national energy policy and the tools and constraints of
achieving those objectives.

The impact of foreign policy developments on the energy situation is
briefly examined in another section of the study. The impact of energy
development on air pollution and land use is considered as well as the
specific impact of coal, oil, oil shale, and nuclear power development on
the environment. Available federal energy resources and the problems of
using them to meet the energy demands of the future are examined, and

the policy options available for the short term, mid-term, and long term are outlined.

Most observers expect the greatest impact of the study to be the finding that economic growth and standard of living can be increased at a rate that is not completely dependent on the growth of energy. One of the arguments that has long been advanced is that there is a simple and direct relationship between economic growth and the growth in energy usage. The finding of the EPP study that this is not necessarily the case is expected to have tremendous impact in Congress and throughout the federal government in formulating policies to meet the energy crisis. Two of the most immediate short-term effects expected are to provide fresh ammunition to those in the federal government who stress the value and importance of energy conservation, and the need to proceed judiciously in the development of energy policies so that social, environmental, and consumer considerations are given the proper priority. In addition, this report from a highly respected and reliable independent research organization is expected by many observers to make it more difficult for the Ford Administration to sell its program of greatly increasing energy supply as the only means of dealing with the energy crisis. The major impact on Congress is expected to be a change in the atmosphere in which such measures as the Emergency Energy Act, the coal stripping regulation legislation, and legislation related to such areas as oil shale development and outer continental shelf drilling are considered. The very fact that choices are available and that a higher standard of living as outlined in the technical fix and zero energy growth scenarios is possible without the increase in energy consumption of the historical growth scenario could do much to reduce the sense of panic with which many observers feel some congressmen tend to view the energy crisis.

In addition, the parts of the study that deal with specific energy sources, such as coal, oil, and nuclear power, are expected by some observers to have an effect on legislation relating to these areas. With regard to coal, for example, the study questions the advisability and long-term need for stripping coal from slopes over 20 degrees. With regard to oil shale, the study points out the great difficulties of revegetating spent shale. The unique problems and uncertainties of nuclear power are also listed briefly in the study.

Ecological Aspects of Exponential Growth of Energy Demand[5]

What we are dealing with, essentially, are the principles of ecology. It has long been known by ecologists that the population of any biologic species, if given a favorable environment, will increase exponentially with time; that is, that the population will double repeatedly at roughly equal intervals of time. From our previous observations, we have seen that this is also true of industrial components. For example, the world electric power capacity is now growing at 8 percent per year and is doubling every 8.7 years (Figure 8-1). Both the miles traveled by automobiles and the miles flown per year by the world's civil aviation scheduled flights are doubling every 10 years. The human population is now doubling in 35 years (Figure 8-2).

FIGURE 8-1   World Electricity-Generating Capacity As an Example of Exponential Growth

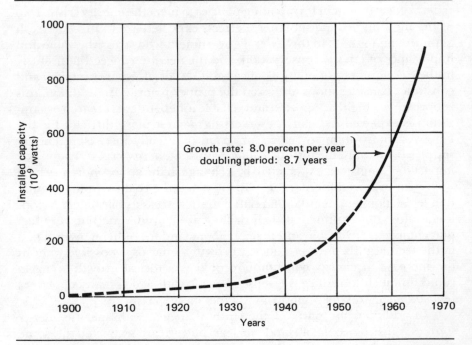

Growth rate: 8.0 percent per year
doubling period: 8.7 years

Source: M. King Hubbert, "World Energy Demands and the Middle East," (Washington, D.C.: Middle East Institute, 26th Annual Conference, 1972); also appearing in "Survey of World Energy Resources," Canadian Institute of Mining and Metallurgy *Bulletin* (July 1973).

The second part of this ecological principle is that such exponential growth of any biologic population can be maintained for only a limited number of doublings before retarding influences set in. In the biological case, these influences may be represented by restriction of food supply, by crowding, or by environmental pollution. The complete biologic growth curve is represented by the logistics curve of Figure 8-3.

That there must be limits to growth can easily be seen by the most elementary arithmetic analysis. Consider the familiar checkerboard problem of packing one grain of wheat on the first square, two on the second, four on the third, and doubling the number for each successive square. The number of grains on the nth square will be 2^{n-1}, and on the last or

FIGURE 8-2   Growth of Human Population Since the Year 1000 A.D. As an Example of an Ecological Disturbance

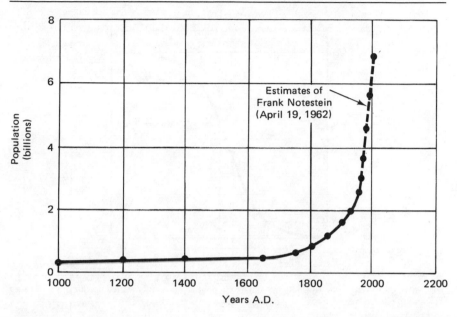

Source: Hubbert, *op. cit.*

64th square, 2^{63}. The sum of the grains on the entire board will be twice this amount less one grain, or $2^{64} - 1$. When translated into volume of wheat, it turns out that the quantity of wheat required for the last square would equal approximately 1,000 times the present world annual wheat crop, and the requirement for the whole board would be twice this amount.

If, instead of wheat grains, one average-size American automobile could be doubled 64 times and if the resulting cars were stacked evenly over all the land areas of the earth, they could form a layer 2,000 kilometers, or 1,200 miles, deep.

From such simple examples, it follows unequivocally that exponential growth, either biological or industrial, can be only a temporary phenomenon because the earth itself cannot tolerate more than a few tens of doublings of any biological or industrial component. Furthermore, most of these possible doublings have occurred already.

After the cessation of exponential growth, any individual component has only three possible futures: (1) it may, as in the case of water power, level off and stabilize at a maximum; (2) it may overshoot and, after passing a maximum, decline and stabilize at some intermediate level capable of being sustained; or (3) it may decline to zero and become extinct.

FIGURE 8-3   Logistic Growth Curve

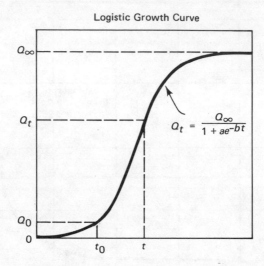

Logistic Growth Curve

$$Q_t = \frac{Q_\infty}{1 + ae^{-bt}}$$

The logistic growth curve showing both the initial exponential phase and the final slowing down during a cycle of growth.

Source: Hubbert, *op. cit.*

Applied to human society, these three possibilities are illustrated graphically in Figure 8-4. What stands out most clearly is that our present phase of exponential growth based upon man's ability to control ever larger quantities of energy can be only a temporary period of about three centuries duration in the totality of human history. It represents but a brief transitional epoch between two very much longer periods, each characterized by rates of change to slow as to be regarded essentially as periods of non-growth. Although the forthcoming period poses no insuperable physical or biological difficulties, it can hardly fail to force a major revision in those aspects of our current culture whose tenets are dependent upon the assumption that the growth rates that have characterized this temporary period can somehow be sustained indefinitely.

The Importance of Conservation
An exhaustive, 19-month study by the House of Representatives Government Operations Committee gives the United States only five years to cut in half its astonishing rate of increase in energy consumption.[6] Otherwise, the quality of American life will significantly deteriorate. The 133-page report optimistically concludes that the necessary cuts can be made and that our standard of living can be maintained. But, the report

FIGURE 8-4   Epoch of Current Industrial Growth in the Context of a Longer Span of Human History

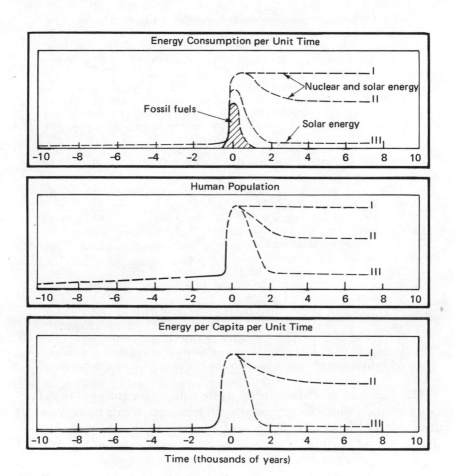

Time (thousands of years)

Source: Hubbert, *op. cit.*

declares, it will take some sacrifice, enormous ingenuity, and, perhaps above all, decisive government leadership.

The report cites a myriad of needed household conservation measures requiring little capital investment, from turning down thermostats to tuning up auto engines. These should be combined with government encouragement for changes in transportation habits, building design, and resource reclamation. The report also cites applaudable, but scattered steps that private industry is now taking. Some of these innovative ideas are listed below.

1. Dow Chemical is using infrared photography to detect heat loss in plants.
2. General Motors and E.I. DuPont deNemours have found that they can manufacture goods with techniques that save 10 to 30 percent energy.
3. Michigan Consolidated Gas has contracted with its gas customers to put up to six inches of insulation in their homes and to add the cost to the gas bill, interest free. The energy savings: 17 percent for houses more than 35 years old, 10 percent for newer homes.

Other dramatic industrial success stories have been seen elsewhere.

1. TRW, Inc. cut its electricity bill for 1974 by more than $120,000 at just one of its plants in Cleveland.
2. The distribution centers of Sears, Roebuck & Co. and J.C. Penney Co. in Atlanta report power savings of as much as 30 percent in recent months, simply by spreading out nonessential loads into time periods of lighter demand and hence lower unit cost.
3. Aetna Life and Casualty of Hartford has figured out a dollar saving of 55 percent on its energy bills through a conservation program.
4. IBM launched an ambitious energy conservation program in 1973 and, in just 10 months, 33 of the company's major plant, laboratory, and headquarter locations across the country reported savings in fuel of 30 percent, the equivalent of enough gallons of oil to heat over 16,000 homes in the Northeast for an entire year.

The stunning fact about such waste-cutting measures is that they require virtually no major capital alterations or operating upheavals. All that is involved is turning lights and equipment off when not in use, reducing lighting in public rooms, setting thermostats at 68 degrees, and other such mundane measures. Although some of the examples above are relatively light energy consumers, significant savings can also be made with energy-intensive industries.

Savings by Industry.   Voluntary conservation measures were responsible for a 7.6 percent median energy reduction per unit of 1974 output. A Commerce Department survey also revealed that conservation practices were in evidence before the Arab oil embargo in fall of 1973. The report indicated that energy savings per unit of output during 1973 improved 4.8 percent over the previous year.[7]

Savings by Federal Agencies.   According to the Federal Energy Administrator, Frank G. Zarb, government agencies reduced overall demand for energy by 24 percent. The original target of 7 percent was easily exceeded because of the energy savings efforts of the Department of Defense (25 percent savings), NASA (24 percent savings), and General Services Administration (21 percent savings). The total dollars saved amounted to 725 million, or more than 90 million barrels of oil.[8]

LAND-USE POLICY ISSUES

Land-use patterns have reached a critical point in the nation's growth cycle. Land has multiple uses for both mankind and the ecosystem. Although the human being is a part of the earth's ecosystem, his treatment of land often ignores this vital web of life. In drastically altering rivers, marshes, lakes, coastal regions, deserts, mountain ranges, prairies, and the unique ecosystems that inhabit these areas mankind is breaking the interdependent links that join the fragile ecosystems. Often the changes not only result in disruption of the environment in the initial sense, but also from subsequent activities flow the toxic pollutants of commerce and urbanization. Moreover, cumulative damages to land surface areas continue to complicate reclamation and restoration.

Land-use policies must skirt sensitive political, social, and economic factors. Balancing these factors will be increasingly difficult if the nation chooses to marshall its remaining finite resources to satisfy exponential growth trends which waste energy, metals, rare earths, fiber, food, etc. We could literally destory our vast open spaces within the next 20 years if raw material acquisition and exponential economic growth become an obsession. With a sound land-use policy, the nation could balance resource acquisition with conservation and maintain a manageable growth rate. Pollution controls and effective zoning of land uses would serve as important stabilizing factors in both the social and ecological sense.

Urban Sprawls

The massive urban growth structure must be managed without destroying the distinctiveness of neighborhoods and communities. The new challenge in land-use management involves developing and maintaining a balanced, creative tension between the forces of development and the forces of conservation. Too often, land-use patterns have reflected social or cultural imbalance and tensions. The migration from suburbia to small towns and rural areas reflects a sense of frustration among many living within urban sprawls.

We are fast reaching the point where there is not really any place for large numbers of people to run and maintain the basic characteristics of the region. Moreover, population shifts represent only one facet of the land-use problem. Industrial requirements for additional land in extracting, processing, and transporting raw materials are growing exponentially.

Fading Green Belts
Unplanned growth of urban sprawls threatens to devour much of the countryside. Many new housing developments are badly planned, poorly constructed, and completely lack basic environmental principles. Many of these developments are modular in the sense that they are subject to rapid obsolescence. Today's typical new residential development often resembles a sterile wasteland—houses built one on top of another—devoid of trees and shrubs and lacking sufficient open space for recreational, spiritual, and esthetic pursuits. Secondary construction brings supportive commercial businesses and industries into new suburban developments; open spaces fill up rapidly. Fragile marshes, estuaries, streams, plant life, and wildlife are destroyed in man's frantic rush to open up new showings or plats.

The Costs of Urban Sprawls
The urban sprawl, with its strip highways and modular-like suburbs, is the subject of a new $150,000 study jointly sponsored by the Department of Housing and Urban Development, the EPA, and the Council on Environmental Quality.[9] The study attempts to place an economic value on unplanned growth. Comparing low-density sprawl, low-density planned development, and planned high density, the report finds these dollar estimates, among others:

1. Total capital costs for a hypothetical high-density community are 56 percent of those for a low-density sprawl development. This translates into a dollar savings of $227.5 million.
2. Given the same two hypothetical communities, savings in land cost for the high-density community amounts to 43 percent, or $12.7 million; savings on streets, 40 percent, or $15.1 million; and savings on utilities, 63 percent, or $39.5 million.
3. Operating and maintenance cost for the high-density planned community would be $2 million less annually, or 11 percent, than for the low-density sprawl community.
4. A more tightly knit roadway system in planned developments not only reduces auto travel, but also pollution (by 20 to 30 percent) and energy expenditure (by 8 to 14 percent).
5. A savings of $1.5 million, or 20 percent, would be realized in building a shopping center in a planned area rather than in a strip development, primarily because of lower land costs.

Minimizing Adverse Impacts
Urbanization will continue for some time to come. Our population is still growing and will continue to grow well into the 21st century. Although

the United States has attained a fertility rate that will eventually produce zero population growth (2.1 children per woman of childbearing age), it must remain at that level for about 75 years before population growth would actually cease. This means that there will be many new households in the years immediately ahead. Demand for housing and supporting facilities should continue strong (although in not the same dimensions as past trends in housing units and facilitating facilities).

There is, however, no need to live in an asphalt jungle or sterile environment. Planners and developers can be taught not only to minimize the adverse environmental impact of their operations, but also to plan for habitat preservation and green belts. With the proper use of open space, careful landscaping, and the right kind of building design, urban and suburban areas can have great esthetic appeal and still support a varied ecosystem complete with wildlife and natural esthetics.[10]

Planned communities are the major means of reversing the destructive effects of urban sprawl (once referred to by an environmentalist as "a melastisizing biological disaster"). New cities such as Columbia, Maryland, and also Reston, Virginia, have pioneered the open space renaissance. In fact, Columbia has placed 28 percent, or better than one-fourth, of its land in permanent open space.

Effective urban land-use planning will require the resolution of the following problem areas of sprawl developments:

1. Incorporating spatial and ethestic land-surface features with even the most impacted urban areas.
2. Restructuring living-working-shopping relationships that de-emphasize distance as a means for achieving life-style requirements.
3. Reclaiming blighted industrial, commercial, and residential slums. This will require new taxing schemes that penalize owners who do not maintain property.
4. Revitalizing infrastructure services that support the health, safety, and the vitality of communities. The inevitable payment of such services must somehow be more equitably borne. Escaping taxation for delivered services is often hidden in lead-lag tax assessments, which penalizes the urban landowners more than owners of newly constructed suburbs, where tax rates often start from lower agricultural rates for farmland.
5. Zoning land use for the total socioeconomic impact which is desired. Too often zoning regulations are punctured by exemptions from influential commercial interests. Strip developments and "leap frog" real estate home building schemes should be discouraged.
6. Altering transportation patterns within urban sprawls. Urban transit facilities represent a critically needed mode of transportation for cities. The greater efficiency and lower pollution levels of mass transit are two obvious advantages. The potential for creating new land use and community patterns (living, working, shopping) are enhanced if fast, efficient mass transit lines are available.

Legislative Land-Use Strategies

Planning land-use requirements for urban regions must, by necessity, employ comprehensive concepts. We must incorporate rural communities in a national land-use policy statement. For purposes of organizational convenience, the federal legislative thrust is incorporated under the *urban* subject heading. Land-use reform may well require the following legislative thrust:

1. Federal assistance in the form of grants-in-aid available to states. The development and administration of comprehensive land-use planning processes are highly emphasized in this category.
2. Creation of an interagency policy and planning board to aid in the management of the grant program.
3. Creation of an office of land-use policy and planning administration in the Department of the Interior.
4. Giving direction to public land management agencies to develop and maintain land-use plans for the public lands.

For land use plans to be effectively designed and implemented, society will be required to evaluate, weigh, and balance the following factors:

1. Upholding the rights of private property—its use, its enjoyment, and its economic value (protection and rights to a reasonable compensation if taken for public purposes).
2. Maintaining reasonable access and use of public lands, monuments, parks, grazing regions, etc. by the public and commercial users of such public lands. This use must be balanced by ecological and esthetic qualities, or uniquely fragile and valuable characteristics of public resources.
3. Satisfying individual life-style choices in context with group conformity pressures.
4. Sustaining the concept of local governments in the face of more centralized federal participation in land-use policy formulation.

Rural Lands

Urban land-use requirements are intensive in most respects. Problems are compressed into relatively small geographical areas. Because most of the American population lives in urban regions, the news-reporting processes emphasize conflicts and crises that confront urban dwellers. But, the quiet, peaceful appearance of vast rural areas throughout most of America is largely illusionary. The developing crisis in rural land-use patterns threatens to revamp farming, recreational, wilderness, and strategically important coastal land resources. These often quiet rural crises go unnoticed in the news headlines, but they involve entire ecosystems and social issues that can determine the eventual fate of the nation.

Since we have discussed most major environmental issues that relate to rural land use in previous sections (another discussion can be found in Case 15), we have simply summarized the major rural land-use issues below.

1. Protecting and enlarging the National Park system.
2. Preserving the integrity of wilderness regions.
3. Retaining the vitality of diverse ecosystems whether they are near urban regions or are located in sensitive or unique natural regions.
4. Controlling pollution levels. Sewer wastes rank at the top of the list of serious pollution problems.
5. Preserving and managing wildlife as an essential web in nature's ecosystem.
6. Sustaining green belts and open agricultural areas even near or within urban sprawls. (Taxation often forces landowners to sell agricultural land near housing developments.

WATER RESOURCE POLICY ISSUES

Water appears to be ubiquitous and bountiful to many persons. Water resources are highly strategic in sustaining nature's many balances in the ecosystem. Water resources interact with the land, the air, and with man's biologic and economic requirements. All of nature's creatures dip from the same source, whether water appears underground, on the surface, or as airborne vapor; and water must be reused.

Water can be polluted and supplies can be completely depleted. The tendencies of nature are to vary the quantity of precipitation that falls over the land surface. Such variations serve to make water a natural resource that requires careful management. As such, it is both a finite resource and a critically important factor in the ecosystem.

National Water Commission Report
Culminating almost 4½ years of effort, during which it met 54 times and prepared 60 background studies, the National Water Commission report concluded that the government is pouring massive amounts of money into channelization and irrigation projects while beneficiaries contribute little toward the cost.[11]

The 570-page landmark report of the seven-man Commission, established by Congress in September 1968, contains 232 specific recommendations for improving future water resources policies to adapt them to future needs. Publication of the report followed field hearings on a draft version of the document made public in late 1972.

The need to protect the environment by coordinating land-use and water-planning functions is emphasized in the report, which also calls for greater reliance on state and local governments and nongovernment groups to implement water-development programs and to improve water quality, better data collection and research and development programs, modifications of laws and institutions that regulate present policies, more economy and efficiency in the use of water, and conservation of energy, which affects water use.

The Commission seeks relief for the American taxpayer, pointing out that the public today carries too large a burden of the cost of many water programs that benefit identifiable segments of American business and industry.

A major thrust of the report indicates that there is presently enough water to meet essential needs but not enough to waste, and that water is no different from any other natural resource except that it is more essential than many others. Water should therefore be considered an economic resource, and the Commission believes that all users receiving an economic return from water should pay full costs of services.

Seven basic themes pervade the 17 chapters of the Commission's report and provide a foundation for conclusions and recommendations it reached:

1. The demands for water in the future are not predetermined, but depend largely on policy decisions that can be controlled by society.
2. Future water programs should shift emphasis from water development to preservation and enhancement of water quality.
3. Planning for water development must be linked to planning for water quality and coordinated with land-use planning.
4. More efficient use of water in agriculture, in industry, and for domestic and municipal purposes is essential to reduce waste.
5. Sound economic principles must be adopted to encourage better use of water resources. The Commission considers consumer willingness to pay to be the most reliable economic indicator of proper water use, if it is coordinated with government regulation of environmental protection.
6. Updated laws and legal institutions are needed if future water policies are to be successfully implemented.
7. Development, management, and protection of water resources should be controlled by the level of government (federal, state, local, or regional) that is closest to specific problems and is capable of fairly representing all interests involved.

About one-fourth of the Commission's 232 recommendations concern land and water planning and relationships among various aspects of water resources programs. Roughly 20 percent of the recommendations deal with changes in legal systems that regulate and control use of water. They include improvement of state laws relating to use of ground and surface waters, changes in state laws to increase recognition of the social values of water, improvement of procedures for recording and transferring water rights, development of permit systems for regulating water use under riparian water law in the Eastern states, and a proposed federal statute to reduce conflicts between federal and state systems of water law.

The Commission's recommendations on cost sharing among federal, state, and local governments and the beneficiaries of water development are among the more controversial portions of the report. In addition to the recommendations for strengthening the role of the federal government in combining water-resources planning and land-use planning, the Commission recommends that identifiable beneficiaries of water programs and projects be required to pay the full costs of developments that give them economic benefits. Adoption of these recommendations would make a drastic change in programs such as inland navigation, flood control, and irrigation, where the federal taxpayer has been bearing from 50 to 100 percent of the cost.

For flood control, the Commission recommends that identifiable beneficiaries be required to bear the full costs of flood control and land drainage programs that benefit them. This is part of a series of recommendations asking for an entirely new approach to flood damage reduction that calls for greater reliance on flood-plain management, flood forecasting, and other non-structural measures for reducing the annual flood-damage toll. Annual flood damages are increasing rapidly despite large federal expenditures for structural measures to control flooding.

No changes are recommended in the existing project for flood control on the lower Mississippi River, where the federal government bears substantially all of the costs of operating and maintaining the levee and floodway system. The Commission believes that since the West has been won 'there is no reason to provide additional interest-free money for new irrigation development in the 17 western states provided for in the federal reclamation laws. The Commission points out that more than three-fourths of the irrigated land in the West has been developed without federal subsidy.

Conservationists are especially pleased that a special section on stream channelization is included in Chapter 2 of the final report. Considerable criticism had been leveled at the Commission during field hearings held last winter because the review draft of the report overlooked the adverse environmental effects of channelization. The report now contains an impartial five-page discussion of channelization, including some excellent "before and after" photographs.

In many cases insufficient weight has been given to the detrimental consequences of channelization and particularly to losses not readily expressed in monetary terms. There seems to be a tendency to more fully weigh all aspects that would result from channelization projects; we should not underestimate or even ignore some operation and maintenance expenses and damages resulting from lowering of groundwater tables, destruction of fish and wildlife habitat, increase in downstream sedimentation and flood damages, and loss of esthetic values.

Three basic study recommendations concerning stream channelization clearly emerge. These recommendations include:

1. All agencies responsible for planning and carrying out channelization projects should broaden and otherwise improve their evaluation procedures, making a special effort to reflect in the cost estimates damages caused by increased downstream flooding and sedimentation, lowering of groundwater levels, and loss of fish and wildlife habitat and esthetic values. The full cost of continuing maintenance should also be reflected.
2. All future proposals for channelization projects should be required to indicate the part of the cost thereof that is properly allocable to increasing the value of lands in private ownership, and no such project should be approved unless and until an appropriate nonfederal entity has agreed to assume that part of the project cost.
3. In considering requests for funds to carry out previously authorized channelization plans, the Appropriations Committees of the Congress should require, from both the agency that would be responsible for the use of these funds and the Council on Environmental Quality, statements on the probable effects of the proposed undertaking on downstream flood and sedimentation problems, on groundwater levels, on fish and wildlife habitat, and on esthetic and other noneconomic values; and these committees should provide for the funding of only those projects for which, in their opinion, the benefits are sufficient to justify both the monetary and nonmonetary costs to the nation.

In the field of water-pollution control, the Commission rejects the zero-discharge goal of the 1972 amendments to the federal Water Pollution Control Act as unattainable, and calls instead for achievement by 1983 of the water-quality standards established under the Water Quality Act of 1965, which could cost as much as $200 billion. The Commission proposes full financing of the federal program of grants for construction of municipal sewage collection and treatment facilities.

Many other provisions of the 1972 amendments are endorsed by the Commission, but clarification of provisions for federal and state responsibilities is recommended in order to provide a sound basis for restoration of American waterways to meet established water-quality standards by the 1983 deadline.

Under the Commission's recommendations, cost of pollution abatement (or process changes to minimize discharge of pollutants) would be paid by the polluters. Deviation from the Commission's "polluter pay" principal is needed for the 10-year period to eliminate the backlog of municipal sewage-treatment facilities needed to meet the stringent standards required under federal water-pollution control legislation.

In offering its recommendations, the Commission recognizes the significant role that federal agencies and programs have played and will continue to play in the American economy. But the Commission believes that as the demands for water approach the upper limits of an essentially fixed supply, it is necessary that the people of the nation, through their representatives in Congress, look at proposed but unauthorized federal water programs. These programs involve expenditures of over $4 billion in the budget for fiscal year 1974. The Commission suggests replacing outmoded and time-worn policies with new ones aimed at meeting the water needs of the future, not the past.

Some of the recommendations in the report are addressed to the president, some to the Congress, and others to various federal and state agencies or to the water industry and the public in general. The Commission hopes that the recommendations will be used by those seeking improvements in policy and procedures as a basis for future legislative and administrative action at all levels of government and throughout the water industry. Some of the policies covered in the recommendations are already being considered by various committees of Congress; for example, legislation designed to improve land-use planning, to establish drinking-water standards, and to modify the scope of the desalting research program.

Case 15
A Case for Clean Air: An Integrative Approach

CLEAN AIR ACT OF 1970

The goal of the Clean Air Act of 1970 is "to protect and enhance the Nation's air quality." Under its authority, the Environmental Protection Agency (EPA) has set "national ambient air quality standards" for six major pollutants: sulfur oxides, particulates, carbon monoxide, photochemical oxidants, hydrocarbons, and nitrogen oxides. *Primary* national standards limit the amount of a pollutant in the air to a level which will ensure protection of our *health. Secondary* standards further limit pollution to levels which protect our *welfare* by reducing the negative effects on visibility, weather, climate, plant and animal life, man-made property and materials, etc. Although EPA knows of many other pollutants in the air, it lacks sufficient information about them to set national ambient standards. Thus, air pollution control promises to be a long, ongoing process.

To achieve the primary and secondary national standards, every polluter has to cut down on its emissions. At the direction of Congress, EPA has set emission limitations on pollution from *mobile sources*—cars,

Thomas L. Kimball, *Conservation Report,* Situation Report No. 1 (February 18, 1975), pp. 1–6.

trucks, buses—as well as *new stationary sources*—power plants, factories, refineries. The states have set limitations for *existing sources*. If all the polluters in a state meet these emission limitations and the air still is not clean enough to achieve the primary and secondary national ambient air quality standards, the state must go further in its cleanup efforts. It must use transportation and land-use controls to discourage auto transportation and restrict construction of new sources.

Each state is required to develop an implementation plan which takes into consideration the pollution levels within its boundaries and the different measures—emission limitations, transportation controls, land-use controls—which must be implemented to ensure the achievement of a statewide air quality that meets the national standards. All provisions of state implementation plans must be approved by EPA. The law and EPA do not specify which particular kinds of pollution controls are to be used. The initial choice is up to the polluters. But EPA approves the selection of controls to make sure they are in compliance with the law.

THE ISSUES

The implementation of the CAA has been a slow, arduous process (with technical problems and legal disputes). The original deadlines for compliance with auto emission limitations have been postponed from 1975 until 1977. Many parts of the country are still short of the monitoring equipment they need to keep tabs on their air quality. According to EPA (at the outset of 1975—the year in which the nation's air was to be cleaned), many of the 247 air quality control regions will not achieve the primary national standards this year. The issues mentioned before—fuel economy, sulfate, tall stacks, scrubbers, significant deterioration, land-use—have a lot to do with the delays in cleaning up our air.

FUEL ECONOMY AND AUTO EMISSIONS

The first issue to draw special attention in 1975 is a proposed five-year modification of the 1977 auto emission limitations. It is intended to facilitate a 40 percent improvement in fuel economy—the mileage we get for the gallons we buy. Right now most of the nation is working on meeting interim auto emission limitations that will lead to compliance with the final 1977 ones. However, California, which led the way in pollution generation in the 1960s, as well as in control research, is working under a stricter set of interim limitations.

Pressures for repealing the 1977 federal limitations and requiring the rest of the country to catch up to California's interim 1975 goals for controlling carbon monoxide and hydrocarbon emissions have surfaced.

In exchange for this postponement in auto pollution control goals, the auto manufacturers have promised to improve the fuel economy of their cars. The average fuel economy for all 1981 model cars must be at least 40 percent better than the average for all 1974 model cars sold. That works out to 19.6 miles per gallon (mpg) in 1981 (or 18.7 mpg for American-made cars and 21.4 mpg for foreigns) compared with the 1974 average of 14.1 mpg. These average fuel economies are based on the number of cars sold, not just manufactured. In other words, if a manufacturer is planning to sell cars which get poor mileage, he must also sell enough automobiles with high fuel economies to bring up the fuel economy average.

Some environmentalists have sharply criticized trading the nation's air quality and health for "promises" from the auto industry. They point out that the industry is two years behind in meeting the emission limitations Congress originally required to be achieved this year, and it is seeking further delays. As for the manufacturers' promises, the government will keep an eye on them. If they do not appear to be living up to their word, the Administration says it will start thinking about seeking legislation to require fuel economy improvements.

Stronger criticisms have been raised on whether it is even necessary to compromise pollution control standards in order to improve auto fuel economy. Last October, EPA and the Department of Transportation (DOT) issued a report entitled "Potential for Motor Vehicle Fuel Economy Improvement." It concluded that at least a 20 percent improvement and possibly a 40 to 60 percent improvement can be achieved without sacrificing the 1977 emission limitations for hydrocarbons and carbon monoxide. Other reports have confirmed this finding.

Economically, the answer is less clear. Opponents argue that the estimated $300 million price increase that will come from meeting both pollution control standards and fuel economy improvements goals will further sour consumer buying. In an economy pushing unemployment rates above 8 percent, that is unacceptable. But the EPA–DOT report says that savings in fuel and maintenance costs resulting from fuel economy improvements are "substantially greater than associated increases in the initial price of cars. The combined effect of these changes on auto sales is not great."

So the apparent reason for changing the auto emission limitations is economics. Unanswered are questions about how much of the continually increasing auto prices will be reduced by not meeting the 1977 standards. Unknown is just how much consumer buying will be influenced by promises of savings in maintenance and operating costs.

SULFATES, DISPERSION, TALL STACKS, AND SCRUBBERS

The EPA took an intensive look at the fuel economy question during a three-week series of technical hearings that concluded on February 7,

1975. In the course of those hearings, a far more disturbing issue arose. Preliminary data developed by the Agency indicate that the oxidation catalyst which most auto manufacturers have selected to control hydrocarbon and carbon monoxide emissions, actually increases sulfate emissions. In fact, EPA speculates that after four years, continued use of the catalyst by cars could begin to pose a net health risk to society—aggravated respiratory conditions, heart and lung diseases, and premature mortalities. But without the catalysts, most cars could not achieve the 1977 emission limitations for hydrocarbons and carbon monoxide unless thoe limitations are revised.

The sulfate problem is especially pertinent due to a long-running, intense dispute over requirements for cleaning up sulfur oxide emissions from power plants and other stationary sources. The power industry contends that dispersing the sulfur dioxide (SO_2) emissions high into the air satisfied the law's requirements. EPA has countered that dispersion leads to the formation of sulfates, which are more dangerous to human health than SO_2 itself. Therefore, EPA asserts, the emissions from the smoke stacks must be reduced. The shortage of low-sulfur oil has heightened the demand for coal combustion, which in turn increases SO_2 emissions.

Here, again, economy has a lot to do with the controversy. To disperse pollutants requires the construction of super-tall stacks plus monitoring equipment to let a plant know when the wind is not strong enough to carry away the emissions. The cost of this kind of dispersion control can run into the millions of dollars. As for actually reducing emissions, flue gas desulfurization systems—better known as scrubbers—are the only substantially proven technology outside of burning low-sulfur fuel. Their cost can run into the tens and hundreds of millions of dollars. That, plus industry contention that the technology is not really proven, have kept the flames of controversy aglow.

EPA has waged a lonely fight for scrubbers. Lacking enough data to set a specific national standard for sulfates, the Agency has concluded that reducing SO_2 emissions is the only alternative to protect public health. The Fifth Circuit Court of Appeals has agreed that abatement, not dispersion, is required by the CAA. The U.S. Court of Appeals in the District of Columbia has confirmed the technical viability of scrubber technology. EPA further substantiated it in its own investigations in the fall of 1973 and the summer of 1974.

Nevertheless, the power industry has fought hard against scrubbers. Its most visible campaign was conducted on the advertisement pages of newspapers and magazines throughout the country when the American Electric Power System spent more than three million dollars making its objections to scrubbers and EPA known to the public.

Although the Nixon White House supported tall stacks and dispersion, neither EPA nor Congress bought them. Congress did pass the Energy

Supply and Environmental Coordination Act to authorize the Federal Energy Administration (FEA) to order plants to convert from natural gas or oil burning to coal combustion. It also authorized EPA to extend compliance schedules for pollution control for converted plants, provided that health standards are met.

The Administration is requesting extension of this authority as well as extension of FEA's authority to enforce conversions until 1985. It also is recommending authorizing EPA to postpone compliance schedules for emission controls on such plants until 1985. Unlike its predecessor, the Ford Administration is not pushing use of tall stacks and dispersion. However, it does favor their temporary use. In certain isolated areas, tall stacks and intermittent controls to disperse emissions would be permitted for up to 10 years. This would affect no more than 20 to 70 power plants, according to EPA. Either scrubbers or low-sulfate fuel combustion would be required everywhere else. EPA says this is a major victory for its scrubber position. Some environmentalists see it as a victory for the American Electric Power System's high-powered ad campaign, since EPA originally expected that scrubbers would be required on about 90 to 100 plants. They also argue that those plants which are permitted to use tall stacks on a temporary basis will have 10 years to continue to pressure EPA and Congress to allow their use permanently.

SIGNIFICANT DETERIORATION AND KEEPING THE CLEAN AIR CLEAN

There is more to pollution control than cleaning up the dirty air. It also involves keeping clean air clean. At least that is what many environmentalists have contended since the Clean Air Act's enactment. The EPA was less convinced at first, and it has taken several court decisions to begin to change its mind. There are really two issues involved: (1) preventing the deterioration of air that is even cleaner than the national primary and secondary standards; and (2) maintaining air quality standards in areas where the dirty air has been cleaned up.

In the first case, litigation went all the way to the Supreme Court in 1973 which upheld a lower-court ruling that EPA must prevent the "significant" deterioration of pristine air quality. Environmentalists rejoiced, and EPA moaned, for neither the courts nor Congress have defined how much deterioration is "significant." After struggling for over a year to come up with a definition, EPA turned it over to the states. Arguing that defining significant deterioration is a subjective matter that will vary from state to state, EPA issued regulations in November which divide the pristine air areas into three classes: Class I—no deterioration; Class II—some deterioration; Class III—as much deterioration as possible without violating primary and secondary national standards.

Initially, all areas have been designated Class II. But any state may redesignate its pristine areas once it has held public hearings on its proposed changes. As a result of these regulations, EPA is back in court again—being sued by environmentalists, power companies, and states who all object to the regulations for different reasons.

The prevention of significant deterioration is not the only case in which the courts have had to tell EPA what the law means. In January 1973, the U.S. Court of Appeals in the District of Columbia informed EPA that the law requires not only the attainment of primary and secondary national standards but also their maintenance. Since then, EPA has identified 147 areas in the country in which there exists a potential for exceeding one or more of the national standards within 10 years unless plans are drawn up to avoid it.

LAND USE

The issues of prevention of "significant deterioration" and "maintenance of air quality" have more in common than court rulings and regulatory hassles. Implicit in both is recognition of the need for land-use planning in ultimately controlling pollution. Cutting back emissions from mobile and stationary sources is an important first step in cleaning up the nation's air. But when enough polluters using controls are located in one area, they still can produce major air pollution problems. At that point, the polluters either have to become nonpolluters or land-use planning has to be implemented to start limiting the number of new polluters.

The Clean Air Act itself recognizes the need for land-use planning in preventing air pollution. Section 110 of the law specifies that state implementation plans should include not only emission limitations, compliance schedules, and timetables but also "land-use and transportation controls." In 1970, Congress realized that if the nation really is going to clean up its air and keep it clean, it has to plan ahead how it will use its resources and redirect growth where it could lead to unsafe air quality.

Transportation controls—charging more for parking or limiting the number of parking spaces in some areas—have received more political attention than anything else on this matter. EPA identified 35 metropolitan areas which will not achieve the primary and secondary standards unless they significantly curtail motor vehicle traffic by discouraging commuting and parking in the city as well as encouraging greater use of mass transportation. Congress itself has had second thoughts about taking the drive out of the American dream. It prohibited parking surcharges when it passed the Energy Supply and Environmental Coordination Act. It then prohibited spending federal monies for parking management plans when it passed EPA's budget for this year. The Administration does not reject the use of transportation controls outright. However, it is calling for more time for their implementation where necessary to avoid economic and social disruption, and extensions of 5 to 10 years have been discussed.

TOPIC QUESTIONS

1. What is the socioecological role of marketing in determining environmental policy for the nation?
2. What are the four major scenarios or options mentioned in the Project Independent Report?
3. What are environmentalists criticisms of the Project Independence Report?
4. After analyzing the legislative policy issues, do you think that the nation must choose between exponential growth or zero growth? What, if any, are the alternatives?
5. What is business doing to conserve energy costs?
6. What new changes are required in order for the nation to have ample clean water supplies by the year 2000?
7. How is a national Land Use policy going to influence the following?
   a. central city cores
   b. suburban sprawls
   c. shopping centers
   d. automobile transportation
8. What broad behavior modification requirements are part of national policy issues?

Case 15

9. Does this case illustrate a basic problem in applying new technological means for controlling air pollution? Is it better to wait until a solution comes along, or to spur industries to seek solutions even if some new techniques eventually fail to resolve a pollution problem?
10. How does the case illustrate trade-off difficulties and limits that decision makers must resolve in deciding the proper balance between consumer interests (price of product) and production incentives (costs and profits)?

RECOMMENDED READINGS

Energy Task Force, *Managing Our Energy Future* (Minneapolis, Minn.: Upper Midwest Council, 1974).

The Cost of Sprawl (Washington, D.C.: U.S. Government Printing Office, Department of Housing and Urban Development, Environmental Protection Agency, and Council on Environmental Quality, 1974).

Project Independence Report (Washington, D.C.: U.S. Government Printing Office, Federal Energy Administration, 1974).

FOOTNOTES

1. According to United States Census Bureau estimates, rural America is experiencing a sharp reversal in the decline of population that began with World War I. During the years 1970 to 1973, an estimated 1,100,000 persons moved into nonmetropolitan areas. Rural population actually increased overall about 4.2 percent. Growth rates in urban areas tapered off to 2.9 percent. In several states the rural population growth exceeded 10 percent. Arizona (+10.3 percent) led in population increases.

2. *Project Independence Report* (Washington, D.C.: U.S. Government Printing Office, 1974), Federal Energy Administration, stock number 4118-00029.

3. *Conservation Report* Situation Report No. 10, (December 23, 1974), pp. 2, 3.

4. *Exploring Energy Choices* (Washington, D.C.: Energy Policy Projects, 1974).

5. The material in this section was derived from M. King Hubbert, *World Energy Demands and The Middle East* (Washington, D.C.: Middle East Institute, 26th Annual Conference, 1972), also appearing in "Survey of World Energy Resources," Canadian Institute of Mining and Metallurgy *Bulletin* (July 1973).

6. As reported in *Conservation News*, Vol. 40, No. 2 (January 15, 1975), pp. 3–5.

7. *The Energy Conservation Program Guide*, (Washington, D.C.: U.S. Commerce Department), 1974.

8. Copies of the Federal Energy Management Program's *1974 Annual Report* may be obtained from Press Room, Office of Communications and Public Affairs, Federal Energy Administration, Washington, D.C. 20461 (202-964-3538).

9. *The Cost of Sprawl* (Washington, D.C.: U.S. Government Printing Office, 1974), sponsored by the Department of Housing and Urban Development, EPA, and the Council on Environmental Quality. The dollar savings were based on funding-construction guidelines in conjunction with projects submitted for federal assistance.

10. For readers interested in an enlightened view of urban life and its environmental relationships, the author recommends two excellent books. Penelope Bonnett, *Nature and the Urban Environment* (Baltimore: New York Press, 1973); Spenser W. Havlick, *The Urban Organism* (New York: MacMillan, 1974).

11. Ken Hampton, "Water Commission Endorses 'User Pay' Concept," *Conservation News* Vol. 38, No. 15 (August 1, 1973), pp. 10–14.

INDEX

(continued)

management, and affluence, 30–37
mix, 32, 143, 147–53
myopia, 130–32
and product development, 144
social, 132
socioecological influences on, 153–54
transvectional view of, 141–43
Mass transit, 123, 220
Mayo, R., 24
McCargo, L., 22
McCormack, M., 70, 71
McDaniel, C. D., 160
McDowell County, 187–91
Meadows, D. H., 63, 76
Meadows, D. L., 76
Media, 210
Mental retardation, 96
Mercury, 170, 186
Mertes, J. E., 49
Microbe, 167
Micromarket, 144
Midwest Research Institute, 192
Migrant worker camp, 16
Mineral resources, 125, 139
Minimum wage, 175
Mining, 139
See also Strip mining
Mississippi River, 213
Mobile home, 142
Mobility, 114, 154
Model society, 52–77
Moisture depletion, 121
Mona, 73–75
Monk parakeet, 156
Montana, 85
Morton, R., 197, 198
Mother Earth News, 41
Motor bike, 36
Mt. McKinley, 45, 46
Multinational corporation, 120, 145
Municipal sewage, 214
Murray, B. B., 49

Nader, R., 32, 49
National Academy of Sciences, 65, 112, 198
National Research Council Committee on Radioactive Waste Disposal, 66
National Air Quality standards, 159
National Association of Homebuilders, 72
National Conference on Flood Plain Management, 20, 22
National Environmental Policy Act, 9, 126
National forest, 125, 138
National park, 125, 138, 139
service, 46, 138
system, 211
National Resources Defense Council, 66
National Rifle Association, 100
National Space Administration, 58–59, 207

National Water Commission Report, 211–15
National Wildlife Federation, 72, 100, 199
Natural filtration, 92
Navigation, 21
Nevada, 124, 125, 126
New York Bight, 185–87
Nixon, R., 75
administration of, 117, 218
No-limits strategy, 5–7
Nomadic society, 86, 112, 114
Nuclear accident, 67, 69
Nuclear power, 130, 199, 200, 201
plant, 134

Obsolescence, 3, 31, 33, 121, 145, 149, 170, 180–81, 208
versus durability, 200
planned, 148
Obsolete scrap, 182
Ocean, 96, 119
dumping, 185, 186
Oil, 199
off-shore, 86, 197
shale, 83, 197, 201
slick, 105
well, 86, 132
Olson, M., 27
Open burning, 166, 167
Open space, 36, 139, 209
Opulence, 54, 55, 59, 62
Oregon, 22, 171
Organic waste, 163, 165
Overconsumption, 120
Overfishing, 97, 119
Overgrazing, 110, 125
Overproduction, 96
Overseas Development Council, 110
Ozone, 158–59

Packaging, 143, 149, 183
Packard, V., 94, 141
Paley Study Commission, 196
Panic, 133, 136
buying, 117, 150
Paper, 33, 166, 181–82
Parking surcharge, 220
Pesticide, 82, 170, 184
Pesticide 2, 4, 5-T, 47–48
Petrochemical complex, 74
Petroleum, 14, 130
Photochemical oxidant, 159
Photosynthesis, 89
Piburn, M., 64, 76
Picker, 164
Plankton, 90
Plant life, 90
Plastics, 163, 184
Plutonium, carcinogenic effects of, 66

(continued)